CUBA

ANATOMY OF A
REVOLUTION

BOOKS BY LEO HUBERMAN
We, The People
Man's Worldly Goods
America Incorporated
The Labor Spy Racket
The Great Bus Strike
The Truth About Unions
The Truth About Socialism

BOOKS BY PAUL M. SWEEZY
*Monopoly and Competition in
the English Coal Trade, 1550-1850*
The Theory of Capitalist Development
Socialism
The Present As History

BOOKS EDITED BY PAUL M. SWEEZY
*F. O. Matthiessen (1902-1950): A
Collective Portrait* (with LEO HUBERMAN)
Karl Marx and the Close of His System
BY EUGEN VON BOHM-BAWERK,
and *Böhm-Bawerk's Criticism of Marx*
BY RUDOLF HILFERDING

Imperialism and Social Classes
BY JOSEPH A. SCHUMPETER

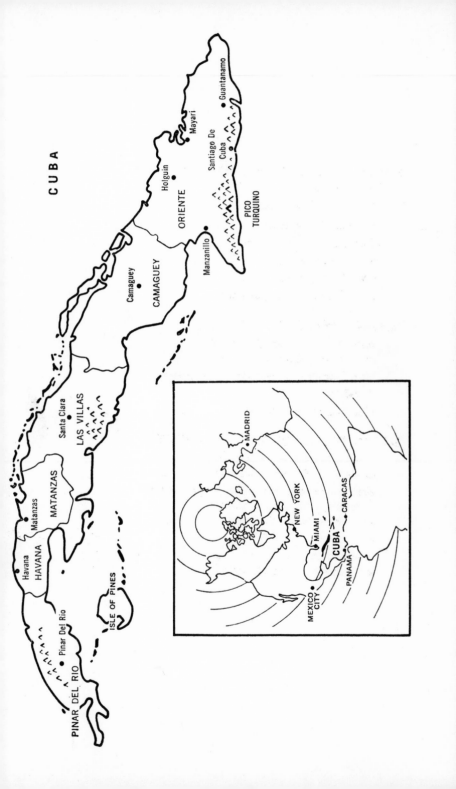

CUBA

ANATOMY OF A REVOLUTION

Leo Huberman
Paul M. Sweezy

SECOND EDITION WITH NEW MATERIAL ADDED

 MONTHLY REVIEW PRESS, *New York 1961*

F
1788
H8

Copyright © 1960
by *Leo Huberman and Paul M. Sweezy*

Second Edition, 1961

Manufactured in the U.S.A.
Library of Congress catalog card number 60-14686

357

The people must be given something more than liberty and democracy in abstract terms. —FIDEL CASTRO

What is going on in Cuba today is no mere palace revolution at the top, in which one oligarchy has ousted another. This is a social revolution involving the masses of the Cuban people, and its aim is not to install a new set of rulers but to work out a new social order. —WALTER LIPPMANN

In my thirty years on The New York Times I have never seen a big story so misunderstood, so badly handled, and so misinterpreted as the Cuban Revolution. —HERBERT MATTHEWS

CONTENTS

Preface

In this work we have attempted to combine the methods of journalism and scholarship to produce a rounded analysis of one of the most original and important social transformations of our time. Since journalism implies speed and scholarship deliberation, the combination necessarily involves a compromise, and we must leave it to the reader to judge whether we have managed to achieve a fruitful one.

We spent approximately three weeks in Cuba, in March 1960. We were received with warm hospitality and given every assistance we asked for. In the course of our inquiries we traveled from one end of Cuba to the other and talked with a large number of people from all walks of life. Some of these encounters and discussions are specifically cited in the text. We refrain from singling out particular individuals in this preface, however, lest we give a misleading impression that they are responsible for or share the views which we have expressed. The interpretation of the Cuban Revolution embodied in this work is our own, and we simply do not know to what extent our Cuban friends may agree with it. We await their comments and criticisms with the greatest interest, in the meanwhile expressing to all of them our heartfelt thanks for their never-failing kindness and patience.

Among the published works on Cuba which we have relied upon for historical facts, background information, and statistical data we would like specially to mention the following:

Ray Brennan, *Castro, Cuba and Justice* (New York, Doubleday & Company, 1959); Fidel Castro, *History Will Absolve Me* (New York, Liberal Press, 1959); Jules Dubois, *Fidel Castro* (Indianapolis, Bobbs-Merrill, 1959); Foreign Policy Association, *Problems of the New Cuba* (New York, Foreign Policy Association, 1935); Waldo Frank, *South of Us* (New York, Garden City Publishing Co., 1940); International Bank for Reconstruction and Development, *Report on Cuba* (Washington, D.C., 1950); Leland H. Jenks, *Our Cuban Colony* (New York, Vanguard Press, 1928); Scott Nearing and Joseph Freeman, *Dollar Diplomacy* (New York, B. W. Huebsch and Viking Press, 1925); Lowry Nelson, *Rural*

Cuba (Minneapolis, University of Minnesota Press, 1950); U.S. Department of Commerce, *Investment in Cuba* (Washington, D.C., Government Printing Office, 1956).

We have drawn freely on these works as well as on standard newspaper and periodical sources. Where we have quoted directly, we have either given the appropriate citation in the text or, where this would have unduly impeded the flow of the narrative, in a special list of "References" beginning on page 208.

We are well aware that it is too early to attempt to pass definitive judgments on the Cuban Revolution and its leaders. And yet no thinking person can turn this undoubted fact into an excuse for failing to take a position on a development of such enormous historical interest and importance. In what follows we have taken our position and tried to explain why. We hope that readers will be both encouraged and assisted to do likewise.

Leo Huberman
Paul M. Sweezy

New York City, June 5, 1960

Preface to Second Edition

Except for correcting a few minor slips and typographical errors, we have made no changes in the main body of the text. Two major misjudgments—that the oil companies would not refuse to refine Soviet oil and that the United States government would not cut the Cuban sugar quota—have been allowed to remain undisturbed because of what seems to us to be their considerable educational value. They testify to a lingering belief in the rationality of those who make United States foreign policy. We would like others to learn from our mistakes, as we hope we have. The important change in this edition is the addition of a chapter entitled "Epilogue—Cuba Revisited" which reports on a three-week trip to Cuba in September and October, 1960. That the few months intervening between the first and second editions have brought exciting and historically important changes in Cuba and Cuba's relations with the outside world, we hope to have demonstrated.

L. H.
P. M. S.

November 20, 1960

PART I

BACKGROUND
OF THE
REVOLUTION

███████████████████████████

CHAPTER 1

Rich Land

When Columbus discovered Cuba on Sunday, October 28, 1492, he was so struck with its charm that he called it "the most beautiful land human eyes have even seen." If he had had time to explore the island he would have learned it was much more than that—Cuba is a rich as well as a beautiful land.

It is the largest island in the West Indies with a total area of 44,218 square miles. Long and narrow, it stretches 745 miles from its western to its eastern tip; in width, it ranges from 125 miles to 22 miles with an average of about 60 miles. It is only 90 miles south of Key West, 112 miles from continental United States, and about 130 miles from Mexico across the Yucatan Channel.

Cuba lies just south of the Tropic of Cancer but its climate is more semi-tropical than tropical with the temperature averaging 75° F. for the year, ranging normally from 70° in the winter to 81° in the summer. Though the humidity is fairly high in both winter and summer, cooling breezes help to make even unpleasantly hot summer days bearable, and at no time is the weather extremely cold. The Cuban farmer never needs to worry about his crops being killed by frost.

What does worry him, on occasion, is lack of rain. Severe droughts do occur, though they are not common. Three fourths of Cuba's annual total rainfall of 54 inches comes down in the wet season from May through October, but only rarely is any month in the dry season, from November through April, without some rain.

Given an equable climate and adequate rainfall, only fertile soil is needed to raise an abundance of crops. Cuba's soil is extremely fertile. More than half of its area is arable land, suitable for growing a diversity of crops. Compared to most other countries this is a very high ratio, and Cuba's land is good not only in terms of its fertility but also in terms of its being level—about three fifths of the island is either flat or gently rolling. The rest is mountains and hills. Much of the nonarable land is suitable for grazing.

The highest and most rugged mountains are the Sierra Maestra, in the easternmost province of Oriente. The Pico Real de Turquino, the highest mountain in this range, rises to a height of 6,496 feet. On the south coast of the province of Las Villas, in the center of the island, are the Trinidad-Sancti Spíritus Highlands which reach a maximum elevation of 3,792 feet; and in Pinar Del Río, the westernmost province, lies the Sierra de Los Organos, a range of highlands paralleling the northern coast for about 112 miles and reaching a maximum elevation of 2,532 feet. The short narrow rivers that flow down from these mountain ranges are generally too shallow to be navigated. But Cuba has 2,175 miles of coastline along which are found excellent fishing grounds and many large pouch-shaped bays forming superb well-protected harbors.

The island has no coal and, to date, very little oil has been discovered. But extensive deposits of iron and nickel exist—so large as to be considered among the most important potential sources in the world. Chrome, manganese, and copper are also found in large quantities.

Four and a half centuries after Columbus, a different type of explorer, after a year's intensive study of Cuba, wrote that it is "without question one of the most favorable spots for human existence on the earth's surface." So it is. The "Pearl of the Antilles," as the island has been known since the time of Columbus, could have become a paradise.

But Cuba, in the middle of the 20th century was not a paradise. Far from it.

CHAPTER 2

Poor People

There were, in 1957, only about 6.4 million Cubans—less than the population of New York City—in an area larger than Denmark, Belgium, and the Netherlands combined. With so few people in a country so rich in natural resources, you would expect them to be well off. But they weren't. Most of the people of Cuba were desperately poor.

In the United States, the section of the country where living conditions are most miserable is the South. And the poorest state in the South is Mississippi. In the years 1950-1954, while the average per capita income for Delaware, the richest state in the nation, was $2,279 it was only $829 for Mississippi. But average per capita income for Cuba, in those same years, was not nearly half as much as Mississippi's—only 312 pesos. (The exchange rate between the peso and the dollar is one-for-one, and the two are used interchangeably throughout this work.)

Three hundred twelve pesos means $6 a week. That's what the average person had to live on in Cuba in those years. It wasn't enough. Actually, most of the people of Cuba got less than that—and their way of living showed it.

The 1953 census divided the population of Cuba into 57 percent urban, 43 percent rural. Housing in the cities was generally much better than in the country districts. In fact, the most common rural dwelling unit is not a house at all but a hut, called a bohío, generally made in whole or part from material obtained from the royal palm tree. The roof is usually thatched, the floor is most often the earth itself. Sometimes there are interior partitions, sometimes not. One of the bohíos we visited in the tobacco district of Pinar Del Río had a single partition which separated the small kitchen from the rest of the hut. Wood chips were used for fuel for cooking. There was no running water, no electric light, no toilet. This was "home" for 12 people.

The extent of sanitary and other conveniences—or rather the appalling lack of them, particularly in the rural districts—is shown in the table below from the 1953 census:

Houses having:	All Cuba	(percent) Urban	Rural
Lights:			
Electric	58.2	87.0	9.1
Acetylene	.9	.3	1.9
Kerosene	40.1	12.3	87.6
Other	.8	.4	1.4
Water:			
Inside piping	35.2	54.6	2.3
Cistern	5.0	5.2	4.6
Outside piping	16.8	22.0	8.1
River, well, or spring	43.0	18.2	85.0
Toilets:			
Water closet, inside	28.0	42.8	3.1
Water closet, outside	13.7	18.9	4.8
Privy	35.1	33.3	38.0
None	23.2	5.0	54.1
Baths:			
Tub or shower	44.4	64.9	9.5
None	55.6	35.1	90.5
Refrigeration:			
Mechanical	17.5	26.5	2.4
Ice	7.3	11.0	1.1
None	75.2	62.5	96.5

Two figures in the above table are of special importance because of their relation to the health of the Cuban people. Note that in all of Cuba, both in the urban and rural areas, only 35.2 percent of the dwelling units have running water, and only 28 percent have inside flush toilets. Note that 54.1 percent, more than half the people in the rural areas, have no toilets at all—not even a privy. With the lack of proper water and sewage systems, with so many Cubans having not enough food or the wrong kind of food because they are poor, with the almost total absence of teaching of the fundamentals of good hygiene, with medical care for the rural masses often unobtainable, it is easy to understand why health conditions in Cuba have been deplorably bad. Though the plagues of yellow fever and typhus which half a century ago took an enormous toll have been eliminated, malaria, tuberculosis, and syphilis have still not been brought fully under control. And malnutrition and parasitic infestation continue to be major health problems. In rural areas, particularly, a large number of children get infected with parasitic worms, suffer miserably, and die a painful death. Ray Brennan, Chicago newspaperman, gives a vivid account of this horror:

Parasites grow and multiply within the bodies of little children. Some of those worms, the size of an ordinary lead pencil, gather in clusters or balls, clog the intestinal system, block elimination, and cause anguished deaths. Such parasites often get into the body through the soles of the feet of children walking without shoes on infected ground. After a child dies the parasites may come slithering from the mouth and nasal passages, searching for a living organism on which to feed. What has been done about it over the years? Nothing.

One of the things that might have been done over the years was to teach the children and their parents simple elementary facts about the causes and cure of the diseases that plagued them. Dietary deficiency was one of the causes. It came from not enough food and from the wrong kinds of food. Many rural families just did not have enough money to buy all the food they needed, but others spent most of what little money they had on starchy foods instead of on green vegetables which contained the vitamins they needed. They could have been taught the right things to eat— but there weren't enough schools to do the teaching. Professor Lowry Nelson, in his excellent study entitled *Rural Cuba,* summarizes the rural school problem in these words:

The most obvious fact about Cuban education is the lack of opportunity for rural children to attend school. In some places there are school buildings, but no teachers, in other places there are teachers, but no school buildings. There has been no systematic plan of school-building construction for rural areas. In some cases, where the local interest in schools is sufficiently strong, parents have constructed school buildings at their own expense, contributing money, labor, or materials for this purpose. In still other cases, buildings have been

constructed but have not been furnished with desks and other necessary equipment, and no books have been provided for the pupils.

The extent and quality of education are a key index of the
state of a society. By that standard, Cuba was a miserable failure.
Cuban law made eight years of school attendance compulsory, but
government officials did not supply the teachers, schools, and
equipment to make enforcement of the law possible. (For the
children of the rich, of course, there were adequate private
schools.) The census of 1943 showed that only 35.1 percent of the
children in the required age group were attending school—almost
two thirds of the children of Cuba were not at school! And those
who did attend did not go all the way. The figures for the drop
in enrollment were appallingly large. The statistics for 1949-1950,
gathered by the Economic and Technical Mission of the International Bank for Reconstruction and Development for its 1950
Report on Cuba, showed that "while 180,370 children start the
first grade, only 4,852 enter the eighth grade."

Those who did not drop out generally went to school only a
few hours a day, and they were taught by teachers whose training consisted of just a four-year course in a normal school upon
completion of only eight years of elementary school training.

The census-takers in 1953 gave a "literacy test" to the persons
they interviewed which consisted of asking whether they could
read and write in any language. They found that 23.6 percent
could not pass the test. Almost one out of every four persons in
Cuba, 10 years of age and over, in 1953, could not read and write!

That one-out-of-four figure is important to remember in
another connection. A careful analysis of employment figures from
the 1953 census showed that on an annual basis only about 75
percent of the Cuban labor force was employed. This meant that
on an average day one out of four Cubans who were able to work
and wanted to work could not find a job. Nor was 1953 a specially bad year. On the contrary, it was a pretty good year: it is safe
to say that this one-out-of-four unemployment figure was normal
in pre-revolutionary Cuba.

The full significance of this startling—and tragic—fact can

be grasped if you remember that in the worst year of the worst depression in United States history there were about 25 percent unemployed. *For Cuba, in respect to unemployment, every year was like the worst year of our worst depression.* And there was no system of unemployment insurance or unemployment relief.

When a country has a "normal" unemployment rate of 25 percent, it is a sure sign that something is wrong with the economic system. So great an imbalance in the economy is found in most nations of the world only rarely, in periods of deep crisis. Cuba's phenomenally large rate of unemployment, year in and year out, was a reflection of the fact that its economy was in a permanent state of crisis.

The trouble was sugar.

Good soil, a warm climate, and considerable moisture are necessary for the growing of sugar cane. Cuba has what is needed. It can produce sugar more cheaply than any country in the world and over the years it became the world's largest producer and exporter of sugar. Its entire economy came to revolve around the amount and the value of the sugar crop.

The quantity of sugar produced determined how many workers would have jobs and for how long they would work, the traffic on the railroads, the activity in the harbors, the sales in the stores, the attendance at the movies.

The trouble was that the economy of Cuba came to center almost exclusively on this single crop; a crop that had to be sold in foreign markets unable to absorb all that could be produced.

The trouble was also that the sugar industry around which the economic life of Cuba revolves is a seasonal industry. If the season of work were long and the season of no work short, then that wouldn't matter too much. But it's exactly the other way around. During the time of the *zafra,* the period when the cane is harvested and brought to the mills, hundreds of thousands of field workers, swinging their machetes, cut down millions of tons of cane stalks, trim off the leaves, and throw the stalks into piles which are loaded into carts to be carried to the mills, or to the railroad cars which run to the mills. The *zafra* is a period of great activity—but it lasts only three or four months. Then comes the *tiempo muerto*—the dead season—when the field workers and most of the mill hands are idle—and hungry. The story was graphically told in the 1935 report of the Commission on Cuban Affairs of the Foreign Policy Association:

> With the sugar crop, activity commences over the island. Families begin to purchase meat and rice to build up the terrific energy which must be expended in the field. Clothing and shoes are bought. Traveling salesmen for firms having warehouses full of imported food and clothing crowd the second-class hotels in the rural towns of the island. Lights appear about the countryside as the families once more have enough money to purchase kerosene. . . . During a normal season everything quickly assumes an air of prosperity. But after two to five months of steady employment the atmosphere begins to change. . . . The cane families begin to reduce their expenditures because they can see the dead season ahead. Each worker is willing to take a lower paid job if he can only have something to do for money. Storekeepers reduce the stocks on their shelves and the traveling salesmen retire to Havana. Gradually the prosperity of the *zafra* passes away and the kerosene lights in the bohíos begin to flicker out. Meat, rice with lard, and beans, which have been the foundations of the *zafra* diet now come fewer times each week. The cane cutter looks about him for substitute foods, turning to plantains, sweet potatoes, *malanga* and *yucca*. Instead of drinking coffee, he begins to depend on cane juice which he manufactures by a crude hand press in his doorway. Gradually, the people reduce their diet. The masses, who do little or no planting of their own, beg and pick up their food as best they can or migrate elsewhere for work if such can be found. The rains begin and with them comes malaria. Yet there is no money for doctors or medicine.

The *zafra's* short period of plenty followed by the dead season's long period of want affected directly a large proportion of the workers of Cuba. The Census of 1953 showed that the sugar industry employed 474,053 workers or 23 percent of the total labor force.

Though the workers in the sugar industry had a miserable life, lots of money was being made by the owners (they had good and not-so-good years but over the long period they did very well), and those who were in a position to do so increased their acreage of land and installed bigger and better machinery in their mills.

The little fellows found it harder to compete and were bought up by big corporations headed by capitalists whose only concern was greater profits, not the welfare of the people of Cuba.

By purchase, or by fraud, or by economic pressure, small farms were added to the acreage of big corporations, and Cuban land which had once been distributed widely became concentrated in fewer and fewer hands.

Virgin lands were added, too. Did it matter that the new tracts of land were covered with forests of good timber? Not at all. Forest lands were a treasure of great value to the nation as a whole but that made no difference to profit-seeking sugar capitalists. So millions of feet of fine mahogany and cedar were cut down and as soon as the trees were dried, the entire area was set ablaze. Thus the land was cleared for more cane. And thus a great natural resource was sacrificed to sugar.

From the beginning of Cuban history there had been, in cattle ranching, enormous tracts of land called *latifundia,* owned by single individuals or groups. Now sugar *latifundia* came into being when the giant sugar corporations acquired large blocks of land, often holding large parts of it as reserves, idle, unutilized.

The extent of the concentration of agricultural land in the hands of the large corporations was revealed in the Agricultural Census of 1946:

One hundred and fourteen farms, or fewer than 0.1 percent of the total number, encompassed 20.1 percent of the land.

Eight percent of the total number encompassed 71.1 percent of the land.

At the other end of the scale, the small farms of less than one acre to under 25 acres, were 39 percent of the total number but they encompassed only 3.3 percent of the land.

By this time, more than half the cultivated area of Cuba was devoted to sugar cane. The constantly growing acreage in cane made heavy inroads into the amount of land in food crops. So great was the subordination of the entire national economy to the production of sugar that Cuba, one of the richest agricultural countries in the world, was not able to feed itself! Only about 70 percent of what Cubans ate was produced in Cuba. One of the principal items in the diet of the people was rice—yet rice had to be imported along with such other staples as lard, pulses, wheat flour, and canned goods.

Attention of the people with capital to invest was so focused on sugar that opportunities for making money in other ways were neglected. Thus the economy tended to get more and more lop-sided. In its *Report on Cuba* the World Bank gave some striking examples:

Numerous available Cuban raw materials are not adequately utilized at home, and some are even exported instead, while the finished products made from identical materials are imported. Though seasonal prices may have something to do with it, the fact is that out of 11,000,000 kilos of tomatoes *exported* annually, an estimated equivalent of 9,000,000 kilos *return to Cuba* in various forms such as tomato sauce, paste, ketchup, etc.

Pancreatic enzymes for the tanning industry are all imported, while the domestic raw material—from cattle slaughter—is thrown into the tankage vats.

For that matter, almost none of the by-products of the meat in-dustry are processed in Cuba, although in the United States and some other countries these represent the main sources of profit to the industry. Large quantities of hide scraps from Cuba's tanneries—as well as the other raw materials used for glue and gelatine—are either exported for processing elsewhere or simply discarded.

The trouble with the economy was sugar.

A warning of the danger of monoculture, of the trend toward a one-crop economy, had been given as far back as 1883 by the greatest of Cuba's heroes. In that year José Martí, revolutionist, orator, poet, philosopher, sounded the alarm: "A people commits suicide the day on which it bases its existence on a single crop."

The warning was justified—death to the economic welfare of the country, death to its national aspirations, were certain to follow if the trend toward monoculture continued.

But in Cuba's case it wasn't suicide. It was murder. In 1883 Cuba was on the road to the top of the cliff, but it was the United States that pushed it over the top.

███████████████████████

CHAPTER 3

Foreign Domination

From the beginning of its history as a nation, the United States was always interested in Cuba. Its closeness to our shores, the possibility that its fine harbors might be used by enemy navies to threaten our Atlantic seaboard or our commerce—this was the reason for our early interest in the island. In later years our interest was renewed as we developed a considerable trade with Cuba, and its strategic military importance in respect to the Panama Canal impelled us to secure a naval base there.

In the early nineteenth century the United States government felt that one day Cuba would become a part of the United States. Until it did, it was better, American statesmen thought, that it remain a colony of Spain. If, like the other colonies of Spain in Latin America, it won its independence, then there was danger that England might seize it—and England's power was something to be feared, Spain's was not. (England had the same attitude vis-à-vis the United States—better that Cuba remain a colony of Spain than win its independence and be annexed by the United States.)

So, though Cubans chafed under Spanish misrule, the United States was happy with the situation. We had only to bide our time and Cuba would be ours. That's precisely what Secretary of State John Quincy Adams wrote to the American Minister of Spain on April 28, 1823:

There are laws of political as well as of physical gravitation; and if an apple, severed by the tempest from its native tree, can not choose but fall to the ground, Cuba, forcibly disjoined from its unnatural connection with Spain and incapable of self-support, can gravitate only toward the North American Union, which, by the same law of nature can not cast her off from its bosom.

A generation later, we were inclined to give nature a shove and push the gravitation process along by buying Cuba from

Spain. The United States Minister in Madrid made a secret offer of $100 million for the island, but Spain turned it down. The fact was that though Cuba was still politically dependent on Spain, it had become commercially more attached to the United States. By the 1850's our exports of $8 million and imports of $12 million represented about one third of Cuba's entire foreign trade. She was doing more trading with us than with Spain. Senator Stephen A. Douglas was roundly applauded when he said, in a speech in New Orleans, on December 6, 1858: "It is our destiny to have Cuba and it is folly to debate the question. It naturally belongs to the American continent."

The Cubans, however, had a different idea of their own destiny. They had the curious notion that Cuba "naturally belonged" to the Cubans. In 1868 they rose in armed rebellion to fight for their independence. The depth of their desire to be free and the intensity of their unsuccessful struggle can be gauged from the fact that the war lasted for ten years, 80,000 Spanish soldiers died, and half a billion dollars were spent by the mother country.

A large part of the Cuban countryside was laid waste, the farmers suffered terrible losses, and some American merchants who had financed Cuban sugar estates were now able to pick up good sugar properties at bargain-basement prices. This coincided with the beginning of a great transformation in the sugar industry.

Formerly there had been a world-wide market for cane sugar, and the Cuban industry grew rapidly. In the 1840's and 1850's, however, beet-sugar production, particularly in France and Germany, was subsidized by governments and soon these countries and others in Europe produced all the sugar they needed:

In 1853, only 14 percent of the sugar produced in the world came from beets; in 1884 cane had been outdistanced, 53 percent was the product of beets. And in following years the output of beet-sugar continued to grow more rapidly than that of cane.

The drop in sugar prices which resulted meant that the old Cuban mills, some still grinding by ox-power, would have to be made more efficient or go out of business. New machinery had to be installed, new lands had to be planted, railroads had to take the place of ox-carts in hauling the cane to the mills. Many Cuban millowners did not have the capital that was necessary—but some Americans did. In the 1880's and 1890's, American capitalists began to invest in sugar plantations in a big way. By 1896, they had about $30 million worth of sugar properties—and 10 percent of Cuba's total production came from American-owned mills.

American capitalists bought mining properties too. Iron ore, manganese, and nickel mines were acquired by Bethlehem Steel and Rockefeller interests. By 1896, American mining properties were worth about $15 million. With another $5 million of American money in tobacco plantations, American investments in Cuba totaled $50 million in 1896.

The Cubans meanwhile were still pursuing their goal of independence from Spain. Spurred on by the writings of Martí, they rose up in arms a second time in 1895. In 1898 they were still waging a successful but as yet undecided war, and their bloody struggle for freedom from Spain won the sympathy of the American people.

In the debates that followed the blowing up of the U.S.S. Maine in the harbor of Havana on the evening of February 15, 1898, the position of those who wanted the United States to intervene in the Cuban-Spanish War because it was our "destiny" to control Cuba was stated again and again. So, too, was the position of those who wanted to intervene for humanitarian reasons, to stop the bloodshed and cruelties going on in Cuba. And there were those who argued for intervention to win independence for the Cuban Republic. In his message to Congress on April 11 advocating "the forcible intervention of the United States as a neutral to stop the war," President McKinley argued that the state of affairs in Cuba was "a constant menace to our peace," that intervention was justified "by the very serious injury to the commerce, trade, and business of our people and by the wanton destruction of property and devastation of the island." He made only a slight reference to the fact that the day before he delivered his message to Congress he had received a cable from the American Minister at Madrid advising that immediate peace in Cuba could be secured by negotiations, that a final settlement could be obtained in which Spain would grant the rebels autonomy, or independence, or cede the island to the United States!

On April 19 Congress passed a war resolution which declared that:

(1) The people of Cuba are, and of right ought to be, free and independent.

(2) Spain shall revoke her sovereignty and withdraw her forces from Cuba.

(3) The President of the United States is empowered to use the naval and military forces of the nation to enforce these demands.

(4) "The United States hereby disclaims any disposition or intention to exercise sovereignty, jurisdiction, or control over said island, except for the pacification thereof, and asserts its determination when that is accomplished to leave the government and control of the island to its people." (The first three articles are paraphrased, the fourth is given in its entirety.)

Very clear. The Cubans who were fighting for independence, for the right of Cubans to have their own government and control of their own island, seemed to have every reason to rejoice. Subsequent events, however, proved they were mistaken.

The war was over in less than four months, with the United States the victor in both the Caribbean and the Pacific. The treaty of peace signed in Paris on December 10, 1898, provided for the independence of Cuba and the cession to the United States of Puerto Rico, Guam, and the Philippines (we were to pay Spain $20 million for the Philippines); it provided also for the protection of private property and the pacification of Cuba by the United States.

On January 1, 1899, the Spanish troops evacuated the island, and American military occupation under General Leonard Wood began the job of pacification. We were pledged, by the fourth clause of the war resolution, to get out of Cuba when that job was completed and "leave the government and control of the island to its people."

That was the promise. Now came a maneuver which made the promise hollow.

On November 5, 1900, General Wood, the American military governor, called a constitutional convention in Havana. The delegates were instructed to write a constitution and frame a treaty outlining the future relations between Cuba and the United States. They wrote the constitution and were working on the treaty when that task was taken from them. On March 3, 1901, the Cuban constitutional convention was handed a set of articles, known as the Platt Amendment, which the United States Congress had passed into law and which were now to be incorporated into the new constitution. The Platt Amendment defined Cuba's relations to the United States. The convention could add its provisions to their constitution—or else. Or else what? Or else the American army of occupation would remain in Cuba.

All the articles in the Platt Amendment were restrictions on the sovereignty of Cuba; the two which were of especial importance are quoted in full:

Article III. The Government of Cuba consents that the United States may exercise the right to intervene for the preservation of Cuban independence, the maintenance of a government adequate for the protection of life, property, and individual liberty, and for discharging the obligations with respect to Cuba imposed by the Treaty of Paris on the United States, now to be assumed and undertaken by the Government of Cuba.

Article VII. To enable the United States to maintain the independence of Cuba, and to protect the people thereof, as well as for its own defense, the Cuban Government will sell or lease to the United States the land necessary for coaling or naval stations, at certain specified points, to be agreed upon with the President of the United States.

Confronted with this ultimatum from the United States what were the Cubans to do? They recognized that the Platt Amendment was a menace to their sovereignty. They protested that real independence for Cuba meant being "independent of every other nation, the great and noble American nation included." They were assured by Secretary of State Root that Article III of the Platt Amendment was not "synonymous with intermeddling or interference in the affairs of the Cuban government."

They didn't believe him, but still they had no choice. On June

12, 1901, by a vote of 17 to 11, the Platt Amendment was added to the Cuban constitution (two years later it was written into a permanent treaty between the two countries), and on May 20, 1902, American military occupation of the island was ended.*

But as the Cubans had feared, in spite of the pious assurances of Secretary Root, that was not the end of meddling in Cuban affairs, or even of further military occupation of the island. American troops intervened for the first time under the Platt Amendment in 1906, a second time in 1912, and a third time in 1917. In 1920 the United States sent a series of political and financial advisors who controlled the Cuban government without benefit of troops.**

American-style "independence" for Cuba was a sham. The predictions of Juan Cualberto Gómez, Negro delegate to the constitutional convention, presented at the time of the debate on the Platt Amendment, were proved all too accurate:

---

* Not entirely, however. The United States, under Article VII of the Platt Amendment, leased from Cuba the land at Guantanamo Bay for a naval station, at a rent of $2,000 per year.

** Cuba was not the only place where the American flag followed the dollar. Government intervention on behalf of United States capitalists was so common after 1898 that the bitter protest against "Yankee imperialism" which arose in Latin America was unquestionably justified. The picturesque testimony of Major-General Smedley D. Butler, who was in a position to know, leaves no doubt on that score:

"I spent thirty-three years and four months in active service as a member of our country's most agile military force—the Marine Corps. I served in all commissioned ranks from a second lieutenant to major-general. And during that period I spent most of my time being a high-class muscle man for Big Business, for Wall Street, and for the bankers. In short, I was a racketeer for capitalism. . . .

Thus I helped make Mexico and especially Tampico safe for American oil interests in 1914. I helped make Haiti and Cuba a decent place for the National City Bank boys to collect revenues in. . . . I helped purify Nicaragua for the international banking house of Brown Brothers in 1909-1912. I brought light to the Dominican Republic for American sugar interests in 1916. I helped make Honduras "right" for American fruit companies in 1903. In China in 1927 I helped see to it that Standard Oil went its way unmolested.

During those years I had, as the boys in the back room would say, a swell racket. I was rewarded with honors, medals, promotion. Looking back on it, I feel I might have given Al Capone a few hints. The best *he* could do was to operate his racket in three city districts. We Marines operated on three *continents.*" (*Common Sense*, November, 1935.)

To reserve to the United States the faculty of deciding for themselves when independence is menaced, and when, therefore, they ought to intervene to preserve it, is equivalent to delivering up the key to our house, so that they can enter it at all hours, when the desire takes them, day or night, with intentions good or ill. . . .

If it belongs to the United States to determine what Cuban government merits the qualification "adequate" . . . only those Cuban governments will live which count on its support and benevolence.

The United States did, indeed, have the key to the Cuban house; it did, indeed, enter at will; and the Cuban governments which it supported had, in the nature of the setup, to be run by politicians who could be relied on to do Washington's bidding.

Of politicians who bend the knee not much can be expected in the way of honest, efficient, or democratic government. Following Tomás Estrada Palma, elected the first President of the Republic of Cuba in 1902, came a succession of Presidents whose terms were characterized by venality, nepotism, incompetence, graft, and despotism. Some were elected to office by ballots, others seized or held power by bullets. Two of the better of a thoroughly bad lot were Dr. Ramón Grau San Martín and Dr. Carlos Prío Socarrás; two of the worst, General Gerardo Machado and Sergeant Fulgencio Batista. Machado, who held power from 1924 to 1933, and Batista, who seized control of the army in September 1933 and of the government the following year, were bloody dictators whose regimes were nightmares of repression, assassination, gangsterism, bribery, and corruption.

The Cuban people, led by brave students of the University of Havana, revolted against Machado, "The Butcher," and he fled the country in August 1933. In the turmoil that followed, Grau became president for a brief period of four months. He introduced a series of necessary reform measures designed to alleviate the miserable conditions of the poor, made worse than ever by the Great Depression. Such reforms were what the island needed—but they were not what the privileged upper class of Cubans or American interests wanted. So the administration of Franklin D. Roosevelt which, to its credit, abrogated the Platt Amendment, withheld recognition from the Grau government and

Grau was ousted from office. The recognition that was denied Grau was granted to Batista when he became the "strong man" of Cuba in 1934, and he stayed in power, to the further debasement of Cuban life, for another ten years. Whether the administration in Washington was reactionary or liberal, whether the Platt Amendment was on the books or not, the long arm of United States power was never absent from Cuba. And the results were always the same—good for North American capitalists, bad for the Cuban people.

But this is to get ahead of our story. With American domination of Cuba complete following the end of the war with Spain, capitalists from the United States could really take hold of the economic life of the island. Their lackeys in government office gave them—for a price of course—all kinds of business favors. Public works contracts, special concessions in swamp lands, timber groves, railway rights, and harbor dredging brought shrewd American operators plunder that was counted in the millions of dollars.

Of much more importance, however, than the money that came from corrupt deals were the profits that came from the entry of American capital into the sugar industry on a big scale. Poor old Spain had neglected its colony in search of the yellow gold of the Andes and Mexico; the Americans didn't make that mistake—they found plenty of white gold in the sugar of Cuba.

Though the sugar industry was in a depressed state after the war, big American corporations were certain it had a profitable future. In 1901 the United Fruit Company bought a vast tract of over 175,000 acres, cleared it of jungle growth, and set up two mills. Other big operators bought extensive acreage and all of them now moved on Washington to arrange a deal whereby their Cuban sugar could enter the United States at a lower duty than foreign sugar. The beet-sugar interests in the United States opposed such a deal, but the Sugar Trust bought heavily into the stocks of the beet-sugar refineries and the opposition died. On December 17, 1903, a reciprocity treaty was approved by Congress. It gave to Cuban imports a tariff reduction of 20 percent, and to American products going into Cuba a tariff reduction of from 20 to 40 percent. The treaty gave to refiners in the United

States sugar cheaper than they could buy anywhere else, and to Cuban sugar producers an opportunity to expand output. The preferential rate on American imports gave American farmers and manufacturers an advantage over foreigners in selling to the Cuban market; at the same time it further distorted the economy of Cuba by making her more dependent on American imports instead of on her own resources.

With American capitalists given a free hand, the development of the sugar industry that followed made all expansion prior to the war seem like nothing at all. Here were operators who did things in a big way. The cane that came from their extensive acreage wasn't brought to their mills on ox-carts; they built 9,000 miles of private railroads to connect their fields with the mills, and they had the Cuban government build another 4,800 miles of public railroads to carry their sugar to the nearest convenient ports. The mills that had been grinding sugar in the past were old, the machinery antiquated; they now built giant mills with the newest machinery that could extract much more juice from the cane. To assure themselves of a steady supply of cheap labor that would work day in and day out and no nonsense, they imported thousands of Haitians and Jamaicans and Chinese coolies and housed them in huge barracks on the plantations.

They produced sugar on a big scale, efficiently and cheap. The small planters and small millowners couldn't compete and were soon at their mercy. The formerly independent owner of sugar lands was no longer independent—he had now to bring his cane to the big mill for processing under terms dictated by the big corporation.

All this meant a change of tremendous importance for Cuba. The difference before and after American capitalists took command of the industry was explained to Leland Jenks by an American friend who had resided in Cuba a long time:

Twenty-five years ago the rural Cuban squatted on the piece of land which produced most of what he needed for food and shelter with perhaps something extra which he could exchange for rice and cloth.

The coming of the sugar industry on a large scale has completely changed his world. He now finds himself a part of a great industrial enterprise from which he receives his wages and which furnishes him a house. It has placed him in the stream of modern industrial progress. But he has no part in directing this industrial giant; he has no voice in its management. Yet to it he must look for education, recreation and bread. He has, willy-nilly, exchanged a simple life, ignorant but virtuous, for a vassalage to a foreign colossus. His future is not his own. It is determined for him in a directors' room in New York.

The "vassalage to a foreign colossus" continued to grow— and with it grew the anger and hatred of Cubans. Then came "The Dance of the Millions," and the take-over by Wall Street was complete.

If you have a product which ordinarily sells for $2\frac{1}{2}$ cents a pound and you find you can sell all you can produce for more than double that price, you will make a lot of money and you will try to increase your output so you will make still more money. That's what happened to people in the sugar industry in Cuba during World War I when there was a world-wide shortage of sugar. When the war was over, the beet-sugar fields in Europe were in ruins, sugar control ended in the United States, and the price of sugar skyrocketed to delirious heights. It had been $5\frac{1}{2}$ cents a pound and there was a big profit at that price; it soared to 10 cents a pound in March 1920; it advanced to 13 cents a pound on April 1—and it looked as though it was still going up! Who could be critical of sugar operators for going on a spending spree, and gambling for high stakes, and building themselves huge mansions, and sending their kids off to Europe with pocketfuls of dollars? And who could blame sugar people for wanting to get more where that came from and going to the banks to borrow money to buy more sugar lands and to install new and better machinery in the mills? The banks were eager to lend the money and the orgy of spending and speculating continued.*

---

* There were some carping critics who thought the workers should have been invited to the "dance of the millions," but they were humanitarians totally unfamiliar with the spirit of capitalism. Lowry Nelson tells us what was happening to the men who did the work in the fields while the owners were doing their dance:

"While the sugar companies were making the profits that financed the

In May the price of sugar was still climbing. It leaped to 22½ cents a pound on May 19. Then, horror of horrors—it started to go down. On July 19, it was 17 cents; on September 28 it had fallen to 9 cents; on November 10 it had plunged to 6 cents; on December 13 it touched bottom at 3¾ cents. The dance was over.

Then came a period of crisis. In such a period the big boys gobble up the little fellows. That's what happened.

Sugar millowners couldn't repay their loans to the banks. The banks couldn't pay their depositors and closed their doors. A large number of Cuban properties were taken over by American corporations. The Banco Nacional and the Banco Español went out and the National City Bank came in. American domination of the island of Cuba was clinched.

In 1896, ten percent of Cuba's total production of sugar came from American-owned mills; in 1914, thirty-five percent; in 1926, sixty-three percent.**

There was no doubt about it. The trouble with the economy of Cuba was sugar—and "the Colossus of the North" had assumed the leading role in the tragedy. That's what Leland Jenks, a great American social scientist, concluded after a profound study of Cuban-American relations:

[American capital's] preoccupation with the sugar industry and with railways principally devoted to carrying sugar and cane, has promoted the unbalanced economy of the island. . . . It has en-

---

spending orgy known as the "dance of the millions," cane cutters were being paid at the rate of twenty-five to sixty cents a day. The spectacular boom that brought unprecedented wealth to the few, who lavished it on luxurious and unseemly high living in the cities, left the masses in a more miserable condition than ever."

** Beginning in 1934, during the depression in the United States, some American interests began to dispose of their sugar holdings to Cubans and today many more mills are Cuban-owned than American. But the American mills that remain are giants. As you will see from the statistics of the year 1955 below, although there were only 1/3 as many American mills as Cuban, their output of sugar was more than 2/3 the production of Cuban-owned mills:

	Cuban	United States	Spanish	Other	Total
Number of mills	118	39	3	1	161
Production (percent)	59	40	1	less than 1	100

couraged expansion, overproduction, ruinous competition in the sugar
industry. It has made it possible for irrevocable decisions vitally affecting most of the Cuban population to be taken in Wall Street. . . .
It has been making of Cuba a sugar estate run by chartered account-
ants and bond salesmen. It has raised seriously the question whether
a country can long endure on the basis of one-crop latifundia managed by absentee proprietors as an adjunct to business war in a foreign
land.

Nor did these absentee proprietors' stranglehold on the Cuban
economy begin and end with sugar. Not at all. Their investments
in other fields were of such magnitude as to give them a firm grip
on other key branches of the economy of Cuba. The United States
Department of Commerce reported in 1956:

The only foreign investments of importance are those of the
United States. American participation exceeds 90 percent in the telephone and electric services, about 50 percent in public service railways, and roughly 40 percent in raw sugar production. The Cuban
branches of United States banks are entrusted with almost one-
fourth of all bank deposits. . . . Cuba ranked third in Latin America
in the value of United States direct investments in 1953, outranked
only by Venezuela and Brazil.

There was in Cuba a group of people who had thought
through to the answer to Mr. Jenks' question of "whether a
country can long endure on the basis of one-crop latifundia managed by absentee proprietors." Their answer to the question was
a firm *no*.

They had an answer to another question that had long
plagued their country—what to do about the succession of corrupt politicians who were lackeys of the foreign investors and who
ran the government not in the interest of the people of Cuba but
for their own enrichment. Their answer was: *get rid of them*.

They were convinced that the land of Cuba should belong
to the people who inhabit it; that, rationally managed in the
interest of all the people, their rich island could become what
Columbus saw, "the most beautiful land human eyes have ever
seen."

In 1952 they dedicated themselves to the task of making their
dream come true.

PART II

MAKING
THE
REVOLUTION

CHAPTER 4

The Assault on Moncada

A Cuban presidential election was scheduled for June 1, 1952. A public opinion poll taken on March 1 showed that of the three candidates, Fulgencio Batista was running last. Ten days later, at 2:43 a.m., Batista walked into Camp Columbia, the largest military fortress in Cuba, and took over the armed forces. If he couldn't win at the polls, he could do what he had done in 1934 —take over the government by force.

A few weeks after the *coup d'état,* a young 25-year-old lawyer who had received his doctorate degree at the University of Havana just two years before, appeared before the Urgency Court in Havana. He submitted a brief showing that Batista and his accomplices had violated six articles of the Code of Social Defense for which the prescribed sentence was 108 years in jail. He demanded that the judges do their duty:

Logic tells me that if there exist courts in Cuba Batista should be punished, and if Batista is not punished and continues as master of the State, President, Prime Minister, senator, Major General, civil and military chief, executive power and legislative power, owner of lives and farms, then there do not exist courts, they have been suppressed. Terrible reality?

If that is so, say so as soon as possible, hang up your robe, resign your post.

Who was this foolhardy Cuban citizen who alone had the audacity to challenge the army cutthroat who had seized power a second time? What manner of man was he?

His name was Fidel Castro.

He was born in Oriente Province on August 13, 1926, on his father's sugar plantation at Mayarí, 50 miles from Santiago de Cuba. His father, Angel Castro, had emigrated to Cuba from Galicia, in northwestern Spain, and had prospered in sugar and lumber. On the death of his first wife who had borne him two chil-

dren, Angel Castro married Lina Ruz Gonzales who gave him five
more—Angela, Ramón, Fidel, Raúl, and Juana. In their early
years, young Fidel and his brothers went hunting, and explored
the mountains nearby. The Castro family was rich but everywhere
about them, in the foothills and the mountains, the boys learned
to know what poverty means; they saw the neighboring farmers
living on the borderline of starvation in miserable hovels without
electric light or running water or plumbing facilities of any kind.

Coming from a Roman Catholic family, Fidel was sent to
parochial schools. In the elementary grades he was a boarding
student in Santiago; for his high school education he went to the
Belén Jesuit school in Havana. He did well in high school, both in
his studies and in extra-curricular activities. He was on the debat-
ing team, played basketball and baseball, and graduated in the top
third of his class. In June 1945, when he graduated, the Colegio
Belén Year Book said of him:

> Fidel distinguished himself always in all the subjects related to
> letters. His record was one of excellence, he was a true athlete, al-
> ways defending with bravery and pride the flag of the school. He
> has known how to win the admiration and the affection of all. He
> will make law his career and we do not doubt that he will fill with
> brilliant pages the book of his life. He has good timber and the
> actor in him will not be lacking.

Nineteen years old, six feet tall and still growing, Fidel
entered the University of Havana in 1945. Students in Latin
American universities, and particularly those in Havana, have
always been politically active and Fidel was no exception. He
jumped into politics with both feet, and his astounding oratorical
gift marked him early as a campus leader in the fight for honest
government and for better conditions for the poor of Cuba.

He took time out in 1947 to join an expeditionary force of
3,000 men whose objective was to invade the Dominican Republic
and overthrow its dictator, Trujillo. When the invasion fleet was
intercepted by Cuban naval vessels, Fidel and two companions,
determined that they would not be caught and put under arrest,
swam three miles to shore.

Back at Law School, Fidel pitched into political life again

by helping to organize a committee to fight racial discrimination at the university where Negro students were barred from official representation on athletic teams. In his junior year he ran for the vice presidency of the student governing body and was elected. Later, when the president resigned, he became president.

On October 12, 1948, Fidel married Mirtha Díaz Balart, a philosophy student at the university. A son was born to them eleven months later. The bride's conservative family kept hoping that their son-in-law's interest in politics was merely youthful idealism which would soon pass. But that didn't happen—Fidel was arrested again and again for his active participation in mass meetings and student protests against corruption in Cuba and other Latin American countries. The marriage ended in divorce in 1955.

The year of his marriage marked the first time Fidel voted in a presidential election. He voted for Eduardo Chibás, candidate of the newly-formed Ortodoxo Party, running on a platform of clean government and social reform. Chibás was a remarkably able, intelligent, and courageous fighter against the corruption which he saw everywhere in government. He had served in both the House and Senate so he knew Cuban politics from the inside. What he had learned he told the people in Sunday night radio broadcasts so filled with a consuming hatred for the plunderers and so daring as to hold his immense audience spellbound. He exposed the crooked schemes of grafting officials, named names, and called for their removal from office. Though he lost the election, he had a profound influence on the thinking of young people. Chibás became one of Fidel's heroes—along with the great patriot, José Martí, whose every word on independence for Cuba he had studied and learned to treasure.

On graduation from the University in 1950, Fidel hung out his shingle as a lawyer in Havana. He had a busy practice, with most of his time spent in defending workers, farmers, and political prisoners. He continued his own activity in politics and was a candidate for Congress on what would have been the winning ticket in the 1952 election—the election that never came off because of Batista's *coup*.

When his petition for the imprisonment of Batista was rejected by the court, Fidel decided that there was only one way in which the usurper could be overthrown—revolution. Only one way to put into power an honest government dedicated to the establishment of economic reform—revolution. Only one way to make real Martí's dream of a truly sovereign Cuba—revolution.

Having decided that revolution was necessary Fidel, with characteristic energy and singleness of purpose, now devoted himself to the task of preparing it. To round up a group of volunteers who burned with a desire to overthrow the tyrant was not enough; only those would qualify who were still willing to join in the struggle after they were made to understand that the odds against their success were tremendous and the penalty for failure was horrible—torture and death. They must be trained in the use of arms, and money for guns and ammunition must be obtained. All preparations had to be made secretly, for Batista's spies were everywhere.

After a year of recruiting, training, plotting, and planning, Fidel was ready. His rebel "army" consisted of some 200 men, and two women. Most of them were students or graduates, and nearly all of them were young people like himself, aged 26, and his brother, Raúl, aged 22.

On the outskirts of Santiago in Fidel's native Province of Oriente stood Fort Moncada, second largest of the country's military fortresses. The plan was to attack Moncada at dawn—to take by surprise the 1000 soldiers quartered there, capture their machine guns, tanks, armored trucks, up-to-date rifles and ammunition; then seize the radio stations and call upon the people of Cuba to support the rebel force against the dictator.

On July 26, 1953, the attack was made. In part it was successful—according to plan; in part it was a failure due to errors in the plan as well as some unlucky breaks. Some of the attackers were killed on the spot; others were captured, horribly tortured, then put in jail to wait trial, or murdered in cold blood; still others, including Fidel and Raúl, got away pursued by Batista's army.

By far the largest number of rebels who lost their lives were murdered after the assault was over. In Santiago there began the sort of blood bath which was to characterize the Batista regime and bring the total number of his victims to 20,000 before he was finally overthrown. Trigger-happy police and army men roamed the streets firing at anybody—children as well as adults; in their search for persons who had in any way helped the rebels, the army arrested innocent as well as guilty—and killed them. Batista's orders were carried out: for each of his soldiers who had fallen in the attack, ten prisoners were to be executed. Civil rights were suspended and rigid censorship imposed.

But the story of the butchery that followed the rebel assault on Moncada could not be suppressed. Too many families in Santiago had seen or heard about the killings of their loved ones, or friends, and they protested. Monsignor Pérez Serantes, Archbishop of Santiago, intervened. He secured a promise from the army commanding officer in the city that the lives of the rebels still at large would be spared if they gave themselves up; they would be brought to trial, not murdered.

That was now the public position of top army officials. But privately they gave orders to their men that the leader of the rebels, Fidel Castro, was not to be taken alive. Now, by one of the strange ironies of history, the army patrol that discovered Fidel and two companions exhausted and asleep in a shack in the foothills of the Sierra Maestra, was headed by Lieutenant Pedro Sarría who had been a student at the university while Fidel was active there. None of the other soldiers in the patrol recognized the prisoner. As he bent over Fidel, ostensibly searching him for arms, Lieutenant Sarría whispered in his ear: "Don't give your right name or you will be shot."

With Fidel in prison Raúl Castro, with his men, came down from their hideout in the mountains and surrendered.

The assault on Moncada had ended in defeat. But this first battle, the opening chapter of the Revolution, was not entirely a failure. For though the fort had not been captured, the attention of the people had been won. Fidel Castro and the July 26th Movement had become known. In Oriente, if nowhere else, the spirit of resistance to Batista tyranny was aroused.

▬▬▬▬▬▬▬▬▬▬▬▬▬▬▬▬▬

CHAPTER 5

"History Will Absolve Me"

Fidel's second encounter with Batista was a clear-cut victory. In this battle it became apparent that he was not, as some believed, merely a hot-headed impetuous youth whose idealism had run away with his judgment. He proved that he was brilliant, courageous, learned; a scholar of distinction in law, philosophy, history; a patriot inspired with love of country and a passion for justice for the dispossessed; a man fired with an inextinguishable desire to bring honor and greatness to a sovereign Cuba.

The battlefield was the courtroom. And just as the prisoner Dimitrov, in a Nazi court in 1933, turned the tables on his jailers and indicted them for their crimes, so Fidel Castro, twenty years later, prisoner in a Batista court, proclaimed his defiance of the tyrant, became the accuser, and proved him guilty of murder and treason.

On September 21, 1953, in the courthouse at Santiago, 122 prisoners, including many persons who had had nothing to do with the attack on Moncada, were brought to trial. All the approaches to the courthouse were blocked by armored cars. Lining both sides of the road from Boniato prison to the courthouse, a distance of six miles, were 1,000 soldiers with automatic weapons at the ready. All the prisoners except Fidel Castro were transported in buses; he was taken in a jeep, handcuffed, escorted by heavily-armed soldiers on every side.

On the stand, Fidel was asked whether he had participated in the attack on Moncada. He proudly admitted that he had. Then he was asked why he hadn't used "civil means" to accomplish his purpose. His answer was sharp and to the point:

Simply because there is no freedom in Cuba, because since the 10th of March nobody can talk. I already said that efforts were made but the government, always intransigent, did not want to give ground.

I accused Batista before the tribunals of justice, but the courts did not resolve the case as we expected.

The prosecution spent a lot of time trying to prove that money and help had been given to the rebels by exiled ex-President Prío and other opposition political leaders. Fidel denied this vehemently. Then the prosecutor asked: "If you had no contact with political leaders in this movement, then what support were you counting on?" Fidel replied:

If we had been able to make contact with the people they would have responded. There is our ally: the people. Our plan was to take the radio stations as soon as possible and to broadcast simultaneously over all of them the last speech delivered by the dead leader Eduardo R. Chibás. We felt that all the opposition leaders of the republic would then have joined us, and, in that way, we would have over-thrown the de facto government, the dictatorship of Batista. . . .

"But that leader is dead!" came from the prosecutor.

Fidel answered, "That doesn't matter. Men do not follow men but ideas, Mr. Prosecutor."

Questioned on whether any leaders of the Communist Party (*Partido Socialista Popular*) had participated in the attack, Fidel said no. Had his companions been reading any books, asked the assistant prosecutor.

"They all like books," was his reply.

"Was a book by Lenin found on Santamaría?"

"It is possible because we read all types of books. Anyone who was never interested in socialist literature is an ignoramus."

Fidel was a witness for two hours in this first session. In his testimony he spoke with pride of the aims of the movement, and how the $20,000 collected for the purchase of arms had been contributed by the young people themselves, some of them giving up everything they owned. What he said about those who had participated and those who had not was corroborated in every detail by the testimony of his companions.

At the second session, the next day, Fidel asked for and was granted permission to leave the witness chair and sit with counsel for the defense. Here, as a lawyer, he would be able to ask questions of the witnesses. He planned, through his questioning, to disprove the lies that had been broadcast about the rebel forces by Batista and his officers, and to bring out the evidence proving them guilty of the crime of torture and cold-blooded murder of some 70 captured rebel prisoners.

After a few witnesses had testified, he was able to get into the record the army officers' responsibility for beating and assassinating helpless prisoners. On the stand was rebel García Díaz who, with his brother, had been captured and slugged by Batista soldiers. Díaz testified that he saw them hang his brother. He himself, though wounded, had succeeded in escaping. "Those soldiers who you say committed the crimes," asked Fidel, "and who beat you, did they act on their own or were they obeying orders of the officer on duty?"

"They obeyed orders," García Díaz answered.

Here the court ordered a two-day recess.

When the third session opened, on September 26, Fidel Castro was not in the courtroom. The captain of the guard handed the chief judge a note which he read aloud. "The accused, Dr. Fidel Castro Ruz will not be able to be present. I have just received a communication from the prison in which it is certified that he is sick and needs absolute rest."

Fidel's questioning in the courtroom had resulted in damage to the government case—and greater damage was still to come as the trial proceeded. What to do? Two doctors were sent to examine the prisoner, then sign a certificate that he was too ill to attend. The trick would have worked—except for the fact that the movement against Batista was headed by master strategists who knew the lengths to which the enemy would go and how to balk their cunning scheme with a dramatic counter-plot that would expose them.

No sooner had the judge announced that under the circumstances the trial would proceed without the presence of the sick man, than a woman's voice shouted: "Mr. President, Fidel Castro is not sick!"

With slow, measured steps, Dr. Melba Hernández, one of the two women who had participated in the attack on Moncada, walked to the bench. "Mr. President," she continued, "here I bring a letter from Dr. Fidel Castro, written in his own hand and addressed to this respectable and honorable court." Then she took out of her hair a tiny piece of paper hidden there and handed it to the chief judge. The three judges on the bench read the paper. This is what they read:

To the Urgency Court:

Fidel Castro Ruz, attorney appearing in his own defense in Cause 37 of the present year before said Court respectfully expounds the following:

1. That efforts are made to impede my presence in the trial, by which the fantastic falsehoods that have been woven around the deeds of the 26th of July would be destroyed, and to prevent the revelation of the horrible crimes that were committed that day against prisoners, which were, I say, the most frightful slaughter ever known in the history of Cuba. Because of that today I have been informed that I will not attend the trial because I am sick, the truth being that I am in perfect health without any physical illness of any kind. Thus they are pretending in that way to abuse the Court in the most shameful manner.

2. That despite repeated communications from the judicial power and the last one that the Court addressed to the authorities of the prison, demanding the end to our isolation, because it is unlawful and criminal, I am totally incommunicado. During the fifty-seven days in which I have been in this prison I have not been allowed to see the sun, to talk to anyone nor to see my family.

3. That I have been able to learn with all certainty that my physical elimination is being plotted, under the pretext of escape, poisoning me or some other similar thing and for that purpose they have been elaborating a series of plans and plots that facilitate the consummation of the deeds. I have repeatedly denounced this. The motives are the same as I expounded in number one of this brief.

Like danger faces the lives of other prisoners, among them two of the girls who are exceptional witnesses of the massacre of the 26th of July.

4. I request the Court to proceed to order immediately my examination by a distinguished and competent doctor such as the President of the Medical Association of Santiago de Cuba. I propose also that a member of that Court, especially appointed, accompany the political prisoners on the trips that they make from this prison to the Palace of Justice and vice versa. That the details of this brief be

communicated to the Local and National Bar Associations, to the Supreme Court of Justice and to as many legal institutions as that Court esteems should know these facts.

The importance and the category of the trial that is being held imposes exceptional obligations.

If it is carried out under the conditions which I have denounced, it will not be more than a ridiculous and immoral farce with the full repudiation of the nation.

All of Cuba has its eyes focused on this trial. I hope that this Court will worthily defend the rights of its hierarchy and its honor which is at the same time, in these moments, the honor of the entire judicial power before the History of Cuba.

The action of the Court up to now and the prestige of its magistrates accredit it as one of the most honorable of the Republic which is why I expound these considerations with blind faith in its virile action.

For my part, if for my life I have to cede an iota of my right or of my honor, I prefer to lose it a thousand times: "A just principle from the depth of a cave can do more than an army."

(Signed) FIDEL CASTRO RUZ

September 26, 1953
Provincial Jail of Oriente

P.S. I appoint Dr. Melba Hernández to present this brief in my name. F.C.

So damaging a blow could not be suffered by the army men in charge without immediate reprisals. All prisoners from then on were thoroughly searched from head to foot before they entered the courtroom; Melba Hernández was put in solitary confinement; Fidel Castro, already in solitary, was sent to the most inaccessible part of the prison. The judges of the court were defied: after two court-appointed physicians examined Fidel on September 27 and certified that he was in perfect health, the judges ordered him returned to the trial sessions—but the regime would not permit it.

The trial went on without Fidel. (In his absence, his companions carried on with bravery, honor, and dignity). Not until October 16 was he permitted to appear before the judges again —and then not in the courtroom, but in the nurses' lounge of the Civil Hospital. To make certain that the Cuban people would not hear the voice of Fidel Castro, his trial was to be held in secret with only the following allowed in the room: the three judges, two prosecutors, six reporters (who were prohibited by the censorship from reporting what he said), and the armed guard of close to 100 soldiers.

Who was on trial, Fidel Castro, or the Batista regime?

Given the opportunity, at long last, to take the stand in his own defense, Fidel spoke for five hours. His speech was not a plea for mercy; on the contrary, it was an indictment of the Batista regime. The argument was bolstered with citations from law, political science, economics, history, and philosophy. It was as learned as it was long; as eloquent as only a dedicated person burning with a vision of glory for his country could be. It was one of the greatest speeches in the history of the fight for freedom anywhere in the world.

The full flavor and sweep of the oration can only be captured from a reading of the complete text. Unfortunately there is space in these pages for just a part. Remember, as you read what follows, that these are the words of a young man just turned 27 years of age, speaking extemporaneously, after being held incommunicado for 76 days in solitary confinement.

Our Justice Is Sick . . . Captive

. . . An unheard-of situation had arisen, Honorable Magistrates. Here was a regime afraid to bring an accused before the courts; a regime of blood and terror which shrank in fear at the moral conviction of a defenseless man—unarmed, slandered, and isolated. Thus, having deprived me of all else, they finally deprived me of the trial in which I was the principal accused.

Bear in mind that this was during a period of suspension of rights of the individual and while there was in full force the Law of Public Order as well as censorship of radio and press. What dreadful crimes this regime must have committed, to so fear the voice of one accused man! . . .

As a result of so many obscure and illegal machinations, due to the *will* of those who govern and the *weakness* of those who judge, I find myself here in this little room of the Civil Hospital—to which I have been brought to be tried in secret; so that my voice may be stifled and so that no one may learn of the things I am going to say. Why, then, do we need that imposing Palace of Justice which the Honorable Magistrates would without doubt find rather more comfortable? I must warn you: it is unwise to administer justice from a hospital room, surrounded by sentinels with bayonets fixed; the citizens might suppose that our justice is sick . . . and that it is captive. . . .

I remind you, your laws of procedure provide that trials shall be "both audible and public"; however, the people have been barred altogether from this session of court. The only civilians admitted here have been two attorneys and six reporters, whose newspapers censorship will prevent from printing a word that I say. I see, as my sole audience, in this chamber and in the corridors, nearly a hundred soldiers and officers. I am grateful for the polite and serious attention they give me. I only wish I could have the whole army before me! I know, one day this army will seethe with rage to wash away the awful, the shameful bloodstains splattered across the uniform by the present ruthless clique in their lust for power. On that day, oh, what a fall awaits those mounted, in arrogance, on the backs of the noble soldiers! —provided, that is, that the people have not pulled them down long before!

Finally, I should like to add that no treatise on penal law was allowed to be brought to my cell. I have at my disposal just this tiny code of law lent to me by my learned counsel, Dr. Baudilio Castellanos, the courageous defender of my comrades. In the same way they prohibited me from receiving the books of Martí; it seems the prison censorship considered them too subversive. Or is it because I named Martí as the instigator of the 26th of July?

I was also prevented from bringing to this trial reference books on any other subject. It makes no difference whatsoever! I carry in my heart the teachings of the *Maestro* and in my mind the noble ideas of all men who have defended the freedom of the peoples of the world! . . .

What Cuban Does Not Cherish Glory?

It was never our intention to engage the soldiers of the regiment in combat, but to seize control and weapons by surprise, to arouse the people and then call the soldiers together. We would have invited them to abandon the flag of tyranny and to embrace the banner of Liberty; to defend the supreme interests of the nation and not the petty interests of a small group; to turn their guns around and fire on the enemies of the people and not fire on the people, among whom are their own sons and fathers; to join with the people themselves, brothers of ours that they are, instead of opposing the people as the enemies the government tried to make of them; to march behind the only beautiful ideal worthy of the sacrifice of one's life—the greatness and the happiness of one's country. To those who doubt that many soldiers would have followed us, I ask: What Cuban does not cherish glory? What heart is not set aflame by the dawn of freedom? . . .

The Honorable Prosecutor was very much interested in knowing our chances for success. These chances were based on considerations of technical, military, and social orders. There has been an attempt to establish the myth that modern arms render the people helpless to overthrow tyrants. Military parades and the pompous display of the machines of war are utilized to perpetuate this myth and to create in the people a complex of absolute impotence. But no weapon, no violence can vanquish the people once they have decided to win back their rights. Both past and present are full of examples. . . .

We Counted on the People

I stated that the second consideration on which we based our chances for success was one of social order because we were assured of the people's support. When we speak of the people we do not mean the comfortable ones, the conservative elements of the nation, who welcome any regime of oppression, any dictatorship, any despotism, prostrating themselves before the master of the moment until they grind their foreheads into the ground. When we speak of struggle, the *people* means the vast unredeemed masses, to whom all make promises and whom all deceive; we mean the people who yearn for a better, more dignified and more just nation; who are moved by ancestral aspirations of justice, for they have suffered injustice and mockery, generation after generation; who long for great and wise changes in all aspects of their life; people, who, to attain these changes, are ready to give even the very last breath of their lives—when they believe in something or in someone, especially when they believe in themselves. In stating a purpose, the first condition of sincerity and good faith, is to do precisely what nobody else ever does, that is, to speak with absolute clarity, without fear. The demagogues and professional politicians who manage to perform the miracle of being right in everything and in pleasing everyone, are, of necessity, deceiving everyone about everything. The revolutionaries must proclaim their ideas courageously, define their principles and express their intentions so that no one is deceived, neither friend nor foe.

The people we counted on in our struggle were these:

Seven hundred thousand Cubans without work, who desire to earn their daily bread honestly without having to emigrate in search of livelihood.

Five hundred thousand farm laborers inhabiting miserable shacks, who work four months of the year and starve for the rest of the year, sharing their misery with their children, who have not an inch of land to cultivate, and whose existence inspires compassion in any heart not made of stone.

Four hundred thousand industrial laborers and stevedores whose retirement funds have been embezzled, whose benefits are being taken away, whose homes are wretched quarters, whose salaries pass from the hands of the boss to those of the usurer, whose future is a pay reduction and dismissal, whose life is eternal work and whose only rest is in the tomb.

One hundred thousand small farmers who live and die working on land that is not theirs, looking at it with sadness as Moses did the promised land, to die without possessing it; who, like feudal serfs, have to pay for the use of their parcel of land by giving up a portion of their products; who cannot love it, improve it, beautify it or plant a lemon or an orange tree on it, because they never know when a sheriff will come with the rural guard to evict them from it.

Thirty thousand teachers and professors who are so devoted, dedicated and necessary to the better destiny of future generations and who are so badly treated and paid.

Twenty thousand small business men weighted down by debts, ruined by the crisis and harangued by a plague of filibusters and venal officials.

Ten thousand young professionals: doctors, engineers, lawyers, veterinarians, school teachers, dentists, pharmacists, newspapermen, painters, sculptors, etc., who come forth from school with their degrees, anxious to work and full of hope, only to find themselves at a dead end with all doors closed, and where no ear hears their clamor or supplication.

These are the people, the ones who know misfortune and, therefore, are capable of fighting with limitless courage!

To the people whose desperate roads through life have been paved with the brick of betrayals and false promises, we were not going to say: "We will eventually give you what you need, but rather —here you have it, fight for it with all your might so that liberty and happiness may be yours!" . . .

The Problems We Must Resolve

The problems concerning land, the problem of industrialization, the problem of housing, the problem of unemployment, the problem of education, and the problem of the health of the people; these are the six problems we would take immediate steps to resolve, along with the restoration of public liberties and political democracy.

Perhaps this exposition appears cold and theoretical if one does not know the shocking and tragic conditions of the country with regard to these six problems, to say nothing of the most humiliating political oppression.

Eighty-five percent of the small farmers in Cuba pay rent and live under the constant threat of being dispossessed from the land that they cultivate. More than half the best cultivated land belongs to foreigners. In Oriente, the largest province, the lands of the United Fruit Company and West Indian Company join the north coast to the southern one. There are two hundred thousand peasant families who do not have a single acre of land to cultivate to provide food for their starving children. On the other hand, nearly three hundred thousand caballerías* of productive land owned by powerful interests remain uncultivated.

Cuba is above all an agricultural state. Its population is largely rural. The city depends on these rural areas. The rural people won the Independence. The greatness and prosperity of our country depends on a healthy and vigorous rural population that loves the land and knows how to cultivate it, within the framework of a state that protects and guides them. Considering all this, how can the present state of affairs be tolerated any longer?

With the exception of a few food, lumber, and textile industries, Cuba continues to be a producer of raw materials. We export sugar to import candy, we export hides to import shoes, we export iron to import plows. Everybody agrees that the need to industrialize the country is urgent, that we need steel industries, paper and chemical industries; that we must improve cattle and grain products, the technique and the processing in our food industry, in order to balance the ruinous competition of the Europeans in cheese products, condensed milk, liquors and oil, and that of the Americans in canned goods; that we need merchant ships; that tourism should be an enormous source of revenue. But the capitalists insist that the workers remain under a Claudian yoke; the state folds its arms and industrialization can wait for the Greek calends.

Just as serious or even worse is the housing problem. There are two hundred thousand huts and hovels in Cuba; four hundred thousand families in the country and in the cities live cramped into barracks and tenements without even the minimum sanitary requirements; two million two hundred thousand of our urban population pay rents which absorb between one fifth and one third of their income; and two million eight hundred thousand of our rural and suburban population lack electricity. If the state proposes lowering rents, landlords threaten to freeze all construction; if the state does not interfere,

---

* A caballería is equal to about 33 acres.

construction goes on so long as the landlords get high rents, otherwise they would not lay a single brick even though the rest of the population should have to live exposed to the elements. The utilities monopoly is no better: they extend lines as far as it is profitable, and beyond that point they don't care if the people have to live in darkness for the rest of their lives. The state folds its arms and the people have neither homes nor electricity.

Our educational system is perfectly compatible with the rest of our national situation. Where the *guajiro** is not the owner of his land, what need is there for agricultural schools? Where there are no industries what need is there for technical or industrial schools? Everything falls within the same absurd logic: there is neither one thing nor the other. In any small European country there are more than 200 technical and industrial arts schools; in Cuba, there are only six such schools, and the boys graduate without having anywhere to use their skills. The little rural schools are attended by only half the school-age children—barefoot, half-naked, and undernourished—and frequently the teacher must buy necessary materials from his own salary. Is this the way to make a nation great?

Only death can liberate one from so much misery. In this, however—early death—the state is most helpful. Ninety percent of rural children are consumed by parasites which filter through their bare feet from the earth. Society is moved to compassion upon hearing of the kidnapping or murder of one child, but they are criminally indifferent to the mass murder of so many thousands of children who die every year from lack of facilities, agonizing with pain. Their innocent eyes —death already shining in them—seem to look into infinity as if entreating forgiveness for human selfishness, as if asking God to stay his wrath. When the head of a family works only four months a year, with what can he purchase clothing and medicine for his children? They will grow up with rickets, with not a single good tooth in their mouths by the time they reach thirty; they will have heard ten million speeches and will finally die of misery and deception. Public hospitals, which are always full, accept only patients recommended by some powerful politician who, in turn, demands the electoral votes of the unfortunate one and his family so that Cuba may continue forever the same or worse. . . .

The future of the country and the solution of its problems cannot continue to depend on the selfish interests of a dozen financiers, nor on the cold calculations of profits that ten or twelve magnates

---

* *Guajiro* is a specifically Cuban word meaning poor peasant or land worker. It is used interchangeably with *campesino.*

draw up in their air-conditioned offices. The country cannot continue begging on its knees for miracles from a few golden calves, similar to the Biblical one destroyed by the fury of a prophet. Golden calves cannot perform miracles of any kind. The problems of the Republic can be solved only if we dedicate ourselves to fight for that Republic with the same energy, honesty, and patriotism our liberators had when they created it.

Program of a Revolutionary Government

It is not by statesmen such as Carlos Saladrigas,* whose statesmanship consists of preserving the status quo and mouthing phrases like the "absolute freedom of enterprise," "guarantees to investment capital," and "the law of supply and demand," that we will solve these problems. Those ministers can chat gaily in a mansion on Fifth Avenue** until there remains not even the dust of the bones of those whose problems required immediate solution. In this present-day world, social problems are not solved by spontaneous generation.

A revolutionary government with the backing of the people and the respect of the nation, after cleansing the various institutions of all venal and corrupt officials, would proceed immediately to industrialize the country, mobilizing all inactive capital, currently estimated at about 1500 million dollars, through the National Bank, the Agricultural and Industrial Bank, and the Development Bank, and submitting this mammoth task to experts and men of absolute competence, completely removed from all political machinations, for study, direction, planning, and realization.

After settling the one hundred thousand small farmers as owners on land which they previously rented, a revolutionary government would proceed immediately to solve the land problem. First, as the Constitution orders we would establish the maximum amount of land to be held by each type of agricultural enterprise and would acquire the excess acres by: expropriation, recovery of the lands stolen from the state, improvement of swampland, planting of large nurseries, and reserving of zones for reforestation. Secondly, we would distribute the remaining land among peasant families with priority given to the larger ones, and would promote agricultural cooperatives with a single technical, professional direction in farming and cattle raising. Finally, we would provide resources, equipment, protection, and useful guidance to the peasants.

A revolutionary government would solve the housing problem by cutting all rents in half, by providing tax exemptions on homes in-

---

* Batista's presidential candidate in the 1944 elections.
** In the swank Miramar residential district of Havana.

habited by the owners; by tripling taxes on rented homes; by tearing down hovels and replacing them with modern multiple-dwelling buildings; and by financing housing all over the island on a scale heretofore unheard of; with the criterion that, just as each rural family should possess its own tract of land, each city family should own its home or apartment. There is plenty of building material and more than enough manpower to make a decent home for every Cuban. But if we continue to wait for the miracle of the golden calf, a thousand years will have gone by and the problem will still be the same. On the other hand, today there are greater than ever possibilities of bringing electricity to the remotest corner of the island. The use of nuclear energy in this field is now a reality and will greatly reduce the cost of producing electricity.

With these three projects and reforms, the problem of unemployment would automatically disappear and the work to improve public health and to fight against disease would be made much less difficult.

Finally, a revolutionary government would undertake the integral reform of the educational system, bringing it in line with the foregoing projects with the idea of educating those generations who will have the privilege of living in a happy land. Do not forget the words of the *Apóstol**: "A serious error is being made in Latin America: where the inhabitants depend almost exclusively on the products of the soil for their livelihood, the education stress, contradictorily, is on urban rather than farm life." "The happiest people are the ones whose children are well-educated and instructed in philosophy; whose sentiments are directed into noble channels." "A well-educated people will always be strong and free." . . .

Where Will the Money Come From?

Where will the money be found for all this? When there is an end to rife embezzlement of government funds, when public officials stop taking graft from the large companies who owe taxes to the state, when the enormous resources of the country are brought into full use, when we no longer buy tanks, bombers, and guns for this country (which has no frontiers to defend and where these instruments of war, now being purchased, are used against the people) when there is more interest in educating the people than in killing them—then there will be more than enough money.

Cuba could easily provide for a population three times as great as it now has, so there is no excuse for the abject poverty of a single one of its present inhabitants. The markets should be overflowing

---

* i.e. José Martí.

with produce, pantries should be full, all hands should be working. This is not an inconceivable thought. What is inconceivable is that anyone should go to bed hungry, that children should die for lack of medical attention; what is inconceivable is that 30 percent of our farm people cannot write their names and that 99 percent of them know nothing of Cuba's history. What is inconceivable is that the majority of our rural people are now living in worse circumstances than were the Indians Columbus discovered living in the fairest land that human eyes had ever seen.

To those who would call me a dreamer, I quote the words of Martí: "A true man does not seek the path where advantage lies, but rather, the path where duty lies, and this is the only practical man, whose dream of today will be the law of tomorrow, because he who has looked back on the upheavals of history and has seen civilizations going up in flames, crying out in bloody struggle, throughout the centuries, knows that the future well-being of man, without exception, lies on the side of duty."

This Movement Is a New Generation

Only when we understand that such high ideals inspired them, can we conceive of the heroism of the young men who fell in Santiago.

The meager material means at our disposal was all that prevented our certain success. When the soldiers were told that Prío had given a million dollars to us, they were told this in the regime's attempt to distort the most serious fact—the fact that our movement had no link with past politicians. The regime was trying to prevent the soldiers from learning that this movement is a new Cuban generation with its own ideas, rising up against tyranny; that this movement is made up of young men who were barely seven years old when Batista committed the first of his crimes in 1934. . . .

"With Death, Life Begins"

For my dead friends, I claim no vengeance. Since their lives were priceless, the murderers could not pay for them with their own lives. It is not by blood that we can redeem the lives of those who died for their country. The happiness of their people is the only tribute worthy of them.

My comrades, furthermore, are neither dead nor forgotten; they live today, more than ever, and their murderers will view with dismay the immortality of the victorious spirit of their ideas. Let the *Apóstol* speak for me:

There is a limit to the tears we can shed at the tombs of the dead. Instead of crying over their bodies, we should go there to con-

template their infinite love for their country and its glory—a love
that never falters, loses hope nor grows faint. For the graves of
the martyrs are the most beautiful altars of our day.
When one dies
In the arms of a grateful fatherland
Death ends, prison walls break—
Finally, with death, life begins.

The Right to Rebellion against Tyranny . . .

. . . The right to revolt, established in Article 40 of the Constitution, is still valid. Was it established to function while the Republic was enjoying normal conditions? No. This provision is, in
relation to the Constitution, what a lifeboat is to a ship on high sea.
The lifeboat is lowered only when, for example, the boat is torpedoed
by enemies in ambush along its course. With our Constitution betrayed and the people deprived of all their prerogatives, there was only
one right left, one right which no power may abolish—the right to
resist oppression and injustice. . . .

The right of rebellion against tyranny, Honorable Magistrates,
has been recognized from the most ancient times to the present day
by men of all creeds, ideas, and doctrines.

In the theocratic monarchies of remote antiquity, in China, it
was in effect a constitutional principle that when a king governed
rudely and despotically he should be deposed and replaced by a virtuous prince.

The philosophers of ancient India upheld the principle of active
resistance to arbitrary authority. They justified revolution and very
often put their theories into practice. One of their spiritual leaders
used to say that "An opinion held by the majority is stronger than
the king himself. A rope weaved of many strands is strong enough to
drag a lion."

The city states of Greece and republican Rome not only admitted
but defended the meting-out of violent death to tyrants.

In the Middle Ages, John of Salisbury in his *Book of the States-
man* says that when a prince does not govern according to law and
degenerates into a tyrant, violent overthrow is legitimate and justi-
fiable. He recommends for tyrants the dagger rather than poison.

Saint Thomas Aquinas, in the *Summa Theologica,* rejects the
doctrine of tyrannicide, and yet upholds the thesis that tyrants should
be overthrown by the people.

Martin Luther proclaimed that when a government degenerates
into a tyranny violating the laws, the subjects are released from their
obligation to obey. His disciple, Philippe Melancthon, upholds the

right of resistance when governments become despotic. Calvin, the most outstanding thinker of the Reformation, with regard to political ideas, postulates that people are entitled to take up arms to oppose any usurpation.

No less a man than Juan Mariana, a Spanish Jesuit during the reign of Philip II, asserts in his book, *De Rege et Regis Institutione,* that when a governor usurps power, or even if he were elected, when he governs in a tyrannical manner, it is licit for a private citizen to exercise tyrannicide, either directly or through subterfuge, with the least possible disturbance.

The French writer, Francois Hotman, maintained that between the government and its subjects there is a bond or contract, and that the people may rise in rebellion against the tyranny of governments when the latter violate said agreement. . . .

John Althus, a German jurist of the early seventeenth century states, in his *Treatise on Politics,* that sovereignty, as the supreme authority of the state, is born from the voluntary concourse of all its members; that governmental authority stems from the people and that its unjust, illegal, or tyrannical function exempts them from the duty of obedience and justifies their resistance or rebellion.

Thus far, Honorable Magistrates, I have mentioned examples from antiquity, from the Middle Ages and from the beginnings of the modern age. I selected these examples from writers of all creeds.

Moreover, as you can see, the right to rebellion is at the very roots of Cuba's existence as a nation. By virtue of a rebellion fifty years ago you are today able to appear in the robes of Cuban magistrates. Would that those garments served the cause of justice!

And to Institute New Government

It is well known that in England during the seventeenth century two kings, Charles I and James II, were dethroned for despotism. These acts coincided with the birth of liberal political philosophy and provided the ideological foundation for a new social class, which was then struggling to break the bonds of feudalism.

Against divine right autocracies this new philosophy upheld the principle of the social contract and of the consent of the governed, and constituted the foundation of the American Revolution of 1775 and of the French Revolution of 1789. These great events ushered in the liberation of the Spanish colonies in the New World—the final link in that chain being broken by Cuba.

The new philosophy nurtured our own political ideas and helped us evolve our constitution from the Constitution of Guáimaro up to the Constitution of 1940. The latter was influenced by the socialist

currents of our time; into it were built the principle of the social
function of property and of man's inalienable right to that decorous
living which large vested interests have prevented him from realizing
fully.

The right of insurrection against tyranny then underwent its final
consecration and became a fundamental tenet of political liberty.

As far back as 1649 John Milton wrote that political power lies
in the people, who can enthrone and dethrone kings and who have
the *duty* of overthrowing tyrants.

John Locke, in his essay on government, sustains that when the
natural rights of man are violated, the people have the right and the
duty of suppressing or changing the government. "The last recourse
against wrongful and unauthorized force is opposition to it."

Jean Jacques Rousseau says with great eloquence in his *Social
Contract*: "While a people sees itself forced to obey and obeys, it
does well; as soon as it can shake off the yoke and shakes it off, it
does better, recovering its liberty through use of the very right that
had been taken away from it." . . .

The Declaration of Independence of the Congress of Philadel-
phia, on the 4th of July, 1776, consecrated this right in a beautiful
paragraph which reads: "We hold these truths to be self-evident,
that all men are created equal, that they are endowed by their Creator
with certain unalienable Rights, that among these are Life, Liberty,
and the pursuit of Happiness. That to secure these rights, Governments are instituted among Men, deriving their just powers from the
consent of the governed. That whenever any Form of Government becomes destructive of these ends, it is the Right of the People to alter
or to abolish it, and to institute new Government, laying its foundation
on such principles and organizing its powers in such form, as to them
shall seem most likely to effect their Safety and Happiness."

The famous French Declaration of the Rights of Man willed
this principle to the coming generations: "When the government
violates the rights of the people, insurrection is for them the most
sacred of rights and the most imperative of duties." "When a person
seizes sovereignty, he should be condemned to death by free men."

I believe I have sufficiently justified my point of view. I have
called forth more reasons than the Honorable Prosecutor called forth
to ask that I be condemned to 26 years in prison. All support men
who struggle for freedom and happiness of the people. None support those who oppress the people, revile them, and loot them heart-
lessly. Therefore, I have had to call forth many reasons and he could
not adduce a single one.

How can you justify the presence of Batista in power, since he gained power against the will of the people and by violating the laws of the Republic through the use of treachery and force?

How can you qualify as legitimate a regime of blood, oppression, and ignominy? How can you call a regime revolutionary when it has combined the most backward men, the most backward ideas, and the most backward bureaucracy? How can you consider legally valid the high treason of a court whose mission was to defend our constitution?

With what right do the courts send to prison citizens who tried to redeem their country by giving their own blood—their own lives?

All this is monstrous in the eyes of the nation and is monstrous according to the principles of true justice. . . .

Justice Twice Raped by Force

Honorable Magistrates, I am that humble citizen who one day came in vain to punish the power-hungry men who had violated the law and had torn our institutions to shreds. Now that it is I who am accused, for attempting to overthrow this *illegal* regime and *to restore the legitimate constitution,* I am held for 76 days and am denied the right to speak to anyone, even to my son; guarded by two heavy machine guns, I am led through the city. I am transferred to this hospital to be tried secretly with the greatest severity; and the prosecutor with the Code in his hand, solemnly demands that I be sentenced to 26 years in prison.

You will answer that on the former occasion the court failed to act because force prevented them from doing so. Well then—confess: this time force will oblige you to condemn me. The first time you were unable to punish the guilty: now you will be compelled to punish the innocent. The maiden of justice twice raped by force!

History Will Absolve Me

I come to the close of my defense plea but I will not end it as lawyers usually do—asking that the accused be freed. I cannot ask freedom for myself while my comrades are suffering in the ignominious prison of *Isla de Pinos.* Send me there to join them and to share their fate. It is understandable that honest men should be dead or in prison in this Republic where the president is a criminal and a thief. . . .

I know that imprisonment will be as hard for me as it has ever been for anyone—filled with cowardly threats and wicked torture. But I do not fear prison, just as I do not fear the fury of the miserable tyrant who snuffed life out of 70 brothers of mine.

Sentence me. I don't mind. *History will absolve me.*

CHAPTER 6

Invasion from Mexico

Fidel Castro was sentenced to 15 years in prison. Raúl got 13 years, and the other defendants shorter terms. In October 1953, they were all together again in the penitentiary on the Isle of Pines.

For seven months there, Fidel was in solitary confinement. Finally, granted regular prison privileges, he set up a school for his fellow-prisoners which he named Abel Santamaría Academy in honor of one of the leaders of the Moncada assault who had been captured, tortured, and murdered. He taught history and philosophy, and in his spare time studied English and re-read the works of Martí.

Batista, meanwhile, was having his troubles. The persistent outcry against his usurpation of power made him uncomfortable. The people were restive, and active opposition to his regime in the form of strikes and demonstrations continued—in spite of the terror. On the wall of the Malecón one day he saw painted in red in letters a foot high "July 26, 1953." He was furious—and his craving for acceptance and respectability grew. Two weeks after the Inter-American Press Association, at a meeting in Mexico City, denounced his censorship, he felt constrained to abolish it. Then he announced his candidacy for President in a "free, open, honest election," to be held on November 1, 1954. His opponent was to be former president Ramón Grau San Martín. But the people were not taken in. In Santiago in the campaign that followed, when the candidates arose to speak, the crowds shouted "Viva Fidel Castro! Free Fidel Castro!"

A campaign for a general amnesty for all political prisoners and exiles was begun. Fidel's fellow members in the Cuban Bar Association became active, and the pressure grew. It continued after Grau's withdrawal from the presidential contest and the inauguration of Batista for a four-year term on February 24, 1955. Elected government officials, under pressure from their constitu-

ents, advised Batista that to grant amnesty was
enhance his popularity and smother the smolderi
This, the dictator had a longing for.

News of a possible amnesty was received by
with joy. But they would not accept it if the off͟e ͟   ͟   ͟ ͟ ͟ ͟ to be
hedged with conditions. They would not compromise with the
tyrant even at the price of their freedom. Fidel made this clear
in a letter to a journalist friend written in March 1955:

It is now proper that we too answer civically the moral demand
made upon us by the regime in declaring that there will be an amnesty if the prisoners and the exiled will show the right attitude and
make a tacit or express agreement to respect the government. . . .

Let the lives of those in power be examined, and it will be found
that they are filled with shady activities, fraud, and ill-gotten for-
tunes. Let them be compared with those who have died in Santiago
de Cuba or are here in prison, unstained by dishonor. Our personal
freedom is an inalienable right as citizens born in a country which
does not acknowledge lords of any kind.

We can be deprived of those rights and of everything else by
force, but nobody will ever succeed in getting us to accept enjoyment
of those rights through an unworthy agreement. Thus, we shall not
yield one atom of our honor in exchange for our freedom. . . .

After twenty months we are as firm and unmoved as on the first
day. We do not want an amnesty at the price of dishonor.

The prisoners dictated the terms of their release to their jailer
—and got away with it! On May 2 the Cuban Congress passed
a bill of amnesty which was signed by Batista 11 days later. On
May 15, 1955, Fidel and all his comrades walked out of the
prison into the waiting arms of their relatives and friends.

The crowds that cheered the train en route to Havana, the
demonstration in the station where university students sang the
Cuban national anthem and carried Fidel on their shoulders to
the platform, the newspapermen and photographers who awaited
his arrival at his sister's apartment, were proof that, in spite of
the censorship, the July 26th Movement had become a legend in
Cuba. But Batista had no intention of letting that legend grow
into a menace. Fidel was news. He was invited to speak on the
radio—but Batista's Minister of Communications would not let

m speak. He had no outlet for getting his message to the people. He was watched constantly. It became clear that the struggle to overthrow Batista had to take another form—a form he had planned while in prison.

In July, 1955, Fidel went to Mexico to gather arms and men for an invasion of Cuba.

Raúl was waiting there for him. Other July 26th fighters soon turned up, and more Cubans came to join the ranks. In the United States—in Tampa, Miami, Union City, Bridgeport, and New York—there were colonies of Cubans to whom the message of a free Cuba could be brought, and from whom money could be raised. Fidel went on a speaking tour. He met with exiled rich Cubans in private, and poor Cubans in big mass meetings. At Palm Gardens in New York he told his audience that his program for Cuba went beyond merely ridding the country of the tyrant:

The Cuban people want something more than a mere change of command. Cuba earnestly desires a radical change in every field of its public and social life. The people must be given something more than liberty and democracy in abstract terms. Decent living must be made available to every Cuban; the state cannot ignore the fate of any of its citizens who were born and grew up in the country. There is no greater tragedy than that of the man capable and willing to work, suffering hunger together with his family for lack of work. The state is unavoidably bound to provide him with it or to support him until he finds it. None of the armchair formulas being discussed today include a consideration of this situation; as though the grave problem of Cuba comprised only how to satisfy the ambition of a few politicians who have been ousted from power or who long to get there.

Fidel returned to Mexico City with his pockets bulging. The tour had netted $50,000 in cash and pledges. Now arms could be bought and the invasion "army" which had grown to 80 men could be trained. Fidel found the ideal person for the training job. He was Colonel Alberto Bayo, a Cuban 63 years of age whose parents had taken him as a child to Madrid where he graduated from both the Infantry Academy and the Military Aviation School. He had had years of experience in guerrilla warfare as a

Captain in the Spanish Foreign Legion fighting the African Moors. He had served in the anti-Franco forces in the Spanish Civil War, then returned to Cuba, and later became an instructor in the Military Air Academy at Guadalajara. When Fidel met him, he was running a furniture factory in Mexico City.

Guerrilla warfare is both a science and an art, and in Colonel Bayo the scientist and artist were combined. While he was looking for a suitable place for field training, he visited the men daily in the ten apartments in which they were housed in different sectors of Mexico City, and gave them theoretical instruction. Fortunately, it wasn't long before he was able to locate the right spot where their training in the field could begin. It was a ranch in the district of Chalco, up in the mountains, six miles long and ten miles wide, covered in part with jungle growth. The expeditionary force moved there with all the arms and ammunition that had been bought. In three months of intense work they learned from Colonel Bayo what it would have taken three years to learn in a military school.

They learned how to shoot with pistols, rifles, and machine guns; how to make bombs—and how to use them in blowing up a barricade or destroying a tank; how to spot and bring down enemy aircraft; how to camouflage and take cover; how to carry a wounded comrade and care for him; how to march through the jungle and see and hear without being seen or heard. All this and much more they learned on forced marches up the mountains and in the jungles, carrying full packs, running, crawling, lying still, marching—for five hours, ten hours, fifteen hours a day. They learned how to harass the enemy, to bewilder him, to attack and withdraw, attack, disappear, return, wear him down. They learned discipline—and comradeship.

When their course was completed, the students were graded by Colonel Bayo. The top student in the class was Ernesto "Ché" Guevara, Argentinian-born physician who had spent a good part of his life fighting for justice and against dictatorship. He had fought against Perón in Argentina and for Arbenz and land reform in Guatemala; in Mexico he had met Raúl, then Fidel, and had enlisted in their army against Batista, as a soldier not as a doctor.

That he was to make an excellent soldier was now confirmed by Colonel Bayo.*

Fidel had taken as much of the field training course as was possible, but his other responsibilities kept him away from Chalco part of the time. On one unhappy occasion, in June 1956, he was en route to the ranch from Mexico City with a car full of weapons when he was halted by the police who were after some thieves who had gotten away. The weapons were found, the ranch at Chalco was raided, and all the arms and ammunition were confiscated. With 23 others, Fidel was clapped into the Mexican immigration jail and held for 23 days.

This was only one of a series of arrests, and jail sentences, and losses of weapons for Fidel while he was in Mexico. The Mexican police had been tipped off—and paid off—by Cuban Embassy officials; Batista spies and secret service agents were after him also and much of his time was spent in eluding them. Nevertheless, on November 15, 1956, to the dismay of Colonel Bayo, he announced his intention to invade Cuba and overthrow the dictator. When Bayo reminded his pupil that one of the military principles stressed in the training school was to keep your plans secret from the enemy, Fidel replied: "You taught me that but in this case I want everyone in Cuba to know I am coming. I want them to have faith in the 26th of July Movement. It is a peculiarity all my own although I know that militarily it might be harmful. It is psychological warfare."

Ten days later, the invasion army, 82 strong, carrying rifles, machine guns, ammunition, medicines, and extra supplies of food were aboard the yacht *Granma* on the way to Niquero, west of Santiago de Cuba. On November 30, they were to be met at their landing place by a rebel farmer named Cresencio Pérez, with trucks and 100 men; they were to proceed to Manzanillo where, with other rebel forces waiting there, they would attack the army. Meanwhile, as a diversion, rebel sympathizers would create confusion by bombings and shooting in Holguín, Matanzas, Santiago, and other places. The invading force, with their newly-acquired

* In 1960, Ché Guevara published a manual on guerrilla warfare entitled *La Guerra de Guerrillas*.

supplies, weapons, and ammunition seized from the army at Manzanillo, would be guided by Pérez to a hideout in the Sierras
where they would outfit the hundreds of volunteers who would
join them there. This would be followed, the invaders hoped, by
a general strike throughout Cuba, leading to the downfall of
Batista.

That was the plan. It didn't work.

The 58-foot yacht designed to carry eight passengers and crew
was overloaded with 82 men, arms, supplies, and extra gallons of
gas. The clutch of the engine had needed fixing, but there had
been no time to do it—now, at high speed it would slip. The seas
were rough and water dashed over the deck; the pump didn't work
and the men, who were miserably seasick, had to bail out water.
The voyage was a nightmare of horror.

On invasion day, November 30, they learned via their radio
which could receive but not transmit messages, that the attack
on Santiago and Holguín had gone off as scheduled—and they
were still at sea!

Early on the morning of December 2, the man at the wheel
fell overboard. The choppy water and the darkness made it impossible to locate him, so a light was turned on, he was found and
pulled on board—and another hour was lost. They cruised along
and at Belie, a small fishing village not far from Niquero, the
yacht went aground and could not be budged. They were near the
shore but the waves were fairly high and the bottom muddy, so
Fidel ordered each man to forget about the extra supplies and
save himself. The heavy equipment, explosives, extra ammunition,
food, and medicines had to be left behind.

The men got ashore—after four hours of sloshing through
the mud. Now they were safe—all 82 of them—but they didn't
know where they were! They knew only that wherever it was, with
that early morning light having pierced the darkness and with the
Granma aground, they had to get away fast, despite their
exhaustion.

"We will go to the mountains," Fidel said, "We have arrived in Cuba, and we will be triumphant."

It didn't seem that way to the men, then or in the perilous

days that followed. The *Granma* had been spotted and now Batista aircraft were flying overhead and army patrols were after them. They had no water, no food, no guides. They had only their training with Colonel Bayo—that was what kept alive those who survived the next few weeks.

They marched by night and rested by day. Occasionally they were lucky enough to come upon a farmhouse where they could get food and drink. (They always paid for what they got—a new experience for the *campesinos* with men in uniform).

On December 5, they arrived at a sugar plantation called Alegría del Pío. They bathed and rested, ate their ration of half a sausage and a cracker, slept, cleaned their rifles. Suddenly they were raked by machine gun fire and bombed and strafed by planes. They rushed into the cane for cover but the firing continued and the field was set afire by fragmentation bombs. Here they suffered their first casualties; several men were killed, others were wounded. Ché Guevara got a bullet in the neck but he continued to fight and to give first aid to the wounded around him. Fidel ordered the men to divide up into small units and get away as best they could.

Some of the groups succeeded in breaking out of the trap only to be caught later and killed. Others escaped and remained alive after enduring terrible hardships. Fidel and two companions got away and remained hidden in other cane fields. They lived for five days without food or water—their only nourishment the juice of the cane. So with Raúl and three men with him—they lived for eight days on cane juice, then found themselves a cave in the foothills of the mountains where a *campesino* brought them water, rice, and beans.

A few days later they stumbled on Fidel's party. René Rodríguez, one of the men with Raúl, later related what happened when the two groups were united.

"The days of the dictatorship are numbered!" Fidel assured the six men. Rodríguez look at him with astonishment.

"This man is crazy," he thought to himself. "I was very mad with Fidel because after all we had just been through, with many of our men lost, Fidel stands there telling us with complete confidence that the days of the dictatorship are numbered."

Twenty-two men survived the expedition. Of these, ten were imprisoned in the Isle of Pines and only twelve reached Pico Turquino, the topmost peak in the Sierra Mountains. They were led there by guides sent by Cresencio Pérez as soon as he learned from the farmers in the Sierra that the government radio reports were lies, that it was not true that the expeditionary force had been wiped out and Fidel Castro killed. The twelve who made it were: Fidel Castro, Raúl Castro, Ché Guevara, Camilo Cienfuegos, Calixto García, Faustino Pérez, Calixto Morales, Universo Sánchez, Efigenio Almejeiras, Ciro Redondo, Juan Almeida, and René Rodríguez.

With these 12 men on the top of the mountain that Christmas of 1956, Fidel Castro still believed he could make his revolution. He had every reason to despair, to accept defeat; instead he was buoyant, optimistic, confident. Perhaps René Rodríguez was right—maybe Fidel Castro *was* crazy?

He *was* crazy—as all the great leaders of history have been crazy. He was crazy with the idea that it was his duty—and his destiny—to free Cuba. What he and his men had just gone through was indeed a sore trial; the death of many of his closest friends was truly a heart-rending affliction. Nevertheless, "the days of the dictatorship are numbered," he said.

And so it was.

CHAPTER 7

The Conquest of Power

Twelve men, each with a rifle and ten cartridges, hidden on a mountain top.

An Army, Navy, and Air Force consisting of 30,000 men equipped with the finest modern weapons—machine guns, cannon, tanks, planes—with millions of dollars available to keep supplies of food and arms flowing in a never-ending stream.

That seemed to be the line-up as the two sides got ready for the showdown. But that wasn't really the way the contending forces shaped up. If that had been the whole picture, the twelve men on the mountain could not possibly have won.

The fact was that they weren't just twelve men alone. They had allies everywhere in Cuba, in the mountains and valleys, in the fields, villages, and cities. Some of these men, women, and children were on their side because they had been inspired by Moncada, or Fidel's speech at the trial, or the heroic march into the mountains. Others were on their side because they had always been against tyranny and for a free Cuba. Students who knew the political score and wanted a revolution were on their side from the beginning.

As time went on and the struggle sharpened, more and more groups went over to their side, some merely as sympathetic friends who helped by contributing money, and others who begged, borrowed, or stole a rifle and joined the fighting forces in the mountains, or enrolled in the underground army where the risks were frequently as great.

In the two-year period from Christmas, 1956, when the twelve men were alone on the mountain top until Batista fled and his army surrendered on January 1, 1959, nearly all classes of the population had identified themselves, in varying degrees, with the July 26th Movement. Some became an integral part of it because they believed in its revolutionary program; others made common cause with it because it had become the most effective force in the struggle to overthrow Batista.

By far the most important class that joined the rebels was the peasants. At the beginning, the *campesinos* merely hid the rebels; before many months had passed, the *campesinos*, as a class, were *backing* the rebels. They changed from passive onlookers to active participants. They became one with the revolutionary army.

There were several reasons for this change. One of the most important was the character and conduct of the revolutionary army. Soldiers who wore the uniform of the July 26th Movement were not like the soldiers the *campesinos* had known before. They were friendly and considerate, not arrogant and brutal. They did not pillage and rape; on the contrary, they paid for everything they took, and the penalty for rape in this army was death. The soldiers respected the *campesinos* and helped them.

When the rebels eventually got the materials to construct a field hospital in the Sierra Maestra to care for their wounded, when, at long last, Dr. Julio Martínez Paéz, famous Havana bone specialist, got an X-ray machine, a sterilizer, instruments, drugs, and medicines, then *campesino* families stricken with illness could go to the hospital for treatment. Never before had there been adequate medical care for *campesinos*.

When Ché Guevara set up a school in the mountains, so many *campesino* adults and children attended regularly that the school could not accommodate all who wanted to learn to read and write. Within two years, there were 30 rebel army schools. Never before had the *campesinos* seen a school in the Sierra.

This was indeed a different kind of army—headed by a different kind of commanding officer. Fidel Castro spent time with them, ate with them, talked with them, continually explained, in terms they could understand, what the rebel program was. And since the theory and the practice went hand in hand it was not difficult for the *campesinos* to comprehend that this program was the answer to their needs.

Most important, of course, in winning the *campesinos* to the

revolution was the agrarian reform. Here again they learned tha
this army's program was not just promises—it was promises fu
filled. As the revolutionary army spread out over more and mor
territory, it introduced agrarian reform measures. Fidel tel
about one of the early instances:

> When we arrived at the Sierra Maestra, we executed a ranc
> foreman who had accused tenant farmers and peasants of being pr
> rebel, and who had increased the holdings of his landlord from 1
> acres to 400 acres by taking the land of those he denounced. So w
> tried him and executed him and won the affection of the peasant

Small wonder that the *campesinos* became the backbone c
the revolutionary army. They joined the fighting forces in larg
numbers and they guided the pack trains loaded with supplies c
food, arms, and equipment up the steep mountain trails.

The working class, too, saw in the program of the revolution
ary army an opportunity for a better life. Men in factories an
mines, and women in offices, led double lives—they worked a
their jobs and they worked for the underground army. Witl
home-made bombs they blew up theaters, busses, freight trains
government warehouses, bridges, homes and business offices o
informers; on mimeograph machines in cellars they ran off leaflet
urging the people to help overthrow the dictator; when Che
Guevara asked for materials to set up a rebel newspaper, they
rounded up the necessary supplies of stencils, paper, and ink, anc
soon they were distributing *Cuba Libre* everywhere; with a dyna
mite explosion they blew up the gas and electric main in Havana
cutting off all gas, light, and telephone service and paralyzing the
city for 54 hours; on secret presses they printed "freedom bonds"
in denominations of $1 and up, sold them in every province of
Cuba, and thus added thousands of dollars each month to the
revolutionary treasury.

Those workers who wanted military action were told they
could join the army in the mountains—if they brought their own
weapons. For those with enough money, that was no problem,
but what could a worker do who didn't have the money? In his
book *Castro, Cuba and Justice*, Ray Brennan tells us how some
of them solved the problem:

In Santiago a young soldier came walking down the street one evening. His uniform and boots were gone. So were his sub-Thompson, his .45 revolver, and four grenades he had carried. He was in his underwear, and his wrists were tied behind his back with stout cord.

"Four civilians jumped me, pushed me into an alley, and robbed me," he said. "Well, they didn't exactly rob me. They gave me back my money. They said they didn't want to deprive me personally but that they were taking away the people's property—my uniform, boots, guns, ammunition, and grenades."

There were similar incidents in Bayamo, Manzanillo, Estrada Palma, and other communities with army installations. Rebel sympathizers around the island grinned happily and said: "We have a new supply sergeant—ex-Sergeant Fulgencio Batista. Isn't he the generous one?"

By an odd dialectical process, Batista was a supplier to the rebel cause, not only of arms, but also of men. His army and police took a leaf out of Hitler's book in their treatment of captured rebel soldiers or arrested underground workers. The beatings and the torture were as gruesome as those of the French in Algeria. Those murdered occasionally included completely innocent people—even doctors whose only crime was that they treated the wounded brought to their office. This Batista terror was designed to crush the resistance. It undoubtedly served its purpose of frightening many Cubans into taking no part in furthering the revolutionary cause, but at the same time it unquestionably so enraged many others that it drove them into the anti-Batista movement.

Widespread revulsion against the graft and corruption which characterized the regime also acted as a spur to enlistment in the anti-Batista underground. The exact figure will probably never be known, but it is estimated that Batista himself stole about $400 million. Even businessmen who thought they could live with the payoff and who in many ways profited from it themselves found it was a veritable Frankenstein which threatened to destroy them—so they gave money and other aid to the rebels.

"Corruption was so rife that many of the people who were honest boasted that they, too, were in on it. They preferred to be called rascals than fools." That's what Dr. René Vallejo told us in Cuba in March, 1960. His own story illustrates why honest professional people also flocked into the anti-Batista movement.

Dr. Vallejo was a surgeon who had had graduate training in the United States and served with the American armed forces in Germany in World War II. After the war he returned to Cuba and for three years was head of the public health service in Manzanillo in Oriente. When he arrived, he found the hospital there dirty, run-down, completely stripped of necessary supplies. Patients were admitted only through "pull." When he tried to remedy the conditions at the hospital, and when he posted signs throughout the city that all sick people, rich or poor, were welcome at the hospital, he ran into trouble from the politicians in charge. His personal experience with corruption, favoritism, and graft sent him into the Sierra where he served with such distinction that he became Comandante Vallejo. When we met him he was Chief of Agrarian Reform in the province of Oriente.

While the underground kept Batista's soldiers and police on the jump everywhere in Cuba, the army in the mountains was being expanded with new volunteers and strengthened with fresh supplies of arms and ammunition brought in by plane on landing strips cleared in the jungle by Fidelistas. The new recruits were given a quick Colonel Bayo course in guerrilla warfare, and from time to time units put their learning into practice with quick hit-and-run forays into cities where there were Batista arms depots to be raided. In the Sierra Maestra, Ché Guevara set up industries to provide necessary supplies: bakeries, butcher shops, a shoe factory, a uniform factory, a knapsack factory, ordnance plants. He supervised the construction of more hospitals while Fidel set up additional schools.

There were many setbacks to the anti-Batista movement in 1957. Some of the best underground fighters were caught and put to death; some of the rebel soldiers were lost in battle; a student attempt at assassination of Batista (not approved by Fidel who thought Batista should be brought to justice after his army was defeated) failed, and some brave young men were shot down; a navy revolt was unsuccessful—though it succeeded in proving that even among the Batista armed forces disaffection was growing. Nevertheless, in spite of the losses, there was no question that the movement was gaining strength each day.

That's what Fidel Castro was soon able to tell Batista night after night, beginning on February 24, 1958, when *Radio Rebelde* began broadcasting "from the Territory of Free Cuba in the Sierra Maestra." The people of Cuba had learned to be suspicious of the nightly lies broadcast over the official government radio, but they could get the truth about the progress of the revolution only from hearsay or from the inadequate rebel newspaper. Now they could get the whole story by tuning in on *Radio Rebelde.* They did. Before long *Radio Rebelde* had more listeners than any other station in Cuba.

As he called the roll of Batista's crimes of torture and murder, and warned him that the end was near, Fidel also made a plea to his listeners to refrain from taking personal vengeance on Batista's hangmen when victory was won. Again and again he promised that there was no need for them to kill the Batistianos —they would be tried as war criminals in military courts when the war was over.

From the Free Territory of Cuba, datelined Sierra Maestra, March 12, 1958, came a "Manifesto From The 26th of July Movement To The People." It was signed by Fidel Castro Ruz, Commander in Chief of the Rebel Forces, and Dr. Faustino Pérez, Delegate from Headquarters. The manifesto called Batista a coward because he refused to allow Cuban newspapermen to go to the Sierra Maestra to report on rebel strength; it called for intensified revolutionary action and announced that a general strike would soon be called; it prohibited, beginning April 1, the payment of taxes to state, provincial, or municipal governments; it called upon members of the Batista armed forces to rebel and join the revolutionary army by April 5; it announced the departure from the Sierra Maestra of Major Raúl Castro Ruz with a rebel force to invade the northern part of Oriente, and an invasion under the command of Major Juan Almeida of the eastern part; it announced "a campaign of extermination" beginning April 5, from which date "the war will be relentlessly waged," and said,

"As from this instant, the country should consider itself in total war against the tyranny."

The manifesto was a reflection of the fact that the rebels were now sure they would win. The announced stepping-up of rebel army activity took place—helped tremendously by the landing on a strip in the Sierra of a C-46 plane loaded with automatic weapons, mortar shells, two 50-caliber machine guns, and eighty thousand rounds of ammunition. It was brought by Fidel's boyhood friend, Pedro Miret, one of the heroes of Moncada who had served time in a Mexican prison for having stored rebel weapons, then set up the Cuban Committee in Exile to raise money for arms, and now had flown to his comrade with his precious cargo.

Tipping off Batista that the general strike was imminent—more of Fidel's "psychological" warfare—alerted government forces and enabled them to frighten many workers out of participating in the walkout; Faustino Pérez, in charge of the strike operation, kept the time so secret that many workers weren't informed; some underground operators who had bomb-throwing assignments didn't get the bombs on time. Running a general strike under the best of circumstances is extremely difficult, and in this one serious errors were made. For a variety of reasons, some due to poor planning, others unavoidable, the general strike was a failure. It succeeded, temporarily at least, in Matanzas, Santa Clara, Camagüey, Holguín, and Santiago; but in the key city of Havana it was only partially successful so that troops from Camp Columbia were available to be flown to the other towns where the rebels had momentarily seized power.

The failure of the general strike was a serious blow, and the Batista terror that followed was worse than ever. Pro-rebel morale was at a low ebb everywhere, and it took all of Fidel's wondrous ability as a speaker and leader to revive the people's hopes. Night after night, over *Radio Rebelde*, he got their attention by telling them in detail what the censored Cuban press and radio did not tell them. Mixing bitterness with grief, he gave a detailed catalogue of the dictatorship's continuing atrocities—thus inflaming them to anger again; with his graphic portrayal of stepped-up, ever

more daring exploits of the rebel army and the
underground, he buoyed up their spirits again.

Fidel's success in awakening once more the people
ness of the glory of the struggle infuriated Batista. 1
was goaded into making a fatal mistake. He announced an all-out
campaign to crush the revolutionary army once and for all. This
was precisely what Fidel had hoped for.

On May 5, 1958, the invasion was launched. Twelve thousand
men, more than a third of the regime's total armed strength, were
thrown into the battle. The army had tanks, jeeps, armored cars,
cannon, bazookas, machine guns—all top-notch equipment, most
of it purchased from the United States; the air force carried, in
addition to its ordinary weapons, napalm bombs bought from
Trujillo, Batista's counterpart in the Dominican Republic. Never
before, in Cuban history, had there been so large a movement of
troops and arms.

The odds were 40 to 1—12,000 Batista soldiers against 300
revolutionists in uniform. To offset this overwhelming superiority
in men and weapons, the revolutionary army had three advantages: (1) the battle was to be on its home grounds, a terrain of
rugged mountains and treacherous jungle made to order for
guerrilla warfare and defensive fighting; (2) unlike the government soldiers, the rebel soldiers weren't paid for fighting—they
fought for something they believed in; (3) their leaders were
men of outstanding ability—inspiring, humane, and master
strategists in guerrilla warfare.

The rebel leaders' humanity—and excellent strategy—were
illustrated in the order to the revolutionary army that captured
soldiers were to be treated with kindness, their wounded given
medical attention. They were not held captive but were turned
over to the International Red Cross to be sent back to their homes.
On *Radio Rebelde* Fidel told why this was done: "We do not wish
to deprive these Cubans of the company of their loving families.
Nor, for practical reasons, can we keep them, as our food, cigarettes, and other commodities are in short supply. We hope that the
people of Cuba will understand our position in this respect."

The people of Cuba did understand the position—and liked

it. And captured soldiers, having been fed lying propaganda by their superiors about the horrible death that awaited them if they were taken prisoner, liked it too. They liked it well enough to volunteer military information of importance and, on one occasion, to turn over to the Fidelistas a portable radio transmitter and receiver and government army code book. This was of great value since it enabled the rebels to learn of enemy troop movements in advance—and to be at the right place at the right time. With the captured radio equipment they were able to give instructions to government pilots to bomb—government positions! And to direct supply planes to release their parachute drops of food into the hands of rebel besiegers instead of to the hungry government besieged.

Batista's soldiers soon found that they had no stomach for this war. Fighting in ordered array on a flat plain with the enemy in front of you was one thing, but endlessly climbing mountains with a heavy pack on your back and bullets coming at you from every direction with the enemy nowhere to be seen, that was something else—something they didn't like. And they liked it less when the rains came down and mud and wet and cold nights made life even more miserable.

The war had been going two months when an important victory on another front was announced. There had been several attempts over the years to unite all the various groups and political parties fighting against Batista. These attempts had failed because Fidel would not agree to any program which did not provide for a new government with no ties to the old one; he was not content with having Batista out and the Batista army still powerful enough to set up a successor government in combination with the same old politicos who had governed Cuba in the past; he wanted the war criminals punished; and he wanted a government that would institute economic measures designed to improve the lot of the common people of Cuba.

The united front programs previously offered to him were too weasel-worded to win his confidence; he saw loopholes in them whereby, after the final victory, the same old army and the same old politicians would be carrying on in the same old way. That was why he had refused to go along. But now, on July 20, 1958, an agreement was announced which met with his approval—he had, in fact, written the final draft himself. Fidel signed it for the 26th of July Movement. Other organizations represented were the Organización Auténtico, Directorio Revolucionario, Labor Unity, Partido Cubano Revolucionario (A), Partido Democràta, Federation of University Students, Ex-Army Officers, Montecristi Group, Civic Resistance Movement.

The Communist Party (*Partido Socialista Popular*) had not been invited to sign, though by this time it was supporting the July 26th Movement. When Fidel had first begun his struggle against Batista, the Communist Party had regarded him as a sort of well-meaning adventurer whose tactics could not succeed. The CP maintained that the overthrow of Batista would come not by force of arms, as advocated by Castro, but by mass action (strikes, demonstrations) of the workers and peasants. When the CP saw that in spite of the failure of the general strike, the people still backed Fidel Castro, it changed its tactics and got behind his movement.

One paragraph of the unity pact was of special importance in the light of later events: "And as we ask the government of the United States of America to cease all military and other types of aid to the dictator, we reaffirm our position in defense of our national sovereignty and the nonmilitary, republican tradition of Cuba."

The struggle against Batista had started on the morrow of his *coup* in March 1952. In the years that followed it seemed plain to people all over the world that Batista was a thief and a murderer who should be shunned by decent persons. It was plain to the people of Cuba who had suffered the loss of 20,000 of their finest sons and daughters at the hands of Batista's torturers. But it was not plain to the United States ambassadors to Cuba who were the dictator's pals; and it was not plain to the State Department which disregarded the pleas of eminent Cubans that it stop the shipment of arms to the unlawful government in power. Not until March 1958 was an embargo on arms declared. By that time Cubans who had seen innocent men, women, and children living in defenseless cities slaughtered by American bombs dropped from planes bought in the United States, were filled with hatred for America's pro-Batista policy.

Even *after* the embargo on arms shipments was declared, rockets were delivered to Batista's air force. "This was merely a rectification of a mistake on an order that had been initiated on March 2, 1956" was the explanation of the State Department after the rebels had put it on the spot with the publication of photostats of a Navy Department requisition, dated May 8, 1958, ordering rockets delivered to Batista. The rebels could not be blamed for thinking the "explanation" didn't explain.

They had a right to be cynical about United States protestations of innocence because even after the arms embargo had been put into effect, United States Military Missions were still training Batista's forces. On August 26, 1958, José Miró Cardona, co-ordinator for the unity group, wrote a letter to President Eisenhower in which he pointed out that the agreement whereby United States Army, Navy, and Air Force Missions were sent to Cuba stipulated "that the said Missions would be withdrawn at any time, and the agreement canceled, whenever one of the two countries became involved in domestic or foreign hostilities." Then he went on to say:

It is well known, and both your government and the Cuban government have so recognized it, that our country has been involved in a bloody civil war for almost two years. Nevertheless, the corresponding Departments maintain those Missions in Cuba, which produces deep resentment, since their maintenance, contrary to the spirit and the letter of the agreement, is proof of the moral and material backing offered by the government of the United States of America to the dictatorial regime in Cuba. The North American Missions (Army, Navy, and Air Force) are under the direct orders of the Chief of Staff of the Cuban army, by the terms of the agreement, and it is obvious that they train and support the armed forces of the dictatorship to kill Cubans and to fight against those who struggle to liberate the Fatherland.

No answer from President Eisenhower. Then, almost two months later, on October 13, 1958, came an answer from the State Department. Did it move to put an end to Cuban wrath by ordering the American Missions home? It did not. While proclaiming adherence to the principle of nonintervention in the affairs of Cuba, it argued that the agreement stipulated not that the Missions *must* be withdrawn but only that they *may* be withdrawn, and the United States Government would not withdraw them. Here are the relevant paragraphs:

We have noted your comments regarding the remarks made by President Eisenhower . . . to the effect that the United States believes firmly in the democratic elective process and the choice by the people, through free and fair elections, of democratic governments responsive to them. At the same time, the United States does follow a strict policy of nonintervention in the domestic affairs of our sister American republics, including Cuba. . . .

In your letter you refer to Article 5 of the mission agreements and state that this article "stipulates that the said missions would be withdrawn at any time, and the agreement canceled, whenever one of the two countries became involved in domestic or foreign hostilities." The actual wording of that article reads that the agreements are "subject to cancellation" (i.e. *may* be canceled) under conditions such as you describe so that withdrawal is permissive rather than mandatory as indicated in your letter.

The mission agreements were negotiated in conformity with discussions which had taken place between the two governments on hemispheric military co-operation. The United States government believes that its missions in Cuba are serving the purpose for which they were established. Governments and administrations change from time to time in both Cuba and the United States but hemispheric defense needs present a constant problem the solution of which calls for a co-operative program carried out on a steady, long-range basis.

The Cuban people could not be expected to believe that "hemispheric defense needs" required that the United States should continue to have its military missions teach Batista's soldiers the best ways to kill. They didn't believe it. This State Department answer to their plea further embittered the men who were on the verge of taking power in Cuba. When you read anti-United States Government statements coming from the heads of the Cuban government, don't just attribute it to "the Latin temperament." There are valid reasons—and one of the most important was the spectacle of the United States cooperating with the killer, Batista, to the very end of his regime.

Batista's "extermination campaign" which began on May 5 ended in a rout three months later. The deserters, captured, wounded, and killed added up to ten percent of Batista's army. And a much larger proportion of its weapons—tanks, bazookas, mortars, machine guns, jeeps, ammunition—had been seized by the revolutionary army. The little band of rebels had eluded, out-maneuvered, outfought, and put to flight the 12,000 men who had been sent to "wipe them out."

On *Radio Rebelde* on August 20, 1958, Fidel reported to the people:

Victories in war depend to a minimum on weapons and to a maximum on morale. . . . War is not a simple question of rifles, bullets, guns, and planes. Maybe that belief is one of the reasons why the forces of tyranny have failed. That phrase of Martí that could have been mere poetry: "What matters is not the quantity of weapons at hand but the number of stars on your forehead," has become a profound truth for us.

"Stars on your forehead" was truly of great importance, but what was inside the forehead was also significant. The rebel leaders were military strategists of the first order. They saw that with the Batista army on the run, they must follow up their advantage immediately. This meant leaving their stronghold in the Sierra Maestra and waging the war in open country. It was not enough to have kept the government army from crushing them in the mountains; they had now to meet and defeat that army wherever it was; they had now to conquer all of Cuba.

Despite the defeat of the government army, the revolutionists were still heavily outnumbered in men and weapons. On the plains, sheer numbers could be decisive; enemy planes that had had difficulty spotting rebel units in the mountainous jungle would have no difficulty in open country. Carrying the war to the other provinces of Cuba was obviously what must be done—but it would be the toughest assignment the rebel army had yet faced.

On August 21, 1958, Fidel gave the job to his most able strategist, Ché Guevara, Colonel Bayo's top student. He was to be

supported by Camilo Cienfuegos who had also distinguished himself as a combat leader. They were to march down from the
mountains, through the plains and swamps of the province of
Camagüey, to the province of Las Villas and into its capital city
of Santa Clara. If and when they took and held Santa Clara, Cuba
would be cut in two and the war would soon be won.

Guevara and Cienfuegos picked 250 veterans, battle-tested,
strong, crack shots. In two columns, one along the main highway,
the other to the north, they started their long march. It was tough
going, as they had realized it would be. They had to march through
swamplands in the rainy season, mostly at night to make it more
difficult for the spotter planes guiding enemy bombers, and they
ran into tough resistance when they attacked some of the enemy
forts. Some of their men were killed in battle, but as they proceeded to their objective they picked up more than enough volunteers
to make up for their losses in dead and wounded, and by the
time they reached their goal their army was larger than when it
started. In the Escambray Mountains, Major William Alexander
Morgan, an American, was training more men who would soon
join the rebel fighting forces. And everywhere all over the island,
the underground was busily carrying on its effective sabotage.

On Christmas Eve the people of Cuba heard a new voice on
the radio: "This is Radio Sancti Spíritus in the free territory of
Cuba." Ché Guevara's forces had taken the city. On Christmas
Day, on the Oriente front, Fidel's troops on their way to Santiago
in an offensive that had started six weeks before, entered Palma
Soriano to the northwest. Raúl Castro's men were marching
toward Santiago from the northeastern part of Oriente where they
had been successfully engaged in a mopping-up operation. In
Pinar del Río, the province farthest west, Batista's army was being
harassed by rebel guerrillas based in the mountains of the Sierra
de los Organos. And in the provinces of Havana and Matanzas
army installations were blown up by underground fighters. Everywhere in Cuba Batista's forces were in trouble. There was no
longer any doubt now that the end was near.

On New Year's Eve Cienfuegos, after taking the army fortress
at Yaguajay, was marching toward Santa Clara to help Guevara

who had seized control of the city and was besieging the enemy
fort. Raúl's columns had captured the towns of Guantánamo and
Fidel's troops were a few miles from Santiago. The war was almost
over. Batista knew it—he made his getaway on a plane at 2:10
a.m. on New Year's Day.

In his letter of resignation, announced by his top general
after he fled, Batista had tried one more trick—he had appointed
Dr. Carlos M. Piedra, the senior justice of the Supreme Court, as
President of the Republic. But Fidel Castro, on hearing the news
at 9 a.m. at the front in Oriente, didn't fall for it. He wasn't going
to have a military junta headed by a Batista appointee take over
the country. He notified his commanding officers on all fronts to
continue fighting, and on the radio he told the people not to be
deceived by the attempted *coup d'état* in the capital. He said the
war would continue until there had been unconditional surrender
of the Batista armed forces, and the people were to start a general
strike as soon as they received word from *Radio Rebelde*.

Later that day Major William Morgan received the surrender
of Batista officers at the Naval Station at Cienfuegos and took
command of the city. In Santa Clara, in the decisive battle of the
war, the Batista forces surrendered unconditionally to Ché
Guevara. Before dawn on January 2, Fidel's army marched into
Santiago, and accepted the unconditional surrender of the Batista
forces at Fort Moncada. The red and black flag of the rebel army
was hoisted over the fort where, on July 26, 1953, Fidel Castro
had lost the first battle of the revolution. The war was over.

Fidel and his bearded, victorious army rode in triumph from
one end of the island to the other. The crowds went wild with
joy. The people of Cuba, almost to a man, shouted their admira-
tion and love for their hero, Fidel Castro, aged 32, undisputed
leader of a nation.

An interesting sidelight on how these history-making events
were reported in the American press and radio: Ray Brennan,
Chicago newspaper correspondent, who had covered the war in

Cuba, much of it in the Sierra Maestra, was flat on his back on a hospital bed in Chicago during the final days of the revolution. He followed the news from Cuba with great interest. From a friend with a short wave radio he got the story of the rebel army victories on New Year's Eve—the victories that had convinced Batista he must flee as soon as possible. But the people of the United States who got their news in the ordinary way did not know that the end had come. Their news from Cuba was upside down. That's what Brennan reports on page 261 of his book, *Cuba, Castro and Justice*:

In the United States the newspaper, television, and radio coverage of Cuba was a strange one that evening. A wire-service dispatch from Cuba reported that Batista was winning—or had won, in effect—the war. There were headlines in many newspapers along the line of "Cuban Rebels Routed." The stories had absolutely no basis in fact.

This was not an isolated instance of Cuban white becoming black when reported in the United States—something to remember when you see or hear the "news" about Cuba. On April 21, 1960, Mr. Herbert Matthews, the first writer to interview Fidel Castro in his hideaway in the Sierra Maestra, a member of the editorial board of *The New York Times*, told the American Society of Newspaper Editors:

In my thirty years on The New York Times I have never seen a big story so misunderstood, so badly handled and so misinterpreted as the Cuban revolution.

Mr. Matthews' indictment was perhaps best illustrated in the slanting of the news on the trials of the war criminals which followed the victory of the revolutionary army. American readers were led to believe that Fidel Castro was a monster who had turned on a blood bath in Cuba. The exact opposite was the case. Fidel *prevented* a blood bath. On the radio after Batista had fled, as he had done before on many occasions over *Radio Rebelde*, Fidel appealed to the people of Cuba to act in a disciplined fashion and not take justice into their own hands. In return, he promised speedy trial and punishment for the war criminals. Had his appeal not been effective, had the people not been restrained from wreaking personal vengeance on the torturers and murderers, then rioting and anarchy would have followed inevitably, and the streets of Cuba would have run red with blood.

This was the considered opinion of Father P. Inaki de Aspiazu, a Basque Catholic priest who escaped from a Franco prison in the Spanish Civil War, and on the advice of his Bishop went into voluntary exile in Argentina. The Franco government has refused to let him return to Spain. In an article entitled "Revolutionary Justice" written on February 8, 1960, on the occasion of his second visit to Cuba, Father Aspiazu wrote:

I have returned to Cuba. For the second time, I have had the impression of having broken through a blockade which encircles the island. A blockade invisible and impalpable, without sentinels and without armies, but closed at all cardinal points. It is a blockade formed by news dispatches, which impede seeing the truth of Cuba from the outside. Behind it, in all of Latin America, I have left numerous friends who received joyfully the victory of the Revolution and today adopt an attitude of doubt and suspicion, when not of hostility.

They are the victims of counter-revolutionary propaganda. . . . I have on my table letters and cables from friends not a little disturbed and even somewhat scandalized by the reports which I send from the encircled island. It is not surprising. Something of the sort occurred to me twenty years ago, when the Basque people struggled to defend their liberty and world opinion, agitated by the news agencies, believed with all sincerity that we had allied ourselves with Communism.

Very few believed what I affirmed against such calumny. In the best of cases, I was considered naive and an unconscious "fellow traveler." Nevertheless the truth about Cuba is in Cuba and not outside of Cuba.

I have a long experience in revolutionary justice. I have seen it and also suffered it in the governmental and rebel zone of Spain during the Civil War; in France, under the Hitlerian oppression and after the liberation, in Italy and in other countries of Europe, without forgetting Nuremberg. These examples of justice, compared to that realized by the Revolution which came out of the Sierra Maestra, are a monstrous inequity. No revolution, nor postwar Europe of this century, can present a complete list of the condemned and of their respective sentences, as can the Revolutionary Government of Cuba.

And it should be noted that the psychological conditions of the country were not very favorable . . . mothers, wives, children of 20,000 assassinated by the most cruel dictatorship in Latin America flocked into the streets. It was to be expected—we all who have had these horrible experiences feared it—that the victims would become avengers, that those who had come out of their hiding places with feline instinct would take direct justice, that houses would be sacked and plazas bloodied by the popular fury. Thanks to the wise campaign directed by Fidel from the Sierra Maestra, seconded by his people in the villages and the cities, the people of Cuba gave a high lesson in civic responsibility—incomparably superior to that of the European peoples. What had been feared did not occur here. The Cubans deposited their confidence in their leaders. They maintained serenity. They left to the tribunals the carrying out of justice. And justice consisted in organizing trials . . . in condemning to death those convicted of assassination, in imprisoning those authors of other grave crimes. There were almost 700 shot, and there are at present some 2,500 prisoners, none of whom was mistreated and whose number descends steadily in the measure that the condemned carry out their sentences.

Their treatment of army prisoners during the war had already proved that Fidel Castro and the other rebel leaders were humanitarians—not the bloodthirsty monsters they were depicted in press and radio following the trials. In fact, it was their very humanity which made them revolutionists in the first place. And it was their very humanity which dictated the program they instituted after their conquest of power—a program designed to alleviate the misery of their less fortunate countrymen.

PART III

THE
REVOLUTION
IN POWER

CHAPTER 8

The Revolutionary Regime

A revolution is a process, not an event. It unfolds through many stages and phases. It never stands still. What is true of it today may be untrue tomorrow and vice versa. Description and analysis cannot possibly do justice to the reality, and there is always the danger that they will falsify the reality. All of these statements apply in full measure to the Cuban Revolution, and we ask our readers to keep them in mind as we embark upon the difficult task of characterizing the new regime which came to power on January 1, 1959. This is the more important since bourgeois reportage and scholarship, which inevitably furnish and at the same time color a large part of the available information, are constitutionally incapable of understanding historical phenomena in their development, that is to say dialectically, and hence must interpret them irrationally, in terms of surprise or catastrophe or both.

To begin with, it needs to be stressed that the regime which came to power on January 1, 1959, is by no means identical with the regime that is in power at the time of writing in May of 1960. In fact, hardly anything about it is the same—its personnel, its organization, its aims, even the personality of its leaders have all undergone more or less radical changes. Fidel Castro himself has learned much and changed accordingly in the brief period of less than a year and a half. Not only must we recognize these changes but even more important we must attempt to understand the forces which have produced them and are still operating. Otherwise, we shall stumble into the usual bourgeois pitfalls: we, too, will see in future developments only a series of surprises and catastrophes.

The power behind the new regime which took over the government of Cuba on January 1, 1959, was the rebel army, and this remains as true today as it was then. To understand what has happened during this period we must therefore first of all understand the character and role of the rebel army. This is, of course, a subject which has already been touched upon and to which we will recur again. For present purposes, three points must be singled out and emphasized: (1) The rebel army was and remains essentially a peasant army. (2) The Cuban peasantry is a remarkably revolutionary force. (3) Fidel Castro is first and foremost the undisputed and absolutely trusted leader of the army* and as such the embodiment of the revolutionary will and energy of the peasantry. Let us comment on these points in turn.

(1) The peasant character of the rebel army was determined by, and in turn shaped, the whole course of the Revolution from the time when Castro and his companions first established themselves in the Sierra Maestra in 1956. The original band was made up of young people, mostly students, drawn from a variety of classes and social milieus, but the recruits who rallied around the revolutionary banner which they raised were overwhelmingly of peasant origin. No exact statistics on this are available, of course, but we found a remarkable consensus among those we were able to question who had been in the Sierra Maestra that three fourths to four fifths of the soldiers who participated in the final victorious campaigns of 1958 were peasants. The proportion was undoubtedly smaller among the officers, but even in the highest ranks we would estimate that the majority were peasants.** Castro himself has repeatedly stressed the peasant character of the rebel army and paid tribute to the vanguard role of the peasants in winning and consolidating the Revolution. For example, speaking in Havana on October 26, 1959, at a huge rally called to protest

---

* Cuban practice is to speak of the present army as either the rebel army or the revolutionary army to distinguish it from the old, and now completely liquidated, army of the Batista dictatorship. It seems justified to omit the qualifying adjectives where the context makes quite clear which army is being referred to.

** The highest rank in the rebel army is *Comandante,* equivalent to Major in our military hierarchy. This is in sharp contrast to the old army which was topheavy with colonels and generals.

the bombing of the capital city by Florida-based planes, Fidel had the following to say:

Peasant detachments are the most efficient units of the army, peasants are the best soldiers of the revolutionary army. The small group of officers who expressed solidarity with the traitor Hubert Matos did not belong to this class of soldiers, were not soldiers and officers of peasant origin, who are the flower and heart of the most efficient, brave, and hard core of our revolutionary army.

To understand the full implication of this, one must recall that Hubert Matos, commander of the garrison in the city of Camagüey, had at that time just been arrested, along with a number of other officers, for conspiring against the regime. Matos had been a school teacher and is reputed to have had large personal ambitions. The arguments which he and his fellow oppositionists advanced were based on the by-now familiar charge that Communists were gaining control of the government. By explicitly denying that these officers were of peasant origin, and at the same time praising the peasant-soldiers as the flower of the revolutionary army, Fidel was in effect proclaiming the peasant character of the regime and declaring his own faith that in any showdown it would be the peasant-soldiers who would safeguard the Revolution against its enemies. Everything we were able to learn in Cuba confirms the correctness of this interpretation.

(2) From the political point of view, the most important thing to keep in mind about the Cuban peasantry is that "those who work for wages make up the bulk of the rural population of Cuba." The Census of 1953 counted a total "economically active population" of 1,972,266. Of this number, 221,939, or 11.3 percent, were listed as farmers and ranchers; and 568,799, or 28.8 percent, were listed as farm laborers. In other words, about 40 percent of gainfully occupied Cubans were in agriculture; and within the agricultural labor force, wage workers outnumbered owners and tenants of various kinds by nearly three to one. These figures do not imply, however, that the typical farm was run by an operator hiring three workers. On the contrary, the vast majority of agricultural units were subsistence farms utilizing family labor exclusively. Judging from the special Agricultural Census

of 1946—the figures are not strictly comparable to those of 1953
—we may safely estimate that before the Revolution no more than
one farmer out of five employed wage workers, and that the vast
majority of workers were employed on the large estates (250 acres
and up) which, as was pointed out on page 9 above, were only 8
percent of the total number of farms but included 70 percent
of the farm acreage.

The typical Cuban agriculturalist, then, is not a peasant in
the usual European sense of the term but rather a landless pro-
letarian who customarily works for wages in groups or gangs
under the direction and supervision of others. Occupying this lowly
economic status, he has traditionally been the forgotten man of
Cuban society. For the most part employed only a few months
during the sugar, tobacco, or coffee harvests, he has barely managed to exist the remainder of the year. He himself is more than
likely illiterate, and before the Revolution there was probably no
school for his children to attend. "It is well known in Cuba,"
Lowry Nelson wrote a decade ago, "that there are extensive
rural areas where no schools exist and where the children grow up
without benefit of any education." Even the Church has consistently neglected him. To quote Nelson again, "In Cuba the
church plays only a minor role among farm people." And he
adds in a significant footnote: "The chapels of both Protestants
and Roman Catholics are located, without exception as far as the
writer could ascertain or observe, in the cities and towns. Yet
Cuban farmers live generally in the open country. Their contact
with churches is therefore minimized. Their attitudes suggest general indifference, a condition which is widely recognized." The
reason for existence of the Cuban peasant under the old order was
thus very simply to be exploited for the benefit of others. Beyond
that, no one—neither his employer nor the state nor the Church—
thought enough about him even to attempt to instill in him the
ruling ideologies and values of Cuban society.

It will be readily seen that this was an almost perfect formula
for making revolutionaries. But there is also an additional factor
tending to revolutionize the Cuban peasantry, a factor which, so
far as we are aware, does not exist to the same extent in any other

country, namely, the existence *in the countryside* of a highly developed *industrial* proletariat composed of the workers in the 161 sugar mills which are located in the middle of cane-growing areas all over the island. The standard statistical sources, in giving the number of sugar workers, fail to distinguish between the field and mill workers, so that it is impossible to say precisely how large the rural industrial proletariat is at the present time. But the Foreign Policy Association's 1935 report cites a figure of 58,500 for that time, and this is doubtless the right order of magnitude still. These workers live in close proximity to the field workers, and there is probably a considerable degree of mobility between the groups; they work in highly mechanized plants; and they have a long record of unionism and militant labor action. We have not run across any study of the relations between mill and field workers, and we had no opportunity to undertake one in the brief time we were in Cuba. Nevertheless, we find it quite plausible to assume that their juxtaposition and their common dependence on the same large corporations, many of them foreign-owned, have had important effects on both groups, raising the level of culture and class consciousness of the field workers and disposing the mill workers—and through them the rest of the labor movement—to cooperate more closely, both economically and politically, with the peasantry.

The foregoing of course relates to revolutionary potential, not to revolutionary action. To be sure, the Cuban peasantry has on various occasions in the past, most notably in the abortive revolution of 1933-34, displayed its capacity for action. But it has never developed or found a leadership of its own, and its hopes for genuine reform or improvement have always been quickly disappointed. This has led to an attitude of apparent passivity and cynicism which has misled many observers into a complete misunderstanding of the real aspirations and potentialities of what is perhaps one of the world's most deeply revolutionary classes. To put the matter in its simplest terms, what the Cuban peasantry needed was Fidel Castro. When it found him it revealed for the first time its true revolutionary nature.

(3) How did it come about that Castro, himself the son of a

fairly big landowner, found his destiny in the leadership of a revolutionary peasant movement? The answer to this question can be divided into three parts. In the first place, Castro clearly has all the natural qualifications of a great leader: he is the kind of person who could have made his mark on history in any age or any country. Second, the political philosophy of equality and social justice and the programmatic ideas stressing agrarian reform and industrialization, which he acquired or worked out during his student days, were precisely suited to the circumstances and needs of the Cuban peasantry. (We have already discussed this aspect of Castro's development in Chapters 4 and 5 above: the reader is particularly referred to the relevant passages quoted from *History Will Absolve Me*.) And third, the revolutionary strategy chosen by or forced on Fidel and his friends—the "invasion" from Mexico and the establishment of a guerilla movement in the Sierra Maestra —was completely dependent for success on their ability to inspire, organize, and hold peasant support. Whether or not he deliberately "planned it that way," there can thus be no doubt that the ideas which Fidel espoused and the strategy he pursued made it inevitable that the more successful he was the more deeply he would be committed to the leadership of a peasant revolution.

The revolutionary marriage between Castro and the peasantry did not take place over night, nor was it of a directly political character in its early stages. The Cuban peasant had been deceived by political thieves and swindlers too many times in the past to fall for mere declarations, however fine-sounding they might be; and Fidel's immediate problems were overwhelmingly of a military nature. As we pointed out in Chapter 7, the early contacts were therefore tentative and practical, having to do with such matters as the provisioning of the guerilla troops. From the outset it was the Fidelistas' policy to pay for everything they acquired and in general to treat the civilian population with the utmost consideration (the inhabitants of the Sierra Maestra, it should be borne in mind, are probably the poorest and most neglected stratum of the Cuban peasantry). Out of these practical dealings, there gradually grew feelings of mutual confidence, and this in turn led the peasants to believe in Fidel's policies and program, not because he said what they wanted to hear (though he did that too) but *because their own experience taught them that he meant what he said*. At no time and in no way has Fidel betrayed this trust which the peasants, first of the Sierra Maestra and later of the whole island, came to repose in him. Agrarian reform, the heart of his revolutionary program, actually began in the Sierra during the period of civil war and was proclaimed for the whole country in a rebel law as early as October 10, 1958. And, as we shall see later, the definitive Agrarian Reform Law of May 17, 1959, constitutes an historic fulfillment of an oft-reiterated pledge dating back to that day in 1953 when Fidel, standing alone on trial in Santiago, declared his faith that, however his judges might decide, history would absolve him.

Having overcome their initial reserve, the peasants in increasing numbers joined the rebel army or organized the various civilian links and services which are so crucial to the success of a guerilla movement. In the circumstances of the time, the distinction between political activity and military activity was completely dissolved. The rebel army governed liberated territory; fought directly against Batista's troops; and, both openly through the propaganda broadcasts over *Radio Rebelde* and clandestinely through the underground, mobilized the population at large for the final struggle against the tyranny. As long as the civil war lasted, in other words, the rebel army was a government, a military force, and a political party all wrapped up in one. Its supreme and undisputed leader was Fidel Castro, and by the time it came down out of the hills to complete the conquest of power in the entire country, there existed between the leader and the peasant officers and soldiers who constituted, in his own words, the "flower and heart" of the army, a truly most remarkable relation of solidarity, trust, and understanding. Nothing that has happened in Cuba since can be properly understood if this basic fact is lost sight of.

With this background we can deal much more briefly with the subject broached at the opening of this chapter, namely, the character of the regime which took over in all of Cuba on January 1, 1959. The real power, we know, was in the rebel army and in Fidel Castro as its supreme commander. Moreover, at that historic juncture, Fidel found himself to be not only the leader of the army but also the fantastically popular symbol and hero of a genuinely national uprising against the monstrous Batista tyranny (by the end all but the hopelessly compromised had turned against the dictator). Nothing would have been easier, or in a sense more natural, than for Fidel and his closest associates to take over the presidency, the prime ministership, and the other leading positions and thus to establish themselves as the provisional government.

This is not what happened, however. Fidel's propaganda had long stressed the theme that he was making the revolution for the good of Cuba and not, in the traditional manner of Cuban politicians, to gain office and line his pockets. While the civil war was still on he had announced that his candidate for President was Manuel Urrutia, a judge who played an honorable role at the time of the attack on Moncada in 1953. He stuck to this decision and seems to have been at least partly guided by Urrutia's wishes in the selection of cabinet personnel. The Prime Minister was José Miro Cardona, head of the Havana Bar Association and Secretary General of the Unity Movement, and the Foreign Minister was Roberto Agramonte who had been Prío's candidate for the presidency in the 1952 election which was never held because of Batista's *coup d'etat*. Other important positions were occupied by Luis Orlando Rodríguez (Interior), a newspaper owner; Humberto Sorí Marín (Agriculture), a lawyer; and Manuel Ray (Public Works), the engineer in charge of construction of the Havana Hilton Hotel. All the members of the new government had been active in one way or another against Batista, some had even been on Fidel's staff in the Sierra, but the most prominent among them were not part of the inner circle which led the rebellion and enjoyed the full confidence of the army. For the most part they seem to have been chosen because they were honest men, well known in their respective businesses and professions. In any case, the aspect which the Cuban Revolution first presented to the world was that of a quite respectable middle-class regime. Not surprisingly, this fact gave rise to many misunderstandings, both then and later.

Whether or not Fidel thought this was a stable or durable situation we do not know. If he did, he was very naive and was soon to learn better. The real power, as we have said, remained in his hands and nothing important could be decided without him. A sort of dual system of government began to emerge, with Fidel on one side and Urrutia and the cabinet on the other. The result, of course, was inefficiency, delay, confusion. Miro soon saw the impossibility of going on this way and offered his resignation as early as January 17, at the same time recommending that Fidel become Prime Minister. But Fidel held back, and it was not until nearly a month later that he finally yielded.

From an organizational point of view, Fidel's accession to the Prime Ministership improved matters, but it went only a little way toward resolving the paradox between the essentially revolutionary character of the regime and the predominantly liberal-to-conservative personnel which represented it before the world. The political history of the first year of the Revolution, officially known as the "Year of Liberation," can be thought of as centering around this problem.

Fidel had made his promises and was determined to carry them out, faithfully and to the letter. In this he had the full backing of the army and of the peasantry behind it, and growing support among urban workers who in increasing numbers were now discovering through their own experience what the peasants had already learned, that when Fidel Castro pledged action in the interests of the people, and not a mere reshuffle of officeholders, he really meant it. To be sure, some of the measures which were put through in the early days commanded widespread approval among most classes of the population, and for this reason caused no sharp divisions in the government. This was especially true of what may be called the price-control laws: rent reductions up to 50 percent for apartments costing under $100 a month, a relatively low ceiling on real estate prices, reductions in telephone and electricity rates and in the price of medicines, and so on. Other measures, too, were relatively uncontroversial, such as those designed to recover for the nation the ill-gotten gains of Batista's henchmen, to root out corruption from government and business, to suppress gambling (except in the luxury hotels and nightclubs), to reform the tax system, and to institute a variety of New Deal-type programs in such fields as education, housing, and health. As long as legislation was confined to such matters as these, no insuperable difficulties arose, though it is clear that friction began to develop quite early between radicals and conservatives, represented chiefly by Fidel on the one side and Urrutia on the other.

That the situation was really untenable only began to appear clearly when the Revolution moved on to measures aiming at basic changes in the Cuban economy and social structure. In this respect, by far the most important event was the passage on May 17, 1959, of the Agrarian Reform Law.* Up to this point, not only were relations within the government reasonably amicable, but (and this is very closely related) relations between Cuba and the United States were correct if not exactly cordial. Cuban liberals and conservatives, like their counterparts all over Latin America, are extremely sensitive to United States attitudes and criticism. For the United States there can be no doubt that the real turning point in relations with Cuba came with the Agrarian Reform. When Fidel went to Washington and New York in April, he was given a friendly reception and even received a good deal of favorable publicity in the press and on TV. After May 17, his stock in United States government and business circles rapidly declined and he was soon assigned the role of *bête noire* (or perhaps red devil would be more accurate) which he still occupies today. This change had its counterpart, and to a degree its reflection, in Cuba. Castro's upper-class and middle-class supporters began to fall away and gradually to move into a posture of opposition where they joined the leftovers of the prerevolutionary regime.

Under these circumstances, the make-up of the government was bound to undergo a drastic alteration. One by one the respectable liberals and conservatives were forced out or resigned, to be replaced by loyal veterans of the Sierra Maestra or trusted leaders of the former underground. There is no need to detail the process

---

* This revolutionary measure will be described and its implications analyzed in Chapter 10 below.

here. Suffice it to call attention to two of the landmarks: Fidel's resignation as Prime Minister in mid-July to force the retirement of Urrutia from the presidency (his successor, Osvaldo Dorticós Torrado, is a loyal Castro supporter); and Ché Guevara's assumption of the presidency of the National Bank in November in place of Felipe Pazos. The process of "radicalizing" the government may be said to have been concluded with the resignation as Minister of Finance in March, 1960, of Rufo López Fresquet and his replacement in that important post by Navy Captain Rolando Diaz Astarain who had been in charge of the recovery of ill-gotten gains. Not that there will be no more changes in the personnel of the top government leadership. No doubt there will be: there may even be defections of government leaders from the revolutionary camp. But what happens from now on will be taking place, as it were, from a new base. López Fresquet was the last of the middle-of-the-roaders who were miscast as revolutionaries in the aftermath of the national uprising which toppled the Batista tyranny in the closing days of 1958.

We have spoken of the radicalization of the government in the months between January, 1959, and March, 1960. This is a perfectly accurate characterization of what happened. But it should not be confused with the radicalization of the regime as a whole. No doubt Fidel and his associates learned a great deal during this eventful period; their courage was tested many times; their resolve to carry through the revolution was steeled; the support of peasants and workers was enlarged and deepened. In all these senses, and more, the regime underwent, and is still undergoing, a process of radicalization. But this is a very different thing from the sloughing off of the middle-class respectability with which it was clothed in its earliest infancy. In essence, as we hope we have made clear in all that we have written up to now, the revolution led by Fidel Castro was always a radical revolution aiming at fundamental social change. And from January 1, 1959, to this day the real power has always been in the revolutionary army, manned and nourished by as radical a social class as any in the world today.

The Revolution in Action

In Chapters 2 and 3 we discussed the conditions that caused the Cuban Revolution—poverty and destitution, illiteracy and disease. Behind these were the glaring inequalities, the chronic stagnation, and the heavy unemployment of a one-crop, semi-colonial economy. Needless to say, these were also the problems that faced the revolutionary regime when it came to power. In addition, it had to repair the depredations of Batista and bind up the wounds of civil war. Many were the observers, both in Cuba and abroad, who shook their heads, sadly or gladly as the case might be, and wrote the whole experiment off as a failure before it had even got started. How could a group of hot-headed young idealists with no practical experience in the affairs of government or business hope to solve problems that had long defied the best efforts of their elders?

This question—and many like it which one hears as frequently and insistently today, even though the revolutionary regime has been in power nearly a year and a half—reflects some of the most deeply rooted fetishes of bourgeois thought. Success in practicing the art of government is supposed to depend on special skills which can be acquired only through long experience. Anyone lacking such skills who attempts to govern is courting certain failure. This theory, which is propagated in a thousand subtle ways by respectable social "science," is the perfect rationalization for reserving the functions of government to a traditional ruling class. For the rest, not only is it false as a generalization but in the case of a country like Cuba—and in this respect the vast majority of the countries of the world are very much like Cuba—it is close to being the exact opposite of the truth.

Experience in government in Cuba has traditionally been experience in mismanagement, exploitation, and stealing. Far from solving the problems of the country, government has itself been one of the worst features of a rotten system. Among the greatest *advantages* of the young men and women who fought and won the revolution were that they had indeed had *no* experience of government, that they despised the hopelessly corrupt class that had had such experience, that they were fired by a consuming ambition to do the simple and obvious things that must be done to rescue their fellow countrymen from the misery in which they lived out their lives. Simple and obvious things like reducing the prices charged by profiteers; giving the beggars and prostitutes and waifs who crowded the streets of the capital city a chance to rehabilitate themselves in decent surroundings; building houses for the homeless, schools for the illiterate, and hospitals for the sick; above all, creating year-round jobs for the unemployed and underemployed and in this way not only raising their material standard of living but also giving them for the first time the price-less sense of full membership in the human brotherhood.

Simple and obvious? Yes, a thousand times yes. It takes no profound economic sophistication, no initiation into the secrets of government or administration, to understand what has to be done. What it does require is a sympathy for human beings, a passion for justice, and a vision unclouded by the fetishes and obfuscations of bourgeois ideology. These qualities the young men and women who made the Cuban Revolution have in full measure. They have other qualities, too, no less important, born of the victorious struggle and an unshakeable conviction of the goodness of their cause: dedication, optimism, enthusiasm, boundless energy. To be with these people, to see with your own eyes how they are rehabilitating and transforming a whole nation, to share their dreams of the great tasks and achievements that lie ahead—these are purifying and liberating experiences. You come away with your faith in the human race restored. And that is about the best thing that can happen to a citizen of the United States, or of Western Europe either, in these years of the decline and fall of world capitalism.

Please do not misunderstand us. We are not saying that the appropriate *methods* of accomplishing the great meliorative tasks of the Revolution are simple and obvious. Often they are anything but. Nor are we saying that expert knowledge and hard-learned skills are of no importance. The very opposite is true. Furthermore, the Cuban revolutionaries themselves are the first to admit and deplore their shortcomings in these respects. But let us be clear about the main point at issue here: for the solution of the problems they have set themselves they have very little indeed to learn from a governing class that for more than half a century has kept Cuba in a state of underdevelopment and the Cuban masses in a state of misery. On the other hand, they have much to learn from the industrially more advanced and developing countries— of both West and East—and this they are both willing and anxious to do to the maximum possible extent. On the basis of what we saw and heard in Cuba, we would venture the opinion that no country is readier to welcome technical assistance of all kinds and from all sources, provided only that it comes as a genuine assistance and not as a disguised form of pressure to force the government to change its policies to suit outside interests. There are already many foreign missions and individuals in Cuba and there will doubtless be many more in the months and years ahead. One of these, an official United States mission to the Ministry of Education, received warm words of commendation from Minister of Education Armando Hart when we visited him in his office. Others include a mission on methods of rice cultivation from Japan and the Cuban mission of the UN Economic Commission for Latin America (ECLA). There are literally dozens of foreign individuals, mostly from Latin American countries, working in and for the government. We met and talked at great length with a group of Chilean and Ecuadorean economists, all of whom had been trained and employed by ECLA at some time in the past. We can testify both to their ability as economists and to their devotion to the ideals and aims of the Cuban Revolution, which they hope to help apply to their own countries in the not-distant future. (Incidentally, we met neither missions nor individual experts from Soviet-bloc countries. They will doubtless come later, their numbers depending mainly on the availability of suitably trained personnel from the United States, Western Europe, and Latin America. For a variety of reasons of historic association and cultural affinity, Cuba will naturally turn to the latter areas first.)

Before we comment on some of the reform programs which the new regime has launched, there is one more bourgeois fetish which ought to be knocked firmly on the head, the ever-recurring notion that ambitious plans for social reform and reconstruction must lead to financial bankruptcy and ruin. A typical expression of this fear—or hope, as the case may be—appears in a *New York Times* dispatch (April 22, 1960) by Tad Szulc from Havana: "There are growing indications," writes Mr. Szulc, "that the Cuban government may have bitten off more than it can now chew in its haste to change the country's economy. . . . But the regime is finding that its available resources are not sufficient to pay the way." From what follows it is apparent that by "available resources" Mr. Szulc means not land and labor and capital and capacity to organize but rather financial revenues. And yet is it not obvious that it is the human and physical factors that set limits to what can be done, and that what happens in the financial sphere is a mere reflection of the underlying processes?

This is not to deny the existence of financial difficulties; it is simply to assert that their importance is symptomatic rather than causal. A sovereign government can always create (either directly or by borrowing from the central bank) whatever financial means it may need. If its spending of created purchasing power leads to no increase of output but only to a larger amount of private spending, then of course there will be inflation, a process that has been going on for literally generations in some Latin American countries. But if its spending of created purchasing power is accompanied by an increase of output or by a reduction of private spending (or some suitable combination of the two), then there need be no inflation and nothing resembling a financial crisis, not to speak of bankruptcy.

The problem, in other words, is not "where is the money coming from," as Mr. Szulc and many others seem to believe, but whether the government has the understanding, the will, and the ability to organize and stimulate production while at the same time applying adequate controls to private spending. If Mr. Szulc had been interested in investigating *these* questions, he would have found that the Cuban government is having plenty of difficulties but also, as we hope to show in Chapter 11 below, that it has impressive achievements to its credit and can be expected to do an increasingly good job as time goes by. As to understanding of financial problems, there is, not unnaturally, a good deal of naiveté and confusion at lower levels of government, and it is said that Fidel himself at one time was something of a "funny money" man. But Fidel has learned a lot in the last year and a half, and all the economists who have advised him with whom we had an opportunity to discuss these matters, report that he now has an excellent grasp of financial problems as he does of economic principles generally. As for the government's top economic officials, Regino Boti, the Minister of Economy, is a Harvard-trained professional economist, for many years on the staff of ECLA and former Professor of Political Economy at Santiago de Cuba; and, as we can testify from personal observation, Ché Guevara, President of the National Bank, has as brilliant, quick, and receptive a mind as is likely to be found in anyone occupying a comparable position in the government of any country in the world. To imagine that leaders like these are going to allow the Cuban Revolution to stagnate in the backwaters of fiscal orthodoxy or sink in the turbulent depths of inflation is simply to betray a complete lack of comprehension of what is happening in that country today. The leaders of the Cuban Revolution are not only very young.* They are also very modern, and what they don't know about both government and economics they are learning fast.

Let us turn now to some of the major reforms which the new regime instituted during its first year in power. In the remainder of this chapter we will discuss education, housing, and social welfare, leaving the more basic agrarian reform for separate consideration in the next chapter.

Two general observations are in order. First is the common-sense character of the reforms. ("We like to think of our government as a common-sense government," said Minister of Economy

---

* The *average* age of the Council of Ministers is 33!

Regino Boti.) But it must be understood, of course, that, like all common sense, the Cuban variety derives from a specific intellectual and moral approach to the world. For lack of a better label we may call this approach rational humanism—a set of values and intellectual attitudes which has developed in the Western world during the last four centuries, more or less, and which in our day finds expression alike in liberalism and in Marxism (and in various intermediate "isms" such as New Dealism, Fabianism, and Social Democracy). Essentially optimistic, it defines the good society in this-worldly, human terms; believes in the improvability, if not perfectibility, of human nature; and rejects all forms of philosophical or theological conservatism. It is, of course, in no sense monolithic, having a Left-Center-Right spectrum of its own and properly claiming as authentic spokesmen such varied figures as Bertrand Russell, John Dewey, and Vladimir Ilyich Lenin. Nevertheless, it has an essential unity, a fact which is correctly understood by its enemies, most notably the Roman Catholic Church. In every period of modern history some variant of it has been the outlook of the "progressives" of the time. In our own day and age the vast majority of the educated younger generation in the industrially less developed three quarters of the world are progressives in this meaning of the term. Philosophically, they speak the same language. They share the same ideals and inspirations. And this means that they have the same conception of common sense.

Now the leaders of the Cuban Revolution are ideal representatives of this large and (in our view) historically decisive sector of the human race. Their whole program derives from and conforms to its common sense. *In Cuba they are actually doing what young people all over the world are dreaming about and would like to do.* We believe this to be an enormously important fact. Not only does it enable us to view the reforms being enacted in Cuba in proper perspective, but even more important it explains why the Cuban Revolution, which at first might appear to be a local incident in a small Caribbean island, is in reality an event of world-shaking significance. Dreams have ever been the stuff of which history is made, and when they are turned into reality

their power is multiplied manyfold. We see no reason to doubt
that the achievements of the young people of Cuba will fire the
imagination and steel the will of young people throughout Latin
America—and far beyond.

Before leaving this subject we should perhaps add that world-
wide sympathy for the Cuban Revolution will certainly not be
universal. Conservatives everywhere, of course, feel very differently, characteristically seeing little in Cuba but chaos and impending
disaster. And, as far as the United States is concerned at any rate,
this aversion extends far beyond traditionally conservative circles.
The reason for this is that despite a time-honored liberal rhetoric
the United States has in practice become the protector of all the
anciens régimes of the world, and this has naturally profoundly
affected the thinking of those who acquiesce in their country's
adopting this course, which as of now means the vast majority of
its inhabitants. It is not that they have any clear philosophic or
moral ideas to put in the place of their predominantly liberal
inheritance. But they have completely lost their traditional belief
in the reality and/or possibility of progress. As a consequence, prevailing attitudes are basically pessimistic and cynical, a fact which
opens up an almost unbridgeable chasm between North Americans
and the younger generation in the underdeveloped countries. Even
North American liberals have for the most part succumbed to
the national mood and find themselves repelled rather than at-
tracted by the energy, optimism, and enthusiasm of the Cuban
Revolution, so reminiscent in many ways of the early days of the
New Deal in the United States. (It was, of course, in no small
measure the disappointment of the hopes of the New Deal that
turned the liberals from optimists into pessimists.) This lack of
sympathy extinguishes both the desire and the ability to understand the Cuban Revolution in its own terms. The best illustration
of what we have in mind is provided by a series of jaundiced and
patronizing articles which Murray Kempton, after a visit to Cuba,
published in the *New York Post* (beginning with the issue of
February 15). Cuban revolutionaries with whom we discussed the
Kempton articles, knowing his reputation as a liberal, were completely baffled (as well as angered) by what, from their point of

view, was his total incomprehension of what is happening in
Cuba. To avoid misunderstanding: not *all* Americans react this
way to Cuba. For example, we ourselves, as veterans of the left-
wing movement, felt thoroughly at home in the intellectual and
moral atmosphere of the Cuban Revolution, much more so than
we do in that of the "affluent society." And we would hazard the
guess that at least one significant segment of the North American
population, the educated Negro youth, would feel the same way.

The second general observation on the character of the Cuban
reforms is of a different order, having to do with something that
struck us again and again during our stay in Cuba, namely, the
extent to which rapid and important results could be obtained
merely by eliminating some of the worst abuses and wastes of the
old order. To put the point in different terms, there was a very
large unused (or abused) potential in the Cuban economy and
society,* and this circumstance has enabled the new regime to
accomplish quickly and relatively easily certain things which in
less favorable conditions might have taken years. This point has
general validity, but nowhere is its relevance more striking than
in the field of educational reform. Let us therefore proceed at once
to that crucially important subject.

Education has quantitative and qualitative aspects, and in
both the Revolution has already brought profound changes. They
were long overdue. According to the census of 1953, 31 percent
of the population of 6 years of age and over had no schooling at
all and another 29.4 percent had 3 years or fewer. For all practical
purposes, in other words, 60 percent were uneducated. Only 3.5
percent had a high-school education, and scarcely more than 1
percent a university education. The quality of the education offered
by the public schools was miserable. Armando Hart, the present
Minister of Education, told us that before the Revolution his had
not been a ministry of education at all but a ministry of instruction, and very bad instruction too. For this reason, all parents who
could afford to sent their children to private schools, then and

* As the United States Department of Commerce put it, "few countries carry
a heavier overhead of underutilized productive facilities." *Investment in
Cuba*, p. 6.

still a big industry in Cuba with some 120,000 students throughout the island. The situation was, of course, much worse in the countryside than in the cities. As already noted in Chapters 2 and 8 (on the excellent authority of Lowry Nelson), there were large parts of rural Cuba that had no schools at all. According to the 1953 census, the rural illiteracy rate among people 10 years of age and over was 41.7 percent. But there is no need to add details since the general picture is clear and denied by no one: the educational system of pre-revolutionary Cuba was woefully deficient in both quantity and quality.

One would naturally be inclined to assume that the sad state of the educational system must have been due to its having been financially starved. But this is definitely not the case. To quote from the United States Department of Commerce report *Investment in Cuba*:

> The Cuban educational system has failed to produce results commensurate with the degree of official sanction which it has received and the percentage of the national budget which has been expended upon it. . . . Almost one fourth of all budgetary appropriations are allotted to education, the sums available in recent years [up to 1956] having amounted to almost 75 million pesos annually.

What was the matter, then? Mismanagement, waste, and graft. There were 1,315 inspectors for 18,000 classrooms. Beautiful buildings had been put up along the Central Highway, and then left largely empty for lack of facilities and teachers (the purpose was boodle, not education). Each school had a bevy of special teachers (for music, physical education, English, etc.) turned out by special training schools and accomplishing almost nothing. Janitorial and maintenance personnel were out of all proportion to need. Perhaps worst of all was the tenure system which gave classrooms to teachers for life and enabled them to retain part of the salary while using the rest to hire a substitute from among the large number of unemployed teachers in the country. Our translator the day we visited the Ministry of Education told us of a teacher she knew who had lived in Miami while employing a substitute to do her work! Lowry Nelson sums up the situation in the following terms:

There are said to be a great many teachers drawing their monthly pay checks who are not actually teaching. . . . Great sums of money are spent on personnel which is not in fact performing any important duties in connection with the educational system. Under such conditions, the meaning of the census figures—which reveal a comparatively adequate supply of primary teachers, but a very low school attendance figure—becomes clear. The money that Cuban people are paying in taxes for education is being spent—and in larger amounts than ever before—but the children are not being educated.

Against this background, it will come as no surprise that the revolutionary government has been able to accomplish a great deal with only a modest increase in the funds allocated to education. Percentagewise, the educational budget has increased by about 10 percent, school capacity by 25 percent, and number of teachers by 30 percent. In the city of Havana, exactly one new school had been built in the 57 years between the establishment of the Republic and the Revolution; in the first year of the Revolution, 37 new schools were added. At the opening of the school year in September, 1959, there were some 18,000 classrooms in operation, and plans were announced to bring this up to a total of 28,000 by September of 1960. When we talked to Minister of Education Hart in March the figure was 25,000, and he had no doubts that the target would be reached.*

In carrying out this expansion program, priority has been given to rural areas where the shortage of both schools and teachers was most acute. This means that from the point of view of the Cuban peasantry *a far-reaching educational revolution has already taken place*. Even if the regime had accomplished nothing else—which, as we shall see, is very far from the case—this alone would be enough to win for it the unshakeable support of the countryside.

---

* Murray Kempton, in the series in the *New York Post* already referred to, reported this as a program to *build* 10,000 new *schools*, rather than *add* 10,000 new *classrooms*. For a variety of reasons, some mentioned in the text above, the number of classrooms added is of course much greater than the number of schools built. Kempton finds in this discrepancy evidence not of his own misunderstanding of the government's plan but of the complete unreliability of its promises! This is unfortunately all too typical of the entire Kempton performance.

It is obvious that such impressive results could be achieved so rapidly only because there was a tremendous amount of waste and slack in the old educational system. Inspectors have been sent into the classroom (their number has declined from 1,315 for 18,000 classrooms to 400 for 25,000 classrooms). Thousands of unemployed teachers have been hired. The jobs of special teachers have been abolished along with the schools that trained them: from now on elementary education will be in the hands of the "integrated" teachers with all-around training. Empty or partly empty school buildings are now used to capacity, often on a two-shift basis (with adult classes in the evenings). Space in non-school buildings has been requisitioned for classroom use. Army headquarters and training centers all over the island—including the Moncada fortress in Santiago and Batista's huge Camp Columbia outside Havana—have been transformed into schools (this act of transformation has become as symbolic of the Revolution as the beard and long hair of the rebel soldier). By such means as these the Revolution has almost overnight brought the blessings of education within reach of a vastly increased proportion of the Cuban population.

Henceforth progress will be slower. Most space suitable for educational purposes is now in use, and nearly all the once unemployed teachers are at work. Further expansion will depend largely on the building of new schools and the training of new teachers. Hart estimates that one hundred percent attendance among children of primary school ages will be achieved in three or four years. (Shortage of equipment such as textbooks, furniture, etc., are a further factor limiting the speed of progress.)

So much for changes in the quantitative aspect of Cuban education. Equally radical changes are under way in the qualitative aspect. Under the old order, as already noted, education was simply instruction; no effort was made to bring it into harmonious relation with the life pattern of the pupil. All that is being changed now. The new regime's philosophy of education, as expounded to us by Armando Hart and his assistant Herminío Almendros, is that which we in the United States have come to identify with the name of John Dewey. Children should learn not only from books and teachers but also from activity, experimentation, and work. Implementing this philosophy, of course, requires a totally new approach to both pedagogy and curriculum. Hart is an enthusiastic crusader for these unorthodox ideas and methods, and as we listened to his eloquent account of great hopes and plans for the future we felt somehow transported back to that distant time, three decades and more ago, when progressive education, still a youthful movement, was being widely hailed as an antidote to the ills of American society. In the United States, of course, the intervening years have brought defeat and disillusionment. Emasculated by the professional educationalists or turned into a caricature of itself by the life-adjusters, progressive education is very much on the defensive in the United States today, and even its remaining champions no longer make the great claims for it they once did. Is a similar fate, we wondered, in store for it in Cuba? The answer, it would seem, depends on what happens to the Cuban Revolution as a whole. We have no doubt that the basic ideas of progressive education are sound and in a favorable environment will produce the good results expected of them, just as we have no doubt that they were bound to be distorted almost beyond recognition and ultimately to fail in a society dominated by the needs and compulsions of giant capitalist corporations. If the Cuban Revolution survives the attempts of its enemies to destroy it—a subject to which we shall return in due course—then it seems likely to us that progressive education will receive its first full-scale test and vindication.

Meanwhile, one cannot but admire the boldness and imagination with which the revolutionary government is applying its educational philosophy. Consider, for example, that most novel and exciting of all educational experiments, the "Camilo Cienfuegos School City,"* situated in the foothills of the Sierra Maestra about 25 miles or so inland from the port city of Manzanillo. We visited the school city and talked at length with Pilar Fernandez,

---

* Camilo Cienfuegos, as noted in Chapter 7 above, was the leader of one of the columns that descended from the Sierra Maestra late in 1958 to complete the conquest of power. Subsequently one of the top leaders of the government, he was lost on an airplane trip in October, 1959—presumably driven out to sea and downed by a storm.

the local representative of the Ministry of Education, and others active in building it and planning its program.

The school city is the answer to a difficult practical problem: how to bring education to the 20,000 children from the ages of 6 to 18 who live in the most inaccessible parts of the 125-mile long and 25-mile wide mountainous region of the Sierra. There are few roads in the Sierra, and up to now there have been no schools either. Many of the inhabitants live in widely scattered households, and not a few are completely isolated. For people living under these conditions, it is not practical to build schools of the usual community type. Previous governments were content to do nothing, which is one reason why the people of the Sierra joined Fidel and became the backbone of the rebel army. If ever there was a "must" for an incoming government it was the obligation of the new regime in Cuba to bring the benefits of the Revolution to all the people of the Sierra, and that meant first and foremost to make it possible for their children to get a decent education. But how?

The school city is the answer. It is in effect a huge boarding school in which a large proportion of the children who live in the Sierra will get a complete education from first grade through high school. Like much else in Cuba today, it is being built—at breakneck speed—by the army. When completed it will consist of 35 units, each unit containing eight classroom buildings, eight dormitories equipped with dining rooms and study halls, and a full complement of sport facilities. In addition there will be a central "sport city" with a large stadium and housing for teachers, administrative personnel, etc. The total population of the city, during the academic year, will be about 25,000 (20,000 students and 5,000 adults)—a "bigger and better city than Manzanillo," Gustavo Casavo, the 24-year-old construction manager, told us.

But this is only part of the story, for the school city will be much more than a gigantic boarding school. It will also be an agricultural and manufacturing center in which the students themselves will produce enough to make the city economically self-supporting. The total area, mostly taken from one large landed estate, will be 500 *caballerías,* or approximately 28 square miles.

Of this the living and study area will take up something under four square miles, while the remainder will be devoted to farms and factories. The self-supporting character of the city will not only relieve the central government of any financial burden in connection with the project but also—and perhaps even more important in the eyes of its creators—it will permit the fullest possible application of the basic principle of progressive education, that the process of learning should combine living, studying, and working. Finally, the students who graduate from the school city will be fully prepared either to continue their education at the university level or to assume productive roles in the nation's economy.

We wondered if the design of the school city, in addition to solving the special problem of education for the Sierra Maestra area, might also reflect a preference for boarding-school education—based on the familiar socialist argument that the social consciousness of children will be more fully developed if from an early age they become accustomed to group rather than individual family life. We raised this question with Armando Hart and received a surprisingly emphatic negative in reply. They do *not* favor boarding schools, and in fact the school city will be the only one in the country. The whole social philosophy of the Cuban Revolution, Hart told us, is strongly oriented toward, not away from, the individual family. So far as possible they want students to live at home. The school city project was adopted solely because it was the only practical way of solving the problem of providing education to the isolated children of the Sierra. Should we confess that we were somewhat disappointed by this reply? Cuba seemed to us to provide a very favorable environment for further experiments in collective living—more so, for example, than the essentially stabilized capitalist society of Israel. We had hoped that the leadership was inclined in this direction and were sorry to learn that this is not the case.

Further evidence of an individualistic strain in the ideology of the Cuban Revolution will be found in the field of housing policy. Here the bias in favor of home *ownership* by each family unit separately is remarkably strong and applies even to dwelling units in large apartment houses. Monthly payments in lieu of rent will add up over a period of years—on the average from 20 to 30 years, the exact period being tailored to the individual buyer's financial circumstances—to the purchase price of the dwelling unit. The payments are low, running to about $25 a month for a house or apartment consisting of living room, dining room, kitchen, two bedrooms, and a bathroom. Most urban families moving into these new homes have been paying up to twice as much in straight rent for accommodations which in many cases were no more than one or two rooms with no separate plumbing at all. Furthermore, the new units, as we can testify from inspecting numerous examples in various parts of the island, are extraordinarily attractive and well located on open land, of which there is an abundance in and around Cuban cities. Where appropriate, housing projects are being supplemented by various community facilities. For example, the large development in East Havana, across the harbor from the downtown area, is being provided with beaches, playgrounds, sports fields, auditoriums, and neighborhood shopping centers. In general the Cuban architects and planners are succeeding in varying the size, style, and layout of buildings in such a way as to avoid the depressing mausoleum-like atmosphere of the typical high-rise urban housing project in the United States.

The housing program is being carried out by two agencies —INRA in the rural areas and INAV (the National Institute of Savings and Housing) in the towns and cities. Large apartment houses are of course not built in the countryside, but aside from this the two agencies seem to have similar policies with regard to ownership, payments, accommodation standards, etc. It is evident from observation in the countryside that the INRA housing program is an ambitious one, but since we have no specific data on it we will confine the analysis here to INAV.

INAV operates through hiring (by public bid) private contractors to do the actual building, and is said to have achieved notable success in bringing down unit costs by encouraging the use of more rational and economical methods than are possible on individual or small-scale projects. INAV has two principal sources of funds, the national lottery and social security pension funds. The lottery, which was a fountainhead of corruption in Batista's time, has been reorganized and has been turned into what is in effect a savings institution. In addition to carrying with it the chance of prizes, each ticket is now a sort of housing bond which can be turned in for amounts ranging from 40 percent of the purchase price in the first year up to 125.4 percent after the ninth year. Through this device it is hoped to make good use of Cubans' long-standing gambling habits and to familiarize them with the benefits of thrift.

INAV has an impressive record of achievement to its credit. It was organized soon after the new regime came to power, and started and/or completed some 10,000 housing units during 1959. Its goal for 1960 is 20,000 units, to cost around $40 million, or about $2,000 per unit. (In judging this figure, one must take into account that the climate is such that no heating or protection against cold is required in Cuba, a fact which reduces the cost of building a house by perhaps as much as 25 percent as compared to most parts of the United States.) When one considers that there was no public housing program at all prior to January 1, 1959, it is indeed clear that the new regime has been and is achieving remarkable results in this field. Foreign visitors to Cuba, and of course Cubans themselves, are almost certain to be impressed by the numerous INAV projects which are to be seen in cities and towns throughout the island.

Nevertheless, it is necessary to maintain a sense of perspective in estimating the extent of success achieved to date. There was already a desperate shortage of decent housing when INAV was founded, and the urban population is increasing by perhaps as much as 75,000 a year. If we allow five persons to a dwelling unit, it is clear that something like three quarters of the 20,000 units to be constructed this year will be required just to keep the shortage from getting worse, leaving only around 5,000 units as an addition to the available supply—and this takes no account of the wearing out of old buildings. (There is almost no private home building in progress now, largely because of the rent control laws and the ceiling prices on real estate.) At this rate, it is all too obvious that very little headway is being made in the fight against inadequate housing. Sooner or later a much more ambitious program will have to be launched if this problem is ever to be really solved.

Is a more nearly adequate program within Cuba's present capabilities? It is obviously impossible for outsiders lacking detailed information to answer this question with any assurance. Still we would like to record our impression for what it is worth that the realistic limits of a housing program have by no means yet been reached. The key point here, of course, is that with private building at a virtual standstill there is a great deal of unemployment and idle productive capacity at all levels of the construction industry. Present limitations on the housing program would therefore seem to be of a financial rather than a physical character, though this statement is subject to qualification to the extent (unknown to us) that additional housing would necessitate additional imports. *Some* imports are certainly needed—e.g. plumbing supplies—and it may be that the state of the foreign exchange reserve and balance of payments will not permit any considerable expansion of the program at this time. If so, it will obviously have to wait until later. But if imports are *not* a limiting factor, it would seem that the problem is simply one of increasing the budget of INAV—either out of general treasury funds or by allocating further specific sources of revenue to INAV. If it be objected that this would increase inflationary pressures, the answer surely is that the appropriate way to handle *this* problem is through general controls on spending (taxation, savings schemes, etc.). Unless such controls are beyond the administrative or political capacity of the government—which we hardly think to be the case in Cuba—it *never* makes sense to hold inflationary pressures down by allowing perfectly good productive resources to remain idle. That is the utterly discredited method of orthodox capitalism.

Let us turn now to the work of another governmental agency created by the new regime, the Ministry of Social Welfare which is under the direction of a beautiful young woman, Raquel Pérez de Miret, a lawyer by training and the only woman member of the Council of Ministers. This Ministry is concerned with what in older sociological literature used to be called "the social problem" —the problem of the destitute, the derelict, the outcast. Since there were literally tens of thousands of people in these categories—the visible evidence was plain to even the most unobserving visitor to Havana in the old days—and since no previous government had ever bothered to do anything to alleviate their plight, it is not surprising that this problem occupied a high place on the agenda of the revolutionary regime. Señora Pérez's Ministry is now operating on a relatively high budget of $24 million a year, and the proof that it has been doing effective work is there for all to see—there are simply no more beggars and prostitutes roaming the streets of Havana. It should be noted, however, that the present important status of the Ministry is in principle a temporary phenomenon. To the extent that (1) it succeeds in its job and (2) the Revolution abolishes the conditions that in the past gave rise to the problems with which it deals, the need for such a Ministry will wither away and eventually disappear. Presumably no one would be happier to work herself out of a job than Señora Pérez: her chief complaint, when we talked to her, was that she never gets time to see her own family.

The welfare program, like other aspects of the new regime's social policy, is strongly family oriented. People requiring assistance are assumed to be the victims of circumstances who, by appropriate measures, can be restored to a normal life, and in Cuba a normal life is a family life. Institutionalization is resorted to only when absolutely unavoidable and then for as brief a time as possible. The methods used are those associated in the United States with the most modern and advanced schools of social work (the young Cubans in this field know the North American literature well and freely acknowledge their debt to it), emphasis being placed not on paternalism but on rehabilitation and self-help. The job of the Ministry is envisaged as the creation of conditions in which the underprivileged and broken human beings will gain (or regain) the ability *and the will* to lead normal productive lives. At the same time, it is fully recognized that in the long run success depends on the elimination of the chronic unemployment that has so long plagued Cuba, and here the work of the Ministry of Social Welfare merges into the major programs and aims of the Revolution as a whole.

We will close this brief discussion of the work being done in the social welfare field with a few notes on the one major project of the Ministry which we had an opportunity to observe at first hand, the complete resettlement of a depressed neighborhood on the outskirts of Santiago. The neighborhood is known as Manzana de Gómez and is situated alongside the Cemetery of Santa Ifigenia in which José Martí is buried. Approximately 650 families live here in conditions which reminded one of us of the slums of an Indian city—hovels, open sewers, naked children, squalor, and filth. But the people do not look down and out the way they do in an Indian slum, and for this there is a very good reason. A short distance away on open land they are building with their own hands an attractive village of cement-block houses, each complete with all conveniences. We watched them at work, and it was easy to see that they had overcome whatever initial skepticism they may have had and were by now convinced that betterment of their condition was not the idle talk of political swindlers but a practical possibility entirely within their own grasp. We discussed the project at length with Amelia García Ponce, the representative of the Ministry of Social Welfare in charge, and got from her a typewritten report on its aims and status. Here are some excerpts from the report:

The program contemplates four basic phases, as follows: (1) Investigation—to know the real condition of this neighborhood in all its aspects: the families, their problems, their needs, their resources, the services at their disposal, their leaders, etc. (2) Analysis and programming—Based on the results of the investigation, a program is worked out dealing with all the aspects considered and encompassing the necessary social preparations, education, work and community development which are essential to it. Likewise taken into account are the types of houses to be constructed, the materials to be used, the different stages of organization of the work, etc. (3) Execution—Realization of the physical and social plan in accordance with the programming. (4) Evaluation—This takes place after the completion of the project and periodically thereafter.

At the present time [March, 1960] the program is in the third phase and is proceeding at a pace which will permit the completion of the new neighborhood by the end of April. In general the organization is as follows: The members of the community, both men and women, work on regular morning, afternoon, and night shifts. For the men, each shift lasts six hours, and the work is divided among workshops and labor teams preparing the materials for use, installing the prefabricated parts, building the houses, putting on the roofs, painting the exteriors, etc. The women work in the dining room of the work area preparing and serving the food, in the sewing center making clothes and other things needed in their homes, and at repairing and painting their furniture, etc.

All are engaged enthusiastically in their work, seeing that the houses where they will live are becoming a reality—hygienic houses, big enough for family needs, provided with necessary services, and situated in an attractive environment. They know that their children will be able to attend the school which is being built on the same land, and that they will also have a medical care center, sports fields, a community house, a shopping center, etc. They work to make all this a reality.

In spite of the basic character of all the foregoing, the ultimate purpose of the program is to fit these men and women to earn their own livings. This is to be achieved not only by means of the preparation which they are now receiving, but also by seeking out jobs for them in work centers already in existence or to be created. Conscious of this necessity, the Revolutionary Government is pushing forward a vast plan of industrialization to create the needed sources of work. But in the meantime, the industrialists, merchants, civic institutions, and the general citizenry of Santiago de Cuba should respond and lend their aid to this effort of the REVOLUTION.

This project is being carried out by the Ministry's Department of Suburban Improvement (as one can readily see, the term "suburb" in Cuba has a very different connotation from what it does in the United States), and it is the first of its kind in the island. Señorita García thinks that for the country as a whole similar projects covering as many as 35,000 families may be needed. She optimistically estimates that it will take three or four years to finish the job.

CHAPTER 10

Structural Reform

What Mark Twain said about the weather is just as applicable to the pre-revolutionary Cuban economy: everybody talked about it but nobody did anything about it. There is this difference, however. Nobody does anything about the weather because nobody knows what to do. In the case of the Cuban economy, on the other hand, anyone who would take the trouble could find out what to do by consulting any one of a dozen or more standard sources.

Consider, for example, the following passage from the report of a World Bank mission to Cuba:

The Mission believes that Cuba can make the greatest and most lasting progress if its development moves toward the following objectives:

1. To make Cuba less dependent on sugar by promoting additional activities—not by curtailing sugar production.

2. To expand existing—and create new—industries producing sugar by-products or using sugar as a raw material. This objective deserves a first priority because progress in these directions will make the sugar sector itself more stable.

3. Vigorously to promote non-sugar exports in order to reduce the emphasis of the country's exports on one product. This will help both to raise total income and employment and also to stabilize it. Among the most promising possibilities for achieving this aim are the promotion of mineral exports and of the export of a variety of crude and processed foodstuffs.

4. To make further progress in producing in Cuba, for domestic consumption, a wide range of foodstuffs, raw materials, and consumer goods now imported.

That was written in 1950-1951 at a time when sugar prices were high and Cuba was relatively prosperous. A great opportunity, the World Bank mission thought, confronted the Cuban people: "They may take advantage of their present opportunity to start to substitute a growing, diversified, and dynamic economy for their present static one, with its single crop dependence." Five years later, the United States Department of Commerce in its detailed report *Investment in Cuba* commented on the recommendations of the World Bank mission and added: "The only developments of importance in the intervening years have been the mechanization of the export cigar industry, with a consequent rise in foreign sales, and the export of sugarcane wax to the United States."

By the time these epoch-making results had been achieved, the sugar boom was over and the Cuban economy once again in the doldrums. Like the World Bank before it, the Department of Commerce once again preached the need for diversification and development—this time presumably under the benevolent aegis of North American capital. Once again nothing of consequence happened. There was no mystery about what had to be done, but still nobody did anything. Why?

The answer, of course, is that those who had the power—the Cuban governing class with its foreign partners and its domestic military accomplices—were simply not interested. The pleas of even their good friends in the World Bank and the Department of Commerce fell on deaf ears. They had done very well out of a stagnant one-crop economy and they had no desire or intention to change it. Hence the *necessity* of the revolution.

When the new regime came to power it knew very well what had to be done and had often proclaimed its intention of doing it. But not every one believed it. Indeed, those members of the upper class who had supported the fight against Batista were quite sure that Fidel was no more serious about basic reforms than all the politicians before him had been. Let the dust settle, they thought, and things would soon revert to normal. The worst excesses and abuses of the dictatorship would be eliminated, a mild land reform and greater protection and encouragement for Cuban capital would be politically expedient and would benefit all but a tiny minority of the biggest latifundists. But that's as far as things would go. Hadn't it been proved again and again in Latin American history—in Mexico, in Venezuela, in Bolivia, and most recently in Guatemala—that any government that stepped out of bounds and threatened the basis of the upper class's privileges would be thrown out by the domestic military, which for this purpose could count on unlimited support from Washington? Surely Fidel Castro knew this and would act accordingly, meanwhile assuring to himself and his companions the normal perquisites and rewards of office holding in Latin America?

They were dead wrong. They didn't understand Fidel Castro. Much more important, they didn't understand that the old military machine had been completely and utterly smashed and that the new peasant army on which Fidel's power rested was a veritable revolutionary dynamo. Previous Latin American revolutionary regimes risked being thrown out by the (old) army if they moved to implement their declared program; Fidel's regime risked being thrown out by the (new) army if it failed to do so.

The turning point came with the adoption of the Agrarian Reform Law in May, 1959. Up to then, the regime had limited itself to correcting abuses and initiating much-needed reforms which, however, did not alter the basic structure of Cuban society. The real test of its intentions was the kind of agrarian reform it would carry through. Would it confine itself to a measure effecting a wider and more equitable distribution of land ownership? If so, as the experience of many countries has shown, nothing essential in the economy or power structure of the country would be changed. Or would it treat agrarian reform in a much more radical way, as the institutional basis for that entire program of economic diversification and development which had so often been recommended but never adopted? If so, a new era not only in Cuban but in all Latin American history would be opened.

From the first "whereas" of the preamble to the law, the answer was perfectly clear. "Whereas," it begins, "the progress of Cuba involves both the growth and diversification of industry in order to facilitate the most effective utilization of its natural resources by its citizens, as well as the elimination of dependence on the one-crop system of agriculture which still basically persists and is one of the symptoms of our inadequate economic development. . . ." Here is the purpose, agrarian reform the means. The remainder of the preamble can be divided into three parts: The first stresses the long line of expert opinion, "especially those [studies] undertaken by the United Nations," that holds agrarian reform to be an essential aspect of an economic development program. The second presents the statistical picture of inequality of land holdings as revealed in the agricultural census of 1946. Here it is noteworthy that the inefficiency of the system is emphasized even more than its injustice, the gist of the argument being that the big estates have been grossly mismanaged and large parts of them allowed to lie idle. The third part of the preamble follows up this argument by asserting, not the necessity of distributing the big estates to individual cultivators but rather that "it is preferable to replace production from large landholdings, which is uneconomical and based on extensive cultivation, by cooperative production based on intensive cultivation and the use of advanced technical methods, which brings with it the advantages of large-scale production." Finally, the preamble makes clear that agrarian reform is not to be a mere reshuffle of titles to property but a continuing process under government guidance and affecting the entire economy. "It is essential," we read, "to establish a technical body that can apply and carry out in every detail the aims of economic development, with the resulting improvement in the standard of living of the Cuban people, in accordance with the letter and the spirit of this law."

The actual body of the law, which runs to 24 pages, contains three main types of provisions: (1) Those laying down the principles and norms of the new system of landholding; (2) those which deal with such matters as compensation of expropriated owners, administration of the law, adjudication of disputes, etc.; and (3) those which establish and define the powers and duties of the "technical body" referred to in the preamble. Let us summarize very briefly what appear to us to be the most important provisions under each heading.

(1) The law is relatively generous in what it allows large landowners to retain. One thousand acres is set as the general ceiling, but exceptions are allowed up to 3,000 acres for farms with very high yields. Any holding of 1,000 acres or less is left

intact provided it is operated by its owner. If there are tenants or squatters, they are to receive title to their land and the owner can keep what is left over. Future sharecropping agreements are prohibited, as is the joint ownership (directly or through corporations) of cane land and sugar mills. On the positive side, a farm of 66 acres of unirrigated fertile land is declared to be the "Vital Minimum" (VM) for a family of five (more or less in other cases according to circumstances). All expropriated land plus land already owned by the state is to be handed over undivided to cooperatives or distributed free of charge in VM-parcels. Any agricultural worker with less than the VM may apply for an allocation from the lands that are available, and the law prescribes the order of priority in which the applications are to be filled. (N.B. that there is no expressed or implied guarantee that all applicants will get land.) In the future, redistributed agricultural lands will be transferable only by inheritance or sale to the state, thus precluding in advance the possibility of building up new latifundia.

So far the law follows a pattern which, allowing for variations in detail, is fairly common in modern land reform statutes. In Chapter V ("Agrarian Cooperation") and Chapter VI ("The National Institute of Agrarian Reform"), however, it deviates radically from this pattern. We shall have more to say about the National Institute of Agrarian Reform (henceforth referred to as INRA) presently. With regard to agrarian cooperation, it may be well to quote the crucial Article 43 in full:

> Whenever possible INRA will promote agrarian cooperatives. The agrarian cooperatives organized by INRA on lands available to it under the provisions of this Law shall be under its direction, and it shall reserve the right to appoint the managers thereof for the purpose of ensuring their better development during the initial stage of this type of economic and social organization and until greater autonomy is granted it by law.

It should be particularly noted that INRA is not simply given the power to establish cooperatives; it is in effect directed to establish them "whenever possible." Evidently, the cooperative is envisioned as the key institution in the new Cuban landholding system. What the term "cooperative" means in this context will be discussed later.

(2) Compensation for expropriated lands is to take the form of 20-year bonds of the national government bearing $4\frac{1}{2}$ percent interest. Valuations are those declared by the owners for tax assessment purposes. Administration of the law is entrusted to INRA which for this purpose is instructed to divide the country into "Agrarian Development Zones." (As of the time of writing there are 28 such zones: from an economic point of view they are on the way to becoming the main subdivisions of the country.) Special Land Courts are set up to expedite legal proceedings, adjudicate disputes, etc.

(3) INRA is created "as an autonomous entity with its own juridical personality for the purpose of applying and enforcing this Law." INRA is thus what we in the United States would call a government corporation; from the legal standpoint it is the exact equivalent of the Tennessee Valley Authority. INRA "shall be governed by a President and an Executive Director, who shall be appointed by the Council of Ministers." (These positions are now held respectively by Fidel Castro and Comandante Antonio Nuñez Jiménez, a former university professor of geography and a veteran of the Sierra Maestra.) The scope, powers, and functions of INRA, as defined particularly in Articles 48-53 but also in various other places throughout the law, are extraordinarily broad and extend to many matters not otherwise touched upon in the law. To cite a few examples: INRA is given responsibilities with respect to rural health, housing, and education; the establishment of centers for providing machinery and other supplies and services to farmers; the gathering and analysis of statistics; research, development, and experimentation in all branches of agriculture; and the provision of credit, especially to cooperatives. In addition to these more or less specific functions, INRA is granted a blanket power "to order and put into practice whatever measures are necessary in order to attain the objectives of the Law." When it is borne in mind that the very first stated objective of the law is "the growth and diversification of industry," the full scope of INRA's activities will be appreciated. It may not have been com-

pletely foreseen by the drafters of the law, but there is nothing either illogical or anomalous in the fact that in practice INRA has become the spearhead and main agency in a vast program to diversify and develop not only the agriculture but also the industries of Cuba.

Before we attempt to summarize what has been done under the Agrarian Reform Law, it may be well to include a few notes and comments which can contribute to a better understanding not only of the law itself but also, and more important, of the nature of the Cuban Revolution as a whole.

The time has not yet come to write the history of the Cuban law, in particular its relation to earlier agrarian reforms in Latin America and elsewhere, nor in any case would we be competent to undertake this important task. But there is one point we believe crucially important to the interpretation of the Cuban Revolution which cannot be passed over, namely, how it came about that the Cuban reform adopted as its chief aim the *direct and immediate* transition to a regime of predominantly cooperative agriculture. We record our own conclusions from numerous discussions with persons concerned in the drafting and administration of the law. Since we were not seeking the views of these people for publication no names are mentioned: responsibility for the views expressed here belongs to us alone.

From the time of the French Revolution through the Stolypin reforms in Russia early in this century and on to the post-World War I reforms in various Eastern European countries, bourgeois land reformers always aimed at the breaking up of large landed estates into small peasant holdings. More radical thought, at least from the time of Marx, has generally rejected this aim on the dual ground that small-scale peasant cultivation of the soil is hopelessly inefficient and that a small peasantry is inevitably a reactionary, counter-revolutionary force. However, the Russian Revolution showed the difficulties which confronted any attempt to go directly from a system of latifundia to some form of collective agriculture. In spite of themselves, the Russian Bolsheviks were forced to distribute the land to millions of small peasants, and it was only much later after fierce and bloody social struggles and frightful agricul-

*A contingent of the Havana University
student militia relives history under the
expert guidance of Fidel Castro*

This was "home" for a tobacco field worker and his family of 12

As members of a cooperative, this will be their new home

Before—not even a privy

The program—
a modern bathroom for every family

The INAV housing project in East Havana

it goes to the mill for grinding . . .

and then is loaded on to ships

Cooperative membe
build new houses
replace the o

A part of the huge
Camilo Cienfuegos School City
in construction

Comandante Dr. Ernesto Ché Guevara

Comandante Dr. René Vallejo, head of INRA in Oriente

Early arrivals at Camilo Cienfuegos School City

Turning over the Moncada fortress to the Ministry of Education

Entrance to the new school

*An enthusiastic audience
welcomes the change from fortress to school*

Henequen cooperative

Building ships for a fishermen's cooperative

Free clinic for peasants

Photographs by INRA and the authors

tural losses that they succeeded in establishing the system of collective and state farms. By the time of World War II it was generally agreed among radical land reformers that the approach to collectivized agriculture in feudal or semi-feudal countries would have to be indirect: first the distribution of land to the peasant cultivators, later the introduction of cooperation and its more or less rapid evolution toward higher forms of collective property and effort. Post-World War II experience in Eastern Europe and China seemed fully to confirm the validity of this view. It seems safe to say that by the mid-1950's it was generally accepted among radicals of all shades of opinion, as much in India as in Soviet Russia. Differences between Communists and others were not concerned with the nature of the process itself but with the speed at which it should proceed and the extent to which it might be necessary and/or justified to use force in hurrying it along.

This was, of course, the general frame of reference within which discussion of land reform proceeded among the Cuban revolutionaries. So far as we can make out, there was pretty general agreement that Cuba would have to follow the same road as others on the way to an efficient and highly developed collective agriculture: it was assumed, in other words, that the Cuban peasants were not ready for cooperative forms of cultivation and would have to go through a more or less lengthy preparatory period during which they would naturally acquire title to the land they tilled. This interpretation is confirmed by the fact, which we learned on the best of authority, that the first draft of the agrarian reform law included no provisions for cooperatives. What was responsible for the complete reversal on this point that occurred between this first draft and the law as finally enacted?

The answer seems to be, very simply, Fidel Castro. When the first draft was submitted to him he rejected it as too conservative. He wanted cooperatives and he believed that most Cuban *campesinos* were ready for them. He insisted and he got his way.

In the light of what has happened since—about which more in due course—it is evident that Fidel was right, that he had a much more profound understanding of the Cuban peasantry than

his more doctrinaire colleagues.* Fidel's view soon became widely
accepted, and it is easy now to forget how daringly original it
was at the time he made his decision regarding the place of cooperatives in the agrarian reform. For our part, we have no doubt
that this decision was one of the most important Fidel will ever
make, a real turning point in the Cuban Revolution. No other
country has ever yet had the enormous advantages of being able
to skip over a phase of predominantly small peasant cultivation and
go directly to a relatively high form of collective cultivation. By
doing so Cuba has been able to put the Revolution on remarkably firm political foundations from the outset and to open up
exciting prospects for the rapid expansion of agricultural and
eventually industrial output. That Fidel Castro could envision
these possibilities and had the courage to act upon them, even
against the apparent lessons of history and the opinion of his
own experts, surely marks him as a political genius and one of
the greatest of revolutionary leaders.

Now a word about INRA and its methods of operation. Laws
and documents are necessary for an understanding of reality, but
they *never* tell the whole story and with respect to an elemental
and pervasive social process such as the Cuban Revolution they
may easily hide as much as they reveal. The first thing to recognize about INRA is that there is no clear dividing line between
it and the army. Many of its key personnel, both in Havana and
in the provinces, are in uniform. The connection was brought

---

* It may be worthwhile in this connection to record a personal incident.
We went to Cuba imagining that the *campesino* would conform to the usual
peasant stereotype and with grave doubts about the feasibility of cooperatives
at this stage of the Revolution. Our eyes were opened by an interview with
half a dozen cane cutters whom we stopped to talk to as they were emerging from a cane field in Pinar del Río. Through our interpreter we asked
them if they were anxious to own their own plots of land. What struck us
was not their answer to the question but that *they didn't understand the
question at all until it had been repeatedly rephrased and explained*. When
they finally understood, they showed no desire for individual ownership but
made it quite clear that what they did want was better houses, more schools,
and steadier work. When we asked them why they were for Fidel, they
answered that it was because they could see with their own eyes that people
like themselves were getting precisely these things. This incident set us to
thinking along fresh lines and led ultimately to the interpretation of the
Cuban Revolution which underlies this work.

home to us by a chat with a Comandante we met while waiting for a plane at the Camagüey airport. He said he was a doctor and psychologist working for INRA and was then on his way to an army post to do some psychological testing (to discover potential leadership ability). Having digested this, we asked the inevitable question: if he was in the army, as he obviously was, and doing testing on army personnel, how had INRA managed to get into the picture? At first he didn't quite get the question and looked puzzled. When it was repeated by the interpreter, he brightened up and shrugged: "Oh, INRA and the army—same thing." Not quite, but there is an essential truth here all the same. And anyone who overlooks it and conceives of INRA in the image of an ordinary bureaucratic agency is sure to go wrong. The fact is, of course, that the army was in the business of requisitioning, taking over, and managing all sorts of things long before INRA was created. Armies always perform such functions in wartime; they do so even more when the war is a civil war; and they do so most of all when the war is a revolutionary war. Moreover, as we have argued before, the army in Cuba was the driving force of the Revolution. It didn't wait for the passage of a law to seize a wide variety of properties belonging to Batista henchmen, latifundists, etc. In one sense, it can be said that INRA was created as a sort of department of the army to take charge of running these properties. This is too simple, too, of course, but it contains another important element of the truth. After INRA was created most of its provincial and zonal chiefs were army men, and for many months their communications with INRA headquarters in Havana were at best somewhat tenuous and uncertain. Much that they did was on their own authority: in a revolutionary situation things do have to get done, and the Cuban rebel army was in no mood to shirk its responsibilities. All of which goes far to account for the kind of thing that has aroused so much comment, usually very censorious, from conservative commentators both in and out of Cuba. To quote the generally accurate and intelligent article which Theodore Draper wrote for *The Reporter* (May 12, 1960) after a visit of several weeks to Cuba:

An INRA delegate, accompanied by a couple of armed soldiers, usually appears at a farm and announces that INRA is taking over everything but a certain portion. He may return later and cut the former owner's allotment in half. Though the law says nothing about farm machinery or cattle, they are also appropriated. The whole transaction is completely informal; there are no hearings, no inventories, no receipts. In some cases, if the owners are willing to accept INRA's offer, they may get paid in cash. No one has yet seen any bonds; the government says they are being printed.

Conservatives find all this most distasteful, but then of course they don't like revolutions anyway. Actually, there is no question that the situation has changed a good deal in the last few months as the government, including both the army and INRA, has improved its own organization, straightened out its lines of authority, and begun the big job of planning the overall development of the economy. There is still a long way to go, as some exasperated INRA department chief in Havana is likely to be the first to tell you, but he will also add, perhaps a bit nostalgically, that if you think *this* is chaos and confusion you ought to have been around a year ago.

Let us now turn to what has been done to realize the objectives of the Agrarian Reform Law. Statistics on land area expropriated or intervened ("intervene" is a legal term meaning to take over provisionally pending final disposition), number of cooperatives established, etc., are to be regarded as no more than informed guesses. This is not said in criticism; it is simply to pass along a warning that was given to us by INRA officials themselves. The situation changes rapidly, headquarters are too busy with other things to make careful or regular counts, and communications with the field are far from perfect. Nevertheless, a considerable amount of information was presented to a meeting which was held around the middle of March in Havana and attended by Fidel, President Dorticós, various Ministers, and all the chiefs and delegates of INRA; and there is every reason to believe that these data give a reasonable idea of the orders of magnitude involved. We have taken the following from the account published in *El Mundo* (March 20) of the report

delivered to this meeting by INRA Executive Dir
Jiménez.

Item: When the agrarian reform is completed, i
affected some 13¼ million acres. *This is 60 percent o, ... total
land area in farms.* As of March, 8.8 million acres had already
been taken over by INRA, and most of the rest was in process
of being taken over, as the *zafra* came to an end. As of the time
of writing, therefore, about three fifths of the agricultural land of
Cuba has come under the control of INRA. Less than one tenth
of this (1.16 million acres) had been paid for in cash or bonds.

Item: Private land titles for farmers numbering 6,908 had
been prepared, of which 576 had been delivered to the new owners.

Item: The number of cooperatives already formed was 764.
Some 500 more (to include 2.7 million acres) were being formed
on cane lands as the latter were taken over. The National Bank
had just loaned INRA $34 million to establish the cane co-
operatives.

Item: INRA had set up 1,400 *tiendas del pueblo*, or people's
stores, on cooperatives and elsewhere in the countryside. (These
stores are a very important part of INRA's program. They bring
the advantages of mass distribution to the peasants in the form of
lower prices and liberal credit privileges. They also provide outlets
for INRA's own agricultural and industrial products, thus alert-
ing INRA to the needs of the people and the state of the market
and greatly facilitating the tasks of rational production programming.)

Item: Up to March 1, INRA had brought approximately
250,000 acres of new (previously uncultivated) land into cultivation (plowed, prepared for planting, and planted). This newly
cultivated land is being largely devoted to crops (rice, corn, peanuts, cotton, and beans) which will directly or indirectly replace
traditionally heavy imports.

Item: As of January 31st, in the field of industry, INRA
owned 81 enterprises worth nearly a quarter of a billion dollars,*

---

* Nuñez Jiménez distinguished between enterprises owned by INRA and those
owned by two specialized credit agencies which had been inherited from
Batista days. Since these agencies were merged into INRA shortly afterward,
we have ignored this distinction.

and administered 28 more (with a value of $13.4 million) which had been intervened by the Ministry of Labor because of labor disputes. (The enterprises owned by INRA became state property in a number of ways, among which two were far and away the most important: first, the recovery of "ill-gotten gains" of the Batista period; and second, the assertion of ownership in the case of enterprises for which the state had in the past provided most of the capital in one form or another.) Other government departments beside INRA own or operate commercial enterprises, the most notable case being the telephone system which is owned by American capital and operated under intervention by the Ministry of Communications. (The question of the probable future size of the public sector will be discussed in Chapter 12.)

These statistics, of course, are far from giving a complete picture of INRA's activities, but they do indicate the overall magnitude of these activities and point to the decisive role which INRA now plays in the Cuban economy. We are entitled to conclude that the Agrarian Reform Law not only provided for a basic change in the system of landholdings, it also established a dynamic agency capable of taking positive action to realize the potential of the new system.

Before leaving the subject of agrarian reform, we must look somewhat more closely at the new cooperative which is taking the place of the old latifundium as the basic Cuban agricultural enterprise. In no case of which we have knowledge has a cooperative yet achieved anything like its final form—physically, economically, socially, or legally. There is as yet no official or accepted theory of the cooperative. Those most closely concerned will tell you that at this stage they are purposely leaving many things open, to be decided in practice or in the light of experience. All this must be kept in mind in judging what follows: we have merely tried to describe some features of what we would judge to be a more or less typical cooperative *in its present stage of development* and to indicate possible lines of further development.

The members are landless workers who bring with them into the cooperatives nothing but a few personal belongings. They have been living in scattered bohíos. Now they are building, or helping to build attractive new houses for themselves. The new dwellings are grouped together around a school and a people's store (after school hours the school will be used for various community purposes). A tobacco cooperative we visited in Pinar del Río will have about 120 families: this is probably larger than average. A cattle cooperative we visited in Camagüey has 90 families. Sizes will presumably vary widely according to circumstances. There is as yet no statute governing the internal organization of the cooperatives. The land belongs to the state, and will presumably continue to do so. The manager is now appointed by INRA, and different managers operate differently. It seems to be agreed among those we asked that if the membership didn't like a manager they could present a complaint to INRA zone headquarters which would investigate and either try to patch up the difference or appoint a new manager. The managers are, of course, obligated to follow INRA directives with respect to area cultivated, crops sown, etc. Members receive wages, often two to three times higher than they used to get, and at the end of the year (or other accounting period) part of the profits, if any, will be divided among them.

Two very important problems have yet to be faced: the problem of landless workers who are not members of a cooperative, and what may be called the problem of rich and poor cooperatives. Most large estates had a group of more or less permanent workers attached to them, and they employed, particularly at harvest time, additional workers, many of them migrants, among whom there has traditionally been a large proportion of Haitians and Jamaicans. When an estate is taken over, it is naturally those who live on it or have an established record of employment on it who form the membership of the new cooperative, and the cooperative equally naturally continues to give employment as and when it can to casual and migratory workers. There might appear to be a danger here of a new class division in the countryside, between cooperative members and unattached agricultural workers. We believe, however, that this problem will tend to solve itself if job opportunities increase as planned over the next few years (more about this later). As the present labor surplus gives way to a labor shortage, the unattached workers will either be absorbed into industry or will be integrated into the cooperatives that need their labor power.

More serious in the long run is the rich-and-poor cooperative problem which arises from the fact that some cooperatives have natural advantages (fertility of the soil, proximity to market, etc.) which others lack. If the more favorably circumstanced are allowed to keep their differential gains, they will be able to develop more rapidly and distribute more income to their members, thus introducing a new element of social stratification into the countryside. The obvious solution to this problem is for the state to remove these sources of inequality by charging "rent" for the use of the land in proportion to its natural advantages, using the proceeds for the benefit of all. We hope that a solution along these lines is sought at a fairly early date; otherwise there is a real danger that stubborn and potentially disruptive vested interests will be created among the members of the more fortunately situated cooperatives.

How does the Cuban cooperative compare with the two basic forms of agricultural enterprise in the Soviet Union, the collective farm (*kolkhos*) and the state farm (*sovkhos*)? The collective farm is formed by the pooling of individual peasant holdings, and remuneration of members takes the form of dividing income (net of material costs) according to work units contributed. Further, the collective is theoretically, and increasingly in practice, an autonomous body which owns its land and capital, elects its own managers, and determines its policies within the framework of the general economic plan. The state farm, on the other hand, is simply a "factory in the field": the land belongs to the state; the management is appointed from above; workers are paid wages; and any income left over after all costs have been met goes to the state. So far as we know there is no element of workers' control in the state farm.

The Cuban cooperative appears to be much closer to the state farm than to the collective. There is no pooling of land (the members never had any to pool); managers are appointed by INRA; wages are the basic form of remuneration. However, the cooperative differs from the state farm in that net income or at least part of it, is to be shared among the members rather than going to the state. In this respect, it bears a resemblance to the collective farm. Furthermore, there is a difference from the state farm implied in the designation, universal in Cuba, of those who belong to the cooperative as "members' rather than simply as workers in the manner of an industrial enterprise. How important is this difference? This is a fundamental question, to which, however, it is not yet possible to give any clear answer. There are those, especially among the critics of the present Cuban government, who maintain that the difference is purely verbal, that in substance the Cuban cooperative is nothing but a state farm. We believe that it is much too early to draw conclusions on this point. While it is difficult for outsiders who do not speak the language to form reliable judgment in such matters, we had a strong sense at all the cooperatives we visited that the members *feel* like members of an organization that belongs to them in a direct and intimate sense, not like employees of an entity as distant and abstract as the "state." If this is so, and if it is not simply a temporary phenomenon connected with the enthusiasm which the early stage of a successful revolution always generates, then we think it likely that the peasants themselves will *make* the co-operative into something quite distinct from the Soviet version of the state farm. Given the fact that the cooperative is completely reshaping their physical environment, raising their cultural level, and transforming their whole way of life, it seems reasonable to expect a degree of involvement and participation far beyond that which characterizes the relationship of the industrial worker to the plant in which he is employed. And, as literacy increases and new skills are mastered, it would indeed be surprising if the members of the cooperative did not find themselves assuming increasing responsibilities for its affairs—including, in addition to the management of its productive and commercial operations, also the government of the new community to which the cooperative is giving rise. Many analysts of Cuban society have noted, usually with regret, that Cubans have almost no tradition of local self-government, and they tend to attribute many of the weaknesses of political democracy as it has operated in Cuba in the past to this cause. It now seems quite possible that the cooperative will change this, not via some lofty constitutional pronouncements but by virtue of the fact that it is the agency which is lifting the Cuban *guajiro* out of his traditional poverty and illiteracy and integrating him into a thoroughly civilized community life. How many of our champions of "pure" democracy through the magic of "free" elections will be ready even to consider the possibility?

In this connection, one is tempted to make comparisons between the Cuban cooperative and two other latter-day collective social institutions, the Chinese commune and the Yugoslav self-governing enterprise. The Cuban cooperative may turn out to be like the commune in combining economic and govermental affairs, and it may develop toward the same goal of self-government that the Yugoslavs have set for their enterprises. However, differences of size (especially between the commune and the cooperative) and historic background make snap comparisons of this kind rather risky. Perhaps it is safest to conclude at this stage that the Cuban cooperative, while bearing a resemblance to various other forms of collective enterprise, is basically an answer to Cuban problems and a product of Cuba's past. It bids fair to take its place as Cuba's most distinctive contribution to the storehouse of institutional inventions from which future revolutions can draw their inspiration and examples.

Whatever position one may take on these admittedly still highly controversial theoretical questions, there can be no question whatever that agrarian reform—and specifically the cooperatives and INRA—has in the short space of one year brought an enormous economic, social, and cultural advance to the Cuban countryside. This is obvious to anyone who will go and look, and it has been attested to time and again by experienced newspaper reporters, even some who are in other respects highly critical of the Castro government. Space limitations prevent our attempting any detailed documentation of this point. Instead we have selected for reproduction in full one dispatch, dealing with what we believe to be a typical situation, by R. Hart Phillips, the permanent *New York Times* correspondent in Cuba:

PARADERO DE DURAN, CUBA, April 8—Adalberto Pena, who lives in this village near the southern coast, about thirty miles from Havana, cannot remember having had a glass of milk until six months ago.

Adalberto, who is 14 years old and looks about 10, said proudly that he had gained twenty pounds in the last six months and that his five brothers and sisters also had put on weight.

"We have a lot to eat now," he said happily, "and everybody drinks milk." Adalberto's father said the children had grown up on a diet of rice and black beans.

The story of Adalberto is the story of most of the children of the eighty members of the René Reina Garcia cooperative farm established by the National Institute of Agrarian Reform in the southern part of Havana Province.

The peasants have lived in the area for many years in small wooden shacks. They worked four or five months a year cutting sugar cane. The rest of the time they eked out a bare existence by doing any work they could find.

The 2,900 acres that form the cooperative were seized by the Institute of Agrarian Reform from the Gomez Mena family. This was part of the land on which cane was grown by the Mercedita Sugar Mill owned by the Gomez Mena family.

The Institute also seized 565 head of cattle from the Gomez Mena dairy, the pumping plants for irrigation, and all equipment.

Armando Cremata, manager of the cooperative, said the property would be paid for with twenty-year bonds at $4\frac{1}{2}$ percent interest as required by the Agrarian Reform Law.

Señor Cremata, a tall, broad-shouldered young man wearing a broad-brim hat, khaki pants, a striped shirt and with a Luger pistol swinging at his hip, showed the cooperative with pride.

This farm is operated in accordance with accepted business methods. Señor Cremata was graduated from a technical school after two years of agricultural study. He worked for several years at the Santiago de las Vegas agricultural experiment station near Havana.

Señor Cremata keeps careful records. He estimates that the farm will produce a gross income of $177,000 this year. Expenses are expected to be $100,000, leaving a profit of $77,000. However, Señor Cremata said he might be a little too optimistic about expenses.

The workers were finishing the harvest of what was said to be about $17,000 worth of lettuce. The big heads were firm, which is highly unusual for lettuce grown in Cuba.

The tomato crop, which brought the farm $25,000, had been harvested. These tomatoes were part of a big shipment the Institute of Agrarian Reform sent to the United States. Carrots were being planted in an irrigated field.

Since crops can be grown throughout the year in Cuba, Señor Cremata said that with increased irrigation from five new wells any kind of vegetable or fruit would give an extraordinarily high yield in the rich black soil of the farm.

Part of the cane crop was plowed under because it was of poor quality. However, the cooperative members have cut $35,000 worth of cane and delivered it to the Mercedita Sugar Mill. Some new cane will be planted so the farm can retain its quota, which is fixed by law, Señor Cremata said.

From 100 to 175 outside day laborers are employed by the cooperative. These are paid $2.67 a day. Each member of the cooperative receives $2.50 a day and part of the profits. The hired workers are housed in barracks and charged $1 a day for food.

The bodega (grocery and bar) owned by the Gomez Mena family's sugar mill was seized. Liquor was banned and a "store of the people" was established.

All cooperative members buy their groceries on credit. Accounts are settled at the end of each month. As is done by the Cuban government in other districts, this store limits its profits to 15 percent.

Señor Cremata said the Institute of Agrarian Reform supplied the tractors and all farm equipment for the cooperative.

Meanwhile, Señor Cremata has piped water into the houses, established a school, cleaned up an old barn for use as a library, and provided movies.

"At first some of our members found it hard to believe all this," Domingo Hernandez, president of the cooperative, said with a wave of his hand toward the growing crops. But the cooperative members are now working enthusiastically and their faces wear the pleased expression of adults who have just been convinced that there really is a Santa Claus.

We have collected a considerable number of similar reports and can confirm their general accuracy from first-hand observation of cooperatives in widely separated parts of the island. To say that the cooperatives are a success is a mild understatement. The truth is that there has probably never been a major social reform in any country at any time that has been accepted more enthusiastically or paid off more handsomely than the agrarian reform in Cuba. Theodore Draper was not exaggerating a bit when he wrote in *The Reporter,* May 12, 1960:

No matter what one may think of the theory behind Cuba's land reform program and no matter how the program turns out in practice, there is no getting around the fact that for the poor, illiterate, landless, outcast *guajiros,* the cooperatives represent a jump of centuries in living standards. They also represent a vast increase of constructive activity in the rural areas that were formerly the most backward and stagnant part of Cuba.

It is necessary to keep these facts constantly in mind when reading the news from Cuba. The upper class is solidly against the new regime, the middle class is sharply divided, there are even waverers among the urban workers. These fissures give rise to spectacular defections, fights among university students, published manifestos, charges and counter-charges—and it is happenings of this sort that make the headlines. The unwary reader could be pardoned for concluding at least once a month, if not oftener, that the regime is about to collapse or be overthrown. When it isn't, when in fact it continues to hew to an uncompromising revolutionary line despite all the threats and shouting, he should remember that its real support has all along been in the rebel army and the peasantry from which the rebel army is largely recruited, and he should also remember that owing to the tremendous achievements of agrarian reform the bond between the regime and the peasantry has never been so strong as it is today.

Turning now to the subject of industry, we find that the conditions that faced the new regime were altogether different from those which gave rise to the land reform. The problem in the industrial field was not so much a basic overhaul of what already existed, for the simple reason that not very much did exist. The problem was rather to create a whole new complex of industries. This of course has been one of the chief proclaimed aims of the revolutionary movement from the very beginning, but in the nature of the case it was not an aim that could be quickly realized. The time required to build a single new factory and provide it with modern machinery and equipment has to be measured not in weeks and months but in years, and this even where all the necessary preconditions exist in the way of availability of personnel with needed organizational and technical experience, adequate financial and material resources, etc. In Cuba these preconditions decidedly did not exist, and the problem was not to build a single factory but to provide the Cuban economy wih a diversified industrial base. Quite inevitably, what has been done along this line to date has been almost wholly in the realm of study, planning, preliminary preparations.*

Paradoxical as it may sound, while this preparatory work was going on, the *need* for industrialization was growing day by day. This was principally owing to two causes set in motion by the vigorous reform activities of the government in other areas:

---

* As far as current industrial operations are concerned, the policies of the new regime have naturally centered upon the problem of getting as much as possible out of already available resources. This is a subject which we must pass over—for lack of space, not because there would be nothing interesting to say. For example, in the case of the American-owned telephone company, there was a difficult problem from the outset. Service is grossly inadequate, as any visitor to Havana can testify. The company had been holding off on improvements for years while trying to get the government to agree to higher rates. Having intervened the company, the new government simultaneously *reduced* rates and launched a program of expanding the number of phones. According to information given us by Minister of Communications Oltuski, the rate reduction cut the company's revenues by $15.5 million in the year March, 1959, to March, 1960. In the same period the number of phones in operation was expanded from 150,000 to 190,000, or by more than 25 percent (there were, however, still 60,000 unfilled orders), and various other investments were made. Nevertheless, the company was still able to earn a return of 6 to 7 percent on the real value of its investment. Oltulski told us in considerable detail of the devices the company had in the past made use of to inflate both its capitalization and its costs: it sounded like a catalogue of the abuses uncovered by the Federal Trade Commission in its famous investigation of the United States power companies in the early 1930's at a time when this country, too, was in a reforming mood.

In this connection it may be interesting to note that the Ministry of Communications is also responsible for regulating the American-owned electric power company, which supplies 90 percent of the island's publicly sold electricity. The electric company has not been intervened but is being carefully investigated, and of course all the same abuses (excessive executive salaries, overpayment for equipment, payment for services allegedly but not actually rendered by affiliated companies, etc., etc.) have been found to exist. When we talked with Oltuski the case was *sub judice* as it were, and he could not comment on what would be done when the investigation was completed. Sooner or later, however, we have no doubt that both the telephone company and the electric company will be nationalized: private ownership in these fields makes no sense even in highly developed capitalist countries (witness the experience of the United States) and even less in underdeveloped countries. The only questions are when and on what terms it will be done.

(1) The upsurge in mass purchasing power consequent on rent and price reductions, wage increases, the establishment of the people's stores, etc. This opened up vast new markets for all kinds of consumer goods at the very time when, for reasons which will be discussed later, imports were necessarily being strictly limited. Some of this enlarged demand, indeed the most important part of it, could fortunately be met at this stage of development through the expansion of agricultural production which was being made possible and promoted by the agrarian reform. (2) But agrarian reform itself created a demand for a variety of domestically produced goods and services, many of which Cuba has never provided before. For example, INRA's plans envisage a rapid increase of cotton production to replace a hitherto imported raw material. But if the cotton is to be produced and used in Cuba it must also be ginned and stored in Cuba, and this requires the creation of a new industry. Similarly, the expansion of output of many other commodities will require additional processing facilities. It will also require increased inputs of various kinds, and these too must for the most part be supplied domestically—e.g. cattle and poultry feeds, chemical fertilizers, etc.

Unless at least the most urgent of these needs for increased industrial output are met within a reasonable time, it is clear that agrarian reform itself, and indeed the whole revolutionary program, will be seriously threatened. The expansion of agricultural output may be limited or its usefulness curtailed; the increased purchasing power of the masses may be dissipated in rising prices instead of rising standards of consumption; the necessity to import necessities may make it impossible to buy the things that are indispensable for longer-run development. Industrialization, in other words, is not something that can be postponed indefinitely. It inevitably takes time, but it is an integral part of a complex process and any unnecessary or undue delay may endanger the whole process, and that means the whole revolution.

This explains why INRA, as the key economic agency of the revolution, has from the beginning been concerned with industrialization. Soon after INRA's own establishment, it organized a Department of Industrialization, and an indication of the importance of this Department may be gathered from the fact that its first director was Ché Guevara, one of the three top leaders of both government and army. When Guevara moved into the presidency of the National Bank last November, his position as head of the Industrialization Department was taken by César Rodríguez, an engineer; but Ché retains his interest in the Department (he told us that he has no taste for the bank job and would prefer his former position as head of the Department of Industrialization to any other in the government), and it remains one of the three or four nerve centers of the revolutionary program. It was the locus of the first genuine comprehensive economic planning activity; and though this work is now increasingly being shifted into the Planning Commission, the Department will continue to play an important, though increasingly technical, role in the whole development process.

At the present time, for reasons which have been alluded to, the industrialization program centers on two types of projects: (1) those needed to complement the agrarian reform, and (2) those that can best contribute to relieving the pressure on the balance of payments. Projects which have longer-range or more ambitious goals are of course being thought about but are still a long way from the action stage, or even the planning stage for that matter. The type and magnitude of projects which stand at or near the top of the priority list are indicated in a number of memoranda which were prepared in the Department of Industrialization in February. Fidel had made a speech the previous month stressing the goal of industrialization and asking the organized workers of the island to contribute 4 percent of their wages for this purpose. The Department of Industrialization was then asked to draw up a list of projects to be financed by the estimated $40 million which the wage deduction would put at the disposal of the government. The Department, finding itself unable to keep within the $40-million limit, submitted instead a list of 27 projects based on criteria of urgency and practicality, suggesting that additional means of financing should be provided. The following table summarizes the proposals:

Sector	Estimated total investment	Maximum employment
Related to agriculture & cattle raising	$16,006,000	2,874
Chemical	32,800,000	645
Metallurgical	76,230,000	2,787
Mining	4,060,000	2,220
Textile	22,750,000	2,244
Totals	151,846,000	10,770

As already indicated, these projects would be aimed chiefly at complementing the agrarian reform and easing the pressure on the balance of payments,* and from the point of view of these objectives it is undoubtedly important that they should be initiated and completed as soon as possible. But they are clearly not of a size or type to effect any basic changes in the structural characteristics of the Cuban economy. Industrialization of *that* kind is still several years away on even the most optimistic calculation.

Lack of space prevents us from discussing these longer-range problems and prospects. We will only add that Cuba's potential is enormous, the problems challenging and exciting, the prospects almost unlimited. It seems clear that sugar cane can become the basis of a wide variety of chemical and manufacturing industries, and as a producer of cane Cuba has natural advantages unmatched anywhere else in the world. Provided with adequate supplies of fertilizer and mechanical equipment, cane production could be greatly expanded while using much less land and labor than at present. Released workers, as well as any that may still be unemployed from other causes, will be available to man the new indus-

---

* Actually, the problem is a good deal more complex than this would suggest. Nearly two thirds of the $152-million investment would have to be paid out for imported materials and machinery, which means that initially the pressure on the balance of payments would be *increased,* with relief coming later when the new plants get into operation. The logical answer, of course, is credits from abroad to cover the import component. Credits for specific projects of this kind are in a real sense self-liquidating, since they make possible the foreign exchange savings out of which they can be repaid. This is unquestionably the type of project to which Cuba will devote whatever foreign credits it can get hold of in the next few years.

tries. In addition, as our own Department of Commerce says
(*Investment in Cuba, p.* 59), Cuba is "one of the world's most
important sources of iron"—not to mention many other mineral
treasures at present locked up in the island's enormous lateritic
ore bodies—so that a great future in mining and metallurgy seems
also assured. Cuba already has the kind of social structure needed
to realize the island's glittering potential. It also has a leadership
with the necessary boldness and imagination. What it still lacks is
above all mastery of modern science and technique, and to overcome this obstacle will take time.

One final subject must be dealt with under the heading of
structural reforms, the establishment of appropriate economic
planning machinery. This was begun with the creation within
INRA's Department of Industrialization of a Section of Planning
and Studies. But INRA, despite its size and key importance, is only
one of a number of government agencies dealing with and having
an effect on the economy, and obviously INRA was in no position
to direct or coordinate the activities of the others. Hence late in
February of this year—nearly 14 months after the new regime
came to power—a Planning Commission (*Junta de planificación*)
was formed at the ministerial level. This Commission consists of
the Prime Minister; the Ministers of Finance, Commerce, and
Public Works; the President of the National Bank; a delegate from
INRA; and the Minister of Economy. The Minister of Economy,
Regino Boti, is *ex officio* Secretary of the Commission and heads
its Secretariat which becomes the government's technical planning
arm. The Secretariat in turn is divided into three Departments—
Planning, which now incorporates the bureau of the budget, formerly a part of the Ministry of Finance; Statistics; and Economic
Organization. The Cuban mission of the UN Economic Commission for Latin America (where Boti worked for many years) is
cooperating in setting up the Secretariat. Aside from getting
organized, which involves bringing in many new young men
(some, who are still studying at the University, on a part-time
basis), the main task of the Secretariat at the present time is
to work out new budgets for all ministries and agencies. Boti told
us that he hoped to have this done for all ministries by July 1

and to have made a beginning on INRA's budget by then. Last year, he said, budgets were uncoordinated, and total government outlays jumped from $420 million in the first half to $830 million in the second half. Receipts rose too—owing to an overhaul in the tax system, the elimination of tax evasion, and an increase in economic activity—but still there was an unplanned deficit for the year of around $100 million.

In the future, we have no doubt, finances will be under much better control. Moreover, the Secretariat of the Planning Commission is beginning to organize a statistical collecting and processing service which will soon be the most advanced in Latin America. And in the offing is the great task of formulating an over-all plan for the development of the Cuban economy for the next three-year or five-year period.

Like many another social revolution before it, the Cuban Revolution has developed its own symbolism—the beard and long hair of the rebel soldier, the peasant with raised machete, the transformation of fortresses into schools, such slogans as "Liberty or Death" and "Revolution Means to Construct." Along this line, the year 1959 was officially dubbed "The Year of Liberation" and 1960 "The Year of Agrarian Reform." If outsiders may be allowed a suggestion, we would propose that 1961 might well be "The Year of the First Economic Plan" and 1962 the first of many "Years of Industrialization."

CHAPTER 11

The Cuban Economy in 1959

In the last three chapters we have attempted to characterize the new regime in Cuba and to describe and explain the major reforms which it has brought to the country's social and economic structure. It is time to pause and ask how the new *system*—for that is what it amounts to—is performing.

Anyone whose knowledge of Cuba comes from the North American press can hardly help believing that during the first year of the Revolution the Cuban economy went from bad to worse and now faces an imminent crisis. We went to Cuba with a fear that this might be the case, and we learned after we got there that it is also a very widely held opinion among Americans and upper-class Cubans inside the country. What are the facts?

Available statistics are neither very complete nor very accurate —the government is the first to admit and deplore it—but they are plenty good enough to enable one to make general comparisons with the past and to paint an overall picture of the present. What they show is the very opposite of a depression-ridden and crisis-threatened economy. The truth is that Cuba experienced an economic boom in 1959. What's more, for the first time in modern Cuban history it was a boom which was *not* based on a strong international demand for sugar, and it occurred in spite of a sharp drop in private home building which has traditionally been one of the island's main economic activities.*

Gross National Product was $2.8 billion in 1957 and declined to $2.6 billion in 1958 owing both to the civil war and the inter-

---

* As indicated above (p. 103), the reason for this decline in private construction was primarily the revolutionary laws reducing rents and putting a ceiling on real estate prices. INAV's public housing program provided nearly as many dwelling units as the private industry had been building earlier but in *value* terms INAV's modest homes were no match for Havana's luxury apartment houses.

national recession of that year. In 1959, the first year of the Revolution, it climbed back up to $2.8 billion. For the same three years, sugar exports and private building behaved as follows:

	Sugar exports		Private building	
	(Value in million $)	(Percent change)	(Value in million $)	(Percent change)
1957	650	—	77.4	—
1958	550	—15.2	74.0	— 4.3
1959	530	— 4.7	33.0	—56.5

At the time of writing the final official figure for value of sugar exports in 1959 is not available to us. In order to have comparable figures for the three years we have therefore computed values by multiplying quantity of exports by the annual f.o.b. price as reported in the *Annuario Azucarero de Cuba* 1959. The figures are rounded so as not to give the impression of exactness. There is no doubt that the order of magnitude of the changes is correctly indicated.

It will be seen that the 1957-1958 pattern is quite "normal." Sugar exports go down by around a hundred million dollars and the economy as a whole contracts by about twice as much. Private building declines as a part of this general contraction. The 1958-1959 pattern, on the other hand, is quite unprecedented. Sugar exports continue to decline, and a tremendous reduction of private building is precipitated by the new regime's rent control and real estate ceiling laws. Nevertheless, Gross National Product recovers to its 1957 level, an increase over 1958 of approximately 7 percent.

The explanation of this seeming paradox is not far to seek. Mass purchasing power was greatly stimulated by the rent reduction and other price roll-backs and by a substantial increase in the wages of lower-paid workers both in the countryside and in the cities. At the same time, public investment by INRA, INAV, the National Tourist Institute (INIT*), and the Ministry of Public Works (chiefly for highways, water supply, and sewage disposal) was vigorously expanded. The stepped-up buying of consumers and public agencies created thousands of new jobs, and these newly

---

* Most of INIT's activities are designed to increase and improve accommodations for *Cuban* tourists and vacationers (public beaches, motels in the countryside, and so on). The luxury hotels, restaurants, and nightclubs of Havana and Varadero which cater to foreign tourists are largely empty because of the reluctance of North Americans to travel to Cuba under present conditions.

employed workers brought additional purchasing power to the market. The result was a cumulative upward movement of effective demand which was more than enough to compensate for the decline in sugar exports and private building. In terms of wages and employment, the results, according to figures given us by the Minister of Labor, Comandante Augusto Martínez Sanchez, were as follows: The total wage bill in 1958 was $723 million; this went up to $1,056 million in 1959, an increase of 46 percent. On January 1, 1959, when the new regime took power, there were 371,000 totally unemployed workers; this went down to 237,000 a year later, a decrease of 36 percent (no estimates of the reduction in partial unemployment were available). Comandante Martínez was confident—and we see no reason to question his confidence— that this rate of expansion of employment can be maintained and that as a consequence *Cuba's traditional scourge of chronic unemployment will give way to a general shortage of labor in three or four years.* If the Cuban Revolution should accomplish nothing else, this by itself would be a history-making achievement.

To what extent was the very large increase in mass purchasing power indicated by these figures dissipated in higher prices rather than higher real incomes? Unfortunately, there is no consumer price or cost of living index on which to base an answer to this question. The only published statistic which purports to provide information relevant to the question is called "Buying Power of the Cuban Peso in Relation to the Cost of Food." With the second half of the year 1937 taken as $1, this stood at 39.1 cents in December, 1958, and at 40.3 cents in July, 1959, the latest figure available to us at the time of writing. This particular index, however, is not highly regarded by the experts and should not be given undue weight. We attempted to approach the matter directly, if somewhat crudely, by asking various people for their impressions of what happened to the cost of living since the new regime came to power. The striking thing about the answers was their disparity. Cooperative members all reported that consumer prices had gone down substantially. Government economists, who as far as their standard of living is concerned may be taken as representative of the urban professional classes, thought the cost of living for them had gone up about 10 percent. And businessmen, among whom we were fortunate to have excellent contacts, reported a catastrophic fall in the purchasing power of *their* pesos.

There is, of course, no contradiction involved in these answers: they were all offered in good faith, and we have no reason to disbelieve any of them. The people's stores have obviously brought prices down in the countryside, and there has unquestionably been some increase in the average city store or market. Really big increases, moreover, have affected many high-quality and luxury goods which are bought by the rich and have traditionally been almost entirely imported. (Many imports have been cut off altogether by a strict licensing system, and others have been subjected to high *ad valorem* taxes. The balance of payments problem which prompted these measures will be discussed below.) We are entitled to conclude that in Cuba today what has happened to the cost of living depends on who you are and what consuming habits you have acquired in the past. And in this, as in all other respects, the chief beneficiaries have been the poor and the chief sufferers the rich.

If we want to get an idea of how much the consumption of the country as a whole has increased, we will do better to turn from income and price data to figures on the production of commonly used commodities. On the industrial side, we have chosen two commodities as being reasonably revealing, namely, electricity and beer. Both are in wide use, and in each case the entire supply is domestically produced. Here are the figures for 1958 and 1959:

	1958	1959	Percent change
Electricity (millions of kwh)	1,463	1,619	+10.6
Beer (millions of liters)	123	156	+26.4

On the agricultural side, we present a complete list of the main crops. These figures are much less useful for judging changes in domestic consumption, since there has traditionally been a large export or import trade in most of them. But they throw a very bright light indeed on the results of the agrarian reform:*

PRODUCTION OF MAIN CROPS
(Thousands of metric tons)

	1958	1959	Percent change
Sugar	5,778.6	5,964.2	+ 3
Tobacco	41.6	41.2	− 1
Coffee	29.1	49.2	+68
Rice (unpolished)	222.7	295.5	+32
Cotton	0	1.4	—
Black and red beans	30.0	35.0	+16
Corn	147.0	190.0	+29
Peanuts	7.0	11.0	+42
Potatoes	101.0	113.0	+11
Pineapples	100.0	98.0	− 2
Oranges	73.0	81.0	+11
Cucumbers	18.0	18.0	0
Tomatoes	69.3	73.1	+ 5

A few notes on this table are in order. The first three crops on the list—sugar, tobacco, and coffee—are Cuba's traditional export crops. The big increase in coffee production is due entirely to the fact that this crop is mainly grown in the parts of Oriente province which were most affected by fighting in 1958: the increase, in other words, is merely a recovery to a more normal level of production. The essentially static condition of sugar and tobacco arises not from any impossibility of increasing production but rather from limitations of the international market. The vitality of Cuban agriculture as revamped by the agrarian reform is seen in the sharp increase in production of commodities of which Cuba has traditionally been a heavy importer, especially rice, cotton, beans, and peanuts. Corn should be included in this list, though here the increase is not so much a matter of import substitution as it is a reflection of a campaign to develop a more intensive and productive form of cattle raising. These are the crops which have been the center

---

* These figures were all provided to us by government economists. Insofar as they are estimates, the main source is the United States Embassy which has in its employ the man who is generally regarded as Cuba's most experienced and reliable crop estimator.

of INRA's planned expansion drive. *Their total volume increased by almost one third in the first year of the Revolution, and there is no doubt that a comparable rate of expansion is being maintained this year.* China, it seems, is not the only country capable of "big leaps forward"! But what other country has ever staged such a leap forward in the very first year of a Revolution and in the midst of a far-reaching agrarian reform? It can be said without exaggeration: in the Cuban Revolution the world is witnessing a process of socio-economic transformation and vitalization that is in many important respects without *any* precedent. Let the world look hard and draw the appropriate conclusions!

One final area of the economy should be mentioned in this all-too brief survey, namely, animal husbandry. Along with sugar and tobacco, this has been the third pillar of Cuba's traditional agrarian economy, but unlike sugar and tobacco its products (chiefly meat and dairy products) have been almost entirely domestically consumed. It is well known that substantial increases in production of animal products take much longer than in other branches of agriculture, and also that it is in this area that radical agrarian reforms have normally been accompanied by the greatest short-term losses. What is surprising about the Cuban experience, therefore, is not that the production increase in 1959 was small—preliminary estimates put it at about two percent—but that there was any increase at all. What might have been expected was that cattle ranchers, faced with the certainty of losing a large part of their lands, would step up the rate of slaughter in an effort to maximize their short-run profits. That this did not happen was due to the prompt action of INRA in intervening the cattle ranches without waiting for formal legal proceedings. This is probably the aspect of the agrarian reform that has aroused the most bitter criticism in the United States. Few of the critics seem to have understood—or, if they did, to allow their understanding to affect their judgment—that such action was in no sense mere arbitrary lawlessness but rather was essential in order to preserve assets of vital importance to the country as a whole.

The relative inelasticity of supply of animal products has given rise to both problems and illusions in Cuba. The problems stem from the fact that as mass purchasing power has gone up, there has been a tremendous increase in the *demand* for animal products. The result, of course, has been *relative* shortages which have had to be met by various devices such as informal rationing by storekeepers, chickenless Wednesdays, meatless Fridays, and so on. These shortages, in turn, have given rise to the illusions: time and again they were cited to us by enemies of the regime as "evidence" of economic chaos and imminent collapse. Actually, of course, they are symptoms of unprecedented well-being for the great mass of Cuban consumers. In our day and age conservatives seem fated to see everything upside down.

By the time we visited Cuba—in March, 1960—the essentially temporary problems of the animal products industry were well on the way to solution. We base this statement not on optimistic forecasts by INRA visionaries but on information given us by a representative of the United Nations Food and Agriculture Organization (FAO) who was working with INRA. According to him, no figures for the whole island were available. But in Havana, which accounts for about 40 percent of total beef consumption, the rate of slaughter in March, 1960, was between 60 and 70 percent higher than a year earlier. Was this not resulting in a depletion of herds, we asked? No, he replied. By then the currently maturing supply of beef cattle had also been sharply stepped up, chiefly owing to better feeding methods (remember the 29 percent increase in corn production). There could be no better evidence than this that (1) the Revolution has already transformed the standard of living of the Cuban masses, and (2) this new and higher standard of living has come to stay.

Looking somewhat farther ahead one is safe in saying that animal husbandry in Cuba has a brilliant future. Most of the old cattle latifundia were miserably backward and wasteful of good land. Actually, Cuba is ideally suited to a technologically modern, capital-intensive cattle culture, and it is along this road that INRA is rapidly moving. It won't be many years before Cuba will not only be supplying all the animal products she needs but will be deriving a large and growing amount of much-needed foreign exchange from this source. There are probably few other fields in which the superiority of planned collective enterprise to chaotic private enterprise is greater or more visible.

Mention of Cuba's need for foreign exchange brings us to the last subject of this chapter, the balance of payments. Since the usual statistical presentation of a country's balance of payments is likely to be more confusing than enlightening to the nonexpert reader we will attempt a somewhat modified exposition.

First, two points which have been stressed more than once in earlier chapters should be recalled: (a) the predominance of sugar and other cane products in Cuba's export trade, normally amounting to between 80 and 90 percent of total exports; and (b) the almost as overwhelming predominance of the United States among Cuba's trading partners (since the war about 60 percent of Cuba's exports have gone to the United States and about 75 percent of imports have come from the United States). Second, while Cuba has normally exported more commodities than she has imported, in no recent year has the export surplus been enough to cover deficits incurred under other headings of what is called the current account. Here is the picture of transactions on current account for the whole seven years of Batista's second dictatorship (1952-1958):

CUBA'S CURRENT ACCOUNT
(Millions of dollars)
Aggregates for seven years, 1952-1958

	Receipts	Expenditures	Balance
1. Merchandise	4,818.1	4,636.4	181.7
2. Tourism	247.7	232.9	14.8
3. Transportation	49.7	480.7	−431.0
4. Insurance	5.5	11.8	− 6.3
5. Dividends & interest	51.7	369.1	−317.4
6. Gov't transactions	12.0	9.7	2.3
7. Other services	138.5	33.8	104.7
8. Gifts	17.1	36.5	− 19.4
9. Total (1 through 8)	5,340.3	5,810.9	−470.6

What this means is that normal business transactions over the seven-year period gave rise to a deficit of nearly half a billion dollars. How was this deficit covered?

For one thing Cuba imported quite a bit of capital from abroad, mostly from the United States. This totaled $120.9 million, leaving $349.7 million to be covered. This was done in two ways. First, at the time of Batista's coming to power, Cuba had large gold and foreign exchange reserves which had been built up during the war and postwar years of strong international demand for sugar. These reserves were systematically drawn upon to cover the deficits of the 1950's. But the total paid out in this way was $513.1 million, which is $163.4 million *greater* than the remaining deficit of $349.7 million. What does this mean?

In the official statistics, this gap is listed under the innocent-sounding heading of "Errors and omissions," which makes it sound like a mere technical detail. Now, there need be no doubt that errors exist throughout the table, and not much can be said about them. But the "omissions" are another matter. We know quite a lot about them—in fact, almost everything except their amount. When one of Batista's buddies brought in an automobile without declaring it at the customs, that was an omission. When another of them, or the dictator himself, sent a million pesos by courier to New York, had them sold there for dollars, and deposited the proceeds in his name in a New York bank, that too was an omission. The omissions from the balance of payments figures, in other words, represent a part of the goods and money stolen by Batista and his henchmen during their eight years of plundering and torturing the Cuban people. We get an idea of how large these depredations were from the fact that they occasioned this drain of $163.4 million on the nation's reserves above and beyond what would have been required to cover the deficit arising from regular business transactions.

Several other things should be noted about these figures. First, we see the relative unimportance of tourism to Cuba's balance of payments. Over the seven year period, Cubans traveling abroad (mostly in the United States) spent almost as much as foreigners traveling in Cuba. Second, the payments of dividends and interest to foreign capitalists is an enormous drain on the balance of payments, second only to the deficit incurred for paying foreigners to transport Cuban goods. When you observe that over $300 million was sucked out of Cuba in dividends and interest, while only $120 million foreign capital was being invested in Cuba, you may wonder about the great blessings that underdeveloped countries are supposed to derive from the beneficent operations of foreign capitalists.

But the main point, of course, is that the balance of payments was consistently unfavorable to Cuba during the whole Batista period, with the result that what had been a very strong gold and foreign exchange position at the outset had deteriorated to the point of imminent crisis by the end. This was in many ways the most difficult and intractable problem the new regime inherited from its predecessors, and early attempts to cope with it met with indifferent success. Progressively stricter import controls were introduced, and in November Ché Guevara was installed as President of the National Bank to administer them. Meanwhile, INRA was, as already noted above, moving as fast as possible to expand production of the main imported crops. Still, 1959 as a whole witnessed a further deterioration of the reserve position. The *Wall Street Journal* of March 28th cites Guevara as authority for the statement that on December 31, 1959, one full year after the new regime came to power, the nation's gold and dollar reserves had dropped from $75 million to $50 million. The calamity howlers were naturally delighted, and in this case they seemed to have something worth crowing about. There is no doubt that a continuation of the drain would soon have brought a serious threat to important parts of the revolutionary program.

With the new year, however, a turning point was reached. The same story in the *Wall Street Journal* reported that the reserves had recovered to $65 million by the end of February. In a TV speech early in May, Fidel announced that they were up to $150 million, and as we write, a communication has just been received from a government economist that as of the middle of May the figure had reached $166 million.

What accounts for this success? On the one hand, stricter and more effective import controls, which in turn are made possible by INRA's solid achievements in the production of crucially important import substitutes. On the other hand, an aggressive policy of pushing sugar exports as early in the year as possible. The following report from the April 25th issue of *The Times of Havana,* English-language biweekly, tells an interesting story:

From January 1 to April 16, Cuban sugar exports have totalled 1,953,449 long Spanish tons compared to 1,049,404 tons in the same period of 1959, for an increase of 904,045 [86.2 percent].

Of this amount, 946,491 tons have been shipped to the U.S. market as compared to 804,169 tons a year ago. This constitutes 40.14 percent of the U.S. quota.

The remainder, or 1,006,958 tons, was shipped to the world market. This compares with 245,235 tons last year.

Bulk sugar shipments this year have risen to 572,926 tons as compared to only 232,081 tons at the same time in 1959.

It appears that the "impractical" and "inexperienced" young men who are running the Cuban economy are making quite a stab at getting things done on time and in good order!

To be sure, this accelerated rate of sugar exports cannot be maintained throughout the year, the annual market for Cuban sugar being narrowly limited by the United States quota on the one hand and Cuba's obligations under the International Sugar Agreement on the other. But it has served its purpose—to banish the specter of national bankruptcy—and with INRA's program of crop expansion now running at full speed, the threat of further foreign exchange crises seems definitely to have receded into the background.

This is not to argue that the balance of payments problem has been solved once and for all. Cuba's need for imports, especially of a wide variety of capital goods, is almost unlimited. This will continue to be the case for years to come, and as long as it is, there will be a balance of payments problem. But the crisis phase is past and the prospects for progressive improvement in the future are bright. In this, as in other aspects of its economic program, the record of the new regime is excellent.

CHAPTER 12

Capitalism, Socialism, Communism?

We have demonstrated not only that the new system in Cuba has introduced the economic and social reforms which have long been advocated but never before acted upon, but also that it is vastly superior in performance to its predecessor. It remains to determine what kind of a system it is.

This question cannot be answered on the basis of any programmatic or ideological texts. Fidel's speeches are replete with advocacy of specific reforms of precisely the kind that have been adopted, but nowhere, so far as we have been able to discover, has he attempted to characterize the social order which either he personally, or the July 26th Movement which he heads, hopes to see created. Measures are adopted either because they seem obviously to be in the interest of the masses or because they are needed to complement other measures that have already been adopted, never because they fit logically into a theoretical framework. Jean Paul Sartre, the French philosopher and playwright who visited Cuba in March, commented on this aspect of the Cuban Revolution as follows:

> In Paris I questioned a certain number of Cubans, but was never able to understand why they refused to tell me if the objective of the Cuban Revolution was or was not to establish socialism. Now I understand why they could not tell me. That is, that the originality of this Revolution consists precisely in doing what needs to be done without attempting to define it by means of a previous ideology.

If the questioner persists, insisting that there must be some name that is appropriate to the new Cuban society, he is likely to be told, as Joseph Newman of the *New York Herald Tribune* was told, that the Cuban government and Revolution "were 'neither capitalist nor Communist' but simply 'Cuban and humanist.' "

Such a statement accurately reflects the nationalist and humanitarian motives of those who made the Cuban Revolution, but unfortunately it does not help us at all to understand what kind of society is being built in Cuba. We know a good deal about feudalism; we know a good deal about capitalism, including several variants (competitive, monopolistic, underdeveloped) of this system; we are rapidly learning a good deal about socialism. It is therefore an enormous advantage, in studying a given society, to be able to identify it as belonging to one or another of these recognized categories: to do so is to bring to our aid a whole body of previous scientific investigation, to expand enormously our understanding of its mode of functioning, and to provide fruitful hypotheses as to its probable future course of development. The "typing" of a given social system is thus by no means an idle parlor game, it is an essential aspect of any serious analytical effort.

The question we must ask about Cuba, therefore, concerns not the motives of those who made, and are making, the Revolution, but rather the objective characteristics of the social order which is emerging from their labors. Does this social order conform in general outline to any of the recognized present-day systems? More specifically, since it obviously is not feudalism, can it be classified as capitalist or socialist? Or must we conclude that it is really something new and unique, with its own structure and laws of development?

For our part, we have no hesitation in answering: *the new Cuba is a socialist Cuba.* This does not mean that all or even the majority of the means of production are now publicly owned. Undoubtedly, they are not. But, as previous chapters have surely made clear, the dynamic and in this sense overwhelmingly decisive sector in the Cuban economy today is the public sector. Furthermore, while no comprehensive economic plan has as yet been formulated, there can be no question that the government's economic policies and actions, far from being haphazard and uncoordinated, are directed by a supreme central authority—now in the process of being institutionalized in the Planning Commission and its Secretariat—with a view to optimizing their effects on the economy as a whole.

A skeptic might reply that this is the situation *now,* at a time when the momentum of the Revolution has swept all before it and the opposition is disorganized and weak. Later, he might maintain, it will be different. The momentum of the Revolution will peter out, as it always has in past revolutions, and then the *permanent* interest of the still quantitatively predominant private sector will reassert itself, eroding reforms, encroaching on the public sector, corrupting the planners and administrators. Cuba will then be seen to be not a socialist society but to conform to a capitalist type which is common enough in the world today, in which the state plays a large role but as the benefactor and handmaiden of vested interests rather than as the responsible agent of the overwhelming majority of the people. According to this reasoning, the present "socialistic" phase in Cuba is essentially transitory and for this reason cannot be taken as a basis for classifying the Cuban social order. As long as the means of production are predominantly in private hands, Cuba is and will remain essentially a capitalist society.

Now, let there be no mistake: this is a very powerful argument. In fact, if the assumption which underlies it were correct, namely, that the private sector will *remain* quantitatively predominant, we would be obliged to agree with it. It is only political ignorance or naiveté, in our judgment, that can assume the *long-run* compatibility between planning in the public interest and the continued existence of a powerful private sector. Sooner or later, the "planning" will be distorted to the service of private ends or the private sector will be so reduced in size and power as to become incapable of dominating the course of events.

We base our view that Cuba is *and will remain* essentially a socialist society on forces at work in Cuba today which are tending rapidly to reduce the relative importance of the private sector. These forces are partly rooted in the present policies of the revolutionary regime and in part result from pressures over which it has no control.

Under the former heading, the main point to be made is that it is established policy that the entire field of *new* industry involving complex or advanced technology and hence requiring (at this stage) imported capital goods and/or technical personnel, will be reserved exclusively for public enterprise. Given the present meager state of industrial development in Cuba and the manifest vitality of the nascent industrialization drive, this factor alone should be enough to ensure the relatively early predominance of the public sector in the field of industry. In addition, it is government policy to encourage and promote cooperation among the small-scale subsistence farmers who make up the bulk of the non-wage-earning population in the countryside. It is too early to say what sort of a response this policy will evoke, but with the example of the successful INRA cooperatives before them it would hardly be surprising if the rest of Cuba's farmers should turn rather quickly into the road to collective agriculture. In any case, the tendency in the countryside will be toward a larger not a smaller public sector. Finally, we may perhaps add, under the heading of deliberate government policy, the strong likelihood that public utilities and railroads still owned by private interests will be nationalized in due course. That they are still private is an anachronism which a government much less radical than the present Cuban one would hardly be likely to leave long uncorrected.

The automatic forces making for an expansion of the public sector at the expense of the private are more complicated, stemming as they do from a specific historical and international constellation of relationships and events. While there is in Cuba what Marxists have come to call a "national" bourgeoisie—that is to say, a bourgeoisie which has no ties to foreign capital and is strongly anti-imperialist—it is relatively small and weak. The bulk of private enterprise is owned by North Americans; agents or partners of North Americans; or those who, because of psychological and social ties of various kinds, identify themselves more closely with the United States than they do with their own country. These people make up the true Cuban upper class, the "big" bourgeoisie.* They are violently counter-revolutionary and almost to a man look to the

* Its mentality is well suggested by a Havana dispatch by Tad Szulc which appeared in the *New York Times* of April 3rd: "A Cuban gentleman stared enviously at the table occupied by a United States family at a restaurant here one night last week. When the family rose to leave, the man got up from his table and intercepted it. With an embarrassed smile he said: 'I am terribly sorry to do this, but I noticed you had American cigarettes. It would be a

United States to intervene in some way or other to restore the (for them) comfortable world which the Revolution has so rudely shattered. It is simply inconceivable to us that they will be either willing or able to collaborate in the revolutionary reconstruction of the country. We expect their counter-revolutionary tendencies to take more and more overt form (conspiring against the regime, sabotaging the economic plan, etc.), and we do not see how the regime can refuse to meet the challenge by progressively taking over (in what precise form matters little) their part of the private sector of the economy.

If the foregoing analysis is sound, it follows that the public sector will grow both absolutely and relatively to the private sector in the months and years ahead, leaving in the private sector only (1) a few industries such as textiles and beverages which are controlled by the national bourgeoisie, and (2) the petty traders and artisans of the cities. There is no way to estimate precisely how large a proportion of the national economy this might be, but it can safely be said that it will be both small and of diminishing relative importance. We have no doubt that the continued existence of a private sector with these particular characteristics is quite compatible with the development of a full-fledged socialist society.

Turning from the question of what kind of society is emerging from the Cuban Revolution to the quite different, even if not unrelated, question of the role of Communism in Cuba today, one enters an area which is so charged with emotional overtones and conflicts that one almost despairs of being able to present the issues undistorted and in sound historical perspective. Nevertheless, the attempt must be made.

To begin with, then, it must be stressed that Communists, unlike Fidel and the July 26th Movement, are ideologically committed to working for a socialist society. Not being blind, they can see that the measures taken by the new regime, though not dictated by

great favor if you would offer me just one to smoke with my coffee.' . . . Almost everywhere in Cuba United States cigarettes have become a badge of distinction and a social asset a bit reminiscent of the days in Europe immediately after World War II. . . . Many Cubans preferred United States cigarettes although Cuba produces excellent cigarettes in addition to its famous cigars. United States cigarettes were one of the many forms of economic and cultural dependence of Cuba upon its big neighbor."

ideological considerations, are objectively leading in that direction. They therefore cannot help supporting the regime and cooperating with it to the best of their ability. This is why, as all observers agree, they are now devoting all their energy, enthusiasm, and organizing ability to promoting and furthering the government's program. They do this from whatever point of vantage they can reach—inside the government, in the labor movement, the cooperatives, etc.—and without putting forward any slogans or demands that go beyond what the leadership has undertaken, voluntarily and on its own. The leadership, for its part, finding that the Communists work hard for the Revolution, not on their own terms but entirely within the framework of policies laid down by the leadership itself, has no objective reason for rejecting their support or quarreling with them—quite the contrary. And having no well articulated ideology of its own, either Communist or anti-Communist, it has no subjective reason either. Add to this the fact that those, both at home and abroad, who most loudly preach the gospel of anti-Communism are *known* to be enemies of the Revolution and you can understand why the regime has been happy to welcome Communist cooperation and has resolutely fought to keep the issue out of Cuban politics. In fact, under constant goading of the anti-Communist cohorts, the leadership has responded by treating any public raising of the issue as *prima facie* evidence of counter-revolution to be dealt with accordingly.

Does all this mean that the Communists are working themselves into a position from which they can "take over" control of the regime? To assume that it does seems to us to imply an ignorance of recent Cuban history and a naive or disingenuous view of politics.

We have no inside information whatever about whether there are or are not Communists among the top leaders of the Cuban Revolution, but judging from the history of the revolutionary movement it would seem most improbable. From 1953 until around the middle of 1958, the Cuban CP was cool to and sometimes strongly critical of the July 26th Movement. They were definitely rivals for the leadership of the Cuban revolutionary forces, and no love was lost between them. As we pointed out in Chapter 7, it was only after Fidel and his rebel army were already well on the way to victory that the Communists sent an emissary to the Sierra offering their support. By that time all the important present leaders of the regime were long-term veterans of the struggle; they owed absolutely nothing to the Communists, and bonds of solidarity, brotherhood, and loyalty had been formed among themselves which were of a kind and strength that only experiences comparable to the incredible sacrifice, suffering, and heroism of Moncada and the *Granma* and the Sierra campaigns can forge among human beings. If Fidel should join the Communists and bring the others with him, that would be psychologically understandable, but that any of the others should do so alone and on his own seems incredible. Since no responsible observer, to the best of our knowledge, has ever suggested that Fidel has done any such thing, we conclude that the hypothesis of Communist infiltration of the leadership is a pure figment of the anti-Communist imagination.

The question then boils down to this: are the Communists getting into a position from which they can wrest leadership of the masses, of the revolutionary movement itself, out of the hands of Fidel and his colleagues in the army and the government? It would seem to us that anyone who answers this question in the affirmative must either have his tongue in his cheek or believe in black magic. There are said to be about 18,000 members of the CP in Cuba. They have a relative handful of their number scattered around in various government departments. They have traditionally been strong in trade unions, and in recent months Fidel himself, doubtless feeling that the Communists are more reliable collaborators than other available leadership material in the labor movement, has actually helped them to positions of greater trade union power. Otherwise, the Communists have little but a daily newspaper, some able (and some not so able) intellectuals among their leading figures, and the usual party apparatus based on individual members grouped into small cells. By what process of political alchemy are these meager assets to be turned into the building blocks of success against Fidel and his colleagues, who are not only revered by the masses in a way that it is hard for outsiders even to imagine, but in addition have to their credit a record of brilliant leadership in one of the world's most successful revolutions?

Once again, to be sure, we may encounter an argument comparable to that examined above in relation to the character of the Cuban system. It may be said that this is the situation *now*, but that as time goes on and the momentum of the Revolution dies down, it will no longer be possible to maintain two-way communications between masses and leadership in the informal and often spontaneous ways that have worked so admirably up to now. (In this connection, the very greatest importance must be attached to Fidel's masterly TV appearances, in which he quite literally talks directly to the masses and uses his superb pedagogic skills to educate them about the problems facing the regime and the policies adopted to solve these problems. In no respect has the foreign press done greater violence to the truth than by depicting Fidel's TV speeches as the mere rantings of a power-drunk demagogue.) If and when that time comes, the argument would run, there will be a need for a cohesive political apparatus as an intermediary between leadership and masses, capable of transmitting (and interpreting) messages in both directions and of providing necessary discipline, organization, and leadership at regional and local levels where centrifugal forces may be expected to be strongest. Under such circumstances, the CP, which, like all CPs, is designed to carry out precisely such tasks, would come into its own, falling heir to the leadership of the Revolution, by default as it were.

This, too, is a powerful argument, and it may well be precisely along these lines that the Communist leaders themselves are thinking. But once again it is based on a premise that seems to us to be untenable, in this case that only the CP will be ready and able to perform the vitally important intermediary role. The truth is that the need for an apparatus is not going to make itself felt all of a sudden one fine day several years hence, whereupon the Communists will step forward and take over. This need is already beginning to be felt in connection with carrying out the many and complicated tasks of the Revolution as it unfolds, and already various ways of meeting the need are being devised, not by the Communists but by the established leadership of the Revolution. This is a difficult and largely unexplored subject which we are not in a position to treat in any extended, let alone definitive, way. We will only call attention to the fact, which we were able to verify from personal observation, that both the army and INRA, or perhaps it would be more accurate to say the army and INRA in partnership, are extending their activities of an essentially political nature far beyond limits which would be normal for military or bureaucratic apparatuses. They publish a wide variety of propaganda and educational materials, organize schools and courses not only to supply their own specialized personnel needs but also to raise the political level of the masses, organize meetings, and so on. In short, wherever needs for action along such lines make themselves felt, the tendency is not to allow them to go unmet but rather to satisfy them by expanding or adding to the multifarious functions already being discharged by the army and INRA. We are not suggesting that this will necessarily be the way the problem will be finally dealt with—if it makes any sense to use the word "finally" in this context. It may well be that new and more appropriate methods will be devised: there is some talk, for example, of trying to turn the July 26th Movement, which is now in the nature of a symbolic and ceremonial association, into a genuine political party. We simply do not know enough to prophesy in this area, and very likely no one else does either. But what we do know is that the leadership of the Cuban Revolution has shown itself to be extraordinarily energetic and resourceful up to now, and we see no reason to assume in advance that it will be unable to create the institutional machinery which the healthy development of the Revolution may require. In our judgment, for what it is worth, the Communists could make no bigger mistake, now or in the foreseeable future, than to challenge Fidel and his close associates for the leadership of the Revolution. They would lose, and in losing they might easily do irreparable damage to the cause of the Revolution, which of course is also their cause. On the other hand, if they continue to pursue their present course, they may play an important, and in some respects perhaps an indispensable, even if subordinate, role in the building of socialism in Cuba.

Two further points about the role of Communists in Cuba:

(1) People in the United States may understand it better if they recall the role of Communists in the United States in the New Deal period. At that time, there were not a few Communists in the lower levels of the national government and even more in the CIO. They worked hard and often effectively, trying of course always to push matters somewhat further to the Left than they would otherwise tend to go. While they won control in some unions, they were never in a position to make a bid for political leadership in the country and never caused any serious problems except in the minds of the right-wing lunatic fringe. Like all other analogies, this one should not be pushed too far, but we believe that it does serve to give an accurate idea of the part that Communists are playing in the Cuban Revolution.

(2) All the charges and accusations concerning the alleged Communist character of the Cuban government and/or Revolution tend to hide what may turn out to be historically one of the most important facts about the Cuban Revolution: this is the first time—ever, anywhere—that a genuine socialist revolution has been made by *non-Communists!* In the past, no self-styled socialist party has ever even made the effort to put through the deeply radical reforms which are essential if capitalism is to be overthrown and replaced by socialism; only Communist parties have had the necessary determination, in the words of Sartre quoted above, "to do what needs to be done"—and, it should be added, it is this fact more than anything else that has made Communism the formidable world movement it is today. Into this picture stepped Fidel Castro and his rebel army, calling themselves neither socialists nor Communists, in fact without any clearly formulated ideology, seized power in Cuba after two years of bloody civil war, and proceeded with élan and dispatch to "do what needs to be done." No one can now foretell the full implications of this startling fact, but no one need doubt that it will open up new vistas not only in the realm of social thought but also in the realm of revolutionary action.

Before we leave the subject of the character of the new Cuban society and the role of Communism, it will be appropriate to say a few words about the kind and quality of freedom that exists in Cuba today. Two specific impressions will illustrate the complexity of the problem. First, we quote from our notes written down immediately after a two-hour talk with a Cuban big businessman who was introduced to us as having been a strong supporter of Fidel in the anti-Batista days:

Unburdened himself. Cuba is "licked." Terrible conditions. Terror. He and his friends do not dare talk at their clubs for fear of being overheard by the help. If what he said to us were reported he could be shot. Did he know of anyone who had been shot for talking? He could cite no actual examples but insisted that anyone talking in public as he talked to us would be arrested as a counter-revolutionary, put in jail, have his property confiscated, etc.

To put this in proper perspective one must know what he said to us, which was, in a nutshell, that Cuba was going Communist (it made absolutely no difference to him whether Fidel or anyone else was a member of the Communist Party or not) and the United States should intervene, immediately and with whatever armed force might be required, to oust the present government and restore law and order. He also said that on a recent business trip to the United States he had told this to the president of the American college of which he was a graduate and to friends in the State Department. In other words, he talked both counter-revolution and treason, and we had no doubt whatever that he was ready to act on his convictions if he thought he could get away with it. At the same time, he had a well-founded fear that if the government should catch him talking along these lines it would crack down hard on him. For him there was no freedom in Cuba today, and we are perfectly frank in saying that we think it is a good thing for Cuba that there isn't.

The other impression is that of an artist from the United States, Douglas Gorsline, who recently spent a ten-day vacation in Cuba and on his return wrote of his experiences in the pacifist magazine *Liberation* (April 1960). We quote:

. . . I was drawing constantly in many parts of Havana. This provided a unique opportunity to meet many categories of its citizens. . . . Cuba positively reeks of freedom. We were caught up in its heady atmosphere almost from the moment of landing. It is an amazing experience for the jaded American to find a country and a people in such a state of euphoria. It was like Paris just liberated or Ghana freed must have been, perhaps even like New York immediately after victory in our own revolution. Only in a liberated city could there be such instant, happy acquaintance. . . . You see a great many long-haired young soldiers and veteran *barbudos* (the bearded ones), each with his hip-slung .45, or tommy gun. Yet you feel no fear, because it is obvious that the Cubans themselves do not fear them. They have the air of guardians of the revolution, not oppressors, and are regarded with affection and pride. At least while we were there, not a shot was fired in anger, nor did we hear personally an anti-American remark. True there were such questions as "Why isn't your government helping us in this difficult time?" and "Don't you realize that this is the first real taste of freedom our generation has ever had?"

We can fully confirm the genuineness of Mr. Gorsline's account from our own personal experience. We would only add that the sense of freedom which one experiences in the city is much *more* intense in the countryside. Clearly, the Cuban masses, the overwhelming majority of the people of the country, have never been so free at any time in the country's history.

How can you *generalize* about freedom under such conditions? For counter-revolutionaries there is none, for revolutionaries it is all but absolute. And as to whether or not you approve of this state of affairs, how can the conclusion be avoided that it depends on which side you are on, that of the Revolution or the counter-revolution?

The situation is somewhat similar in relation to the problem of elections. No competent observer has any doubt that if elections were to be held now, the government would win an overwhelming majority. Yet the enemies of the Revolution, joined by some liberals who make a fetish of political forms, insistently clamor for elections. Why? Is it because of a passion for pure democracy? Or is it because elections would break the rhythm of the Revolution, revive moribund political rivalries and quarrels, and give the counter-revolution the occasion and opportunity to re-group and prepare a comeback before the great social reforms of the last year have had time to transform Cuba into a society from which both privilege and poverty have been abolished? Once again, it seems to us impossible to avoid the conclusion that whether you are for or against elections at this time depends on which side you are on, that of the Revolution or the counter-revolution.

This does not mean, of course, that those of us who are against elections now want to see the formal machinery of democracy permanently scrapped, or that we are unaware of the dangers inherent in any political system which dispenses with the electoral process. What we do maintain is that the Revolution itself gives the government a far more democratic mandate than the freest of free elections ever could, and that it is the sacred duty of the government to *carry out* the oft-announced platform of the Revolution before it comes back to the people asking for either approval or further instructions.

In the meanwhile, let no man of good will be taken in by the counter-revolutionary propaganda that Cuba is some sort of totalitarian dictatorship. The Revolution will resolutely defend itself against its enemies, both internal and external, and every democrat whose principles reach beyond the realm of empty phrases will heartily applaud. But among honest revolutionaries there is absolutely no fear, no suppression of full and free discussion, no demand for conformity to a dogmatically defined and interpreted line or ideology. For them, and that means for the vast majority of the people of the island, Cuba is indeed a land that "positively reeks of freedom."

CHAPTER 13

The Future of the Revolution

It is almost impossible to imagine a revolution with better prospects of success than the Cuban Revolution. Cuba is such a naturally favored land that despite ruthless exploitation from abroad and criminal mismanagement at home, it was, even before the Revolution, one of the richest underdeveloped countries in the world.* When the Revolution came, the heavy burden of idle manpower and unused resources which the country had been forced to carry for many decades, turned into a priceless asset. Cuba was able to stage a great leap forward during the very first year of the Revolution and will soon be entering the path of industrialization which leads not only to rapidly rising material standards of living but also to the possibility of a genuinely cultured and civilized society.

Yet these very successes and the brilliant future which they foretell are the source of the gravest threat to the Revolution and even to the very existence of Cuba as an independent country. The reasons for this apparent paradox are not far to seek.

The successes of the Revolution have already all but eliminated the possibility of a victorious internal counter-revolution. Backed by a well-equipped and battle-tested army and enjoying the overwhelming support of the peasants and the workers, the regime has little to fear from its domestic enemies in the big bourgeoisie and the urban middle classes. So far as one can now judge, their choices have been narrowed down to three: make the best of what is from their point of view a bad situation,

---

* In a recently published work, Paul Hoffman, former administrator of the Marshall Plan, classified 100 underdeveloped countries of the world into four categories by average per capita income. Fifty-two fall in the under-$100-a-year category, 23 in the $100-$199 category, 16 in the $200-$299 category, and 9 in the $300-$699 category. Cuba is one of the top 9. (P. G. Hoffman, *One Hundred Countries, One and One Quarter Billion People,* Committee for International Economic Growth, Washington, 1960.)

emigrate from the country, or stay and fight the Revolution with a high probability of being caught and punished. If there were no prospect of support and assistance from abroad, most of them would probably take either the first or the second course. Under these circumstances, the activities of the counter-revolutionaries would be at most an annoyance to the regime.

Unfortunately, however, there is a very good prospect of support and assistance from abroad, which will undoubtedly swell the number of active counter-revolutionaries and in effect turn them into agents of a foreign power or coalition of powers. The real threat thus comes from abroad, and *the successes of the Revolution, far from undermining the strength or sapping the resolve of the foreign interests concerned, serve only to alarm them and to strengthen their determination to crush the Revolution.*

Who and what are these foreign interests?

First, of course, the North American capitalists who are losing their properties in Cuba. Second, the remainder of the owning and governing class in the United States which sympathizes with its injured members, and fears, quite correctly, that the Cuban Revolution is in reality merely the first phase of a Latin American Revolution which would (a) cost American capitalists many billions of dollars in expropriated property; (b) force the United States to pay fairer (i.e. much higher) prices for imported raw materials; (c) undermine the entire structure of United States imperialism both in the Western Hemisphere and indirectly in the rest of the world as well; and thus (d) give a powerful impetus everywhere to the historical transition from world capitalism to world socialism. Third, the governing oligarchies of the Latin American countries whose interests and status are essentially like those of their now-defeated counterpart in Cuba, and who feel, again quite correctly, mortally threatened by the success and potential spread of the Cuban Revolution.

These, then, are the main foreign forces opposed to the Cuban Revolution. Their recognized and natural leader, of course, is the government of the United States, securely under the control of the Big Business interests which are already suffering losses as a result of the Cuban Revolution and stand to lose so much more from its spread to the rest of Latin America. The coalition as a whole is a formidable one indeed, and the whole history of United States-Latin American relations compels the conclusion that it will not scruple to use any and all methods to attain its ends. We have no hesitation in saying that he who doubts this is either an ignoramus or a fool. The only effective deterrent to the use of any given method of fighting the Revolution will be a well-founded belief that the method will not work.

Let us inquire what some of the possible methods are, and let us attempt, however tentatively, to assess their chances of working. They can be classified as political, economic, and military. For the sake of an orderly exposition we shall treat them separately, though it must be recognized that they merge into each other and that a variety of methods can and doubtless will be employed simultaneously.

First, then, the political methods. Here the main objectives are to confuse and divide the supporters of the Revolution inside Cuba, to isolate Cuba diplomatically, and to discredit the Revolution in the eyes of supporters or potential supporters abroad. Maximum success would be achieved if the ground could be prepared in this way for a successful counter-revolution. But in any case it would be hoped that the position of the revolutionary regime would be weakened and its ability to resist economic or military attacks diminished. The chief weapons of political warfare of this kind are propaganda and diplomacy, which nowadays are closely tied together. And it is clear that in the struggle against the Cuban Revolution both propaganda and diplomacy will be concentrated first and foremost on the theme of anti-Communism.

Anti-Communism serves both internal and international purposes, and the two are intimately related. The way it works was perfectly demonstrated in the case of the overthrow of the Arbenz government in Guatemala in 1954. Guatemala was at the time in the early stages of what promised to be a genuine social revolution. Communists were of course active, especially in the trade unions where they performed excellent organizational work, but they were certainly no more in control of the government than they are in Cuba today. Nevertheless, a great campaign to pin the Communist label on Guatemala was launched in the United States. At the same time, counter-revolutionary exiles in Nicaragua and Honduras were encouraged and armed, while the government was denied the right to buy arms from the United States or countries allied to the United States. When Guatemala then bought a shipload of arms from Czechoslovakia, this was adduced as "proof" of its Communist character. Next the problem was made the center of attention at a meeting of the Organization of American States (OAS), and the famous Caracas Declaration against Communism in the Americas was passed, with its scarcely concealed threat of collective military action against Guatemala. By this time the opposition to the Arbenz regime inside Guatemala was emboldened, and the political coalition which supported it was wracked with dissension and alarm. Thus the ground was prepared by political means for the final military denouement, which in the event turned out to be of no more than token character. Castillo Armas invaded the country with a handful of mercenaries, and the Guatemalan army, after a short period of wavering, deserted the government and installed him as a military dictator of the familiar Latin American type—soon, of course, to be duly legitimized by "free" elections of an equally familiar type.

Can this performance be repeated in Cuba? The answer is, certainly not. The Castro government, enjoying as it does the 100-percent support of a peasant-worker army, is infinitely stronger than the Arbenz government and has far more impressive achievements to its credit. It is no pushover, and it may be assumed that Washington is fully aware of this. Nevertheless, the anti-Communist card is being played for all it is worth in an attempt to achieve maximum division in the ranks of the government's supporters, to promote the diplomatic isolation of Cuba, and to prepare the ground for the employment of as yet undecided economic and military weapons.

So far, the Cuban leadership has parried this strategy with determination and skill. It has, of course, quite properly and firmly rejected the Communist label. Fidel has explained his own and his government's position on this many times: they are not

Communists, but neither are they anti-Communists; they welcome the cooperation of anyone who proves by deeds that he is for the Revolution; and internationally they will conduct mutually advantageous business relations with any country that is prepared to respect Cuba's sovereignty and independence. Beyond that they have not gone. Above all, they have correctly recognized that to attempt to "prove" their non-Communism is to set foot on the road to disaster. This is how it works: You begin by denying that you are a Communist. Your baiter counters with a statement to the effect that "that's what you *say*, but you cooperate with Communists and follow policies of which they approve. How do I *know* you are not a Communist? You must prove it." If you accept this challenge you are lost. The first step is to refuse to cooperate with Communists, and in order to carry this through you have to establish political tests to determine who is a Communist. The witch hunt is on. Next, you must alter your policies to differentiate yourself from them, and the best way to achieve this is to become once again a client of the United States. But for Latin America this means precisely embracing the *status quo ante,* renouncing all possibility of "doing what needs to be done." The Cuban leadership has quite rightly seen the trap that was being set and has resolutely refused to walk into it. Far from trying to prove its anti-Communism by degrading and servile maneuvers, it has in fact gone over to the counter-attack, pinning the label of counter-revolution on the anti-Communists and thus isolating them from the masses who are, above all else, ardent supporters of the Revolution.

It is in this context that we must view the anti-imperialist and anti-United States propaganda campaigns ceaselessly conducted by the Cuban regime. In a political sense they are the precise counterpart of the anti-Communist campaigns conducted by the United States against Cuba. Internally, their object is to convince the Cuban people of what is undoubtedly true, that the main danger comes from the colossus of the North, and to burn the brand of traitor and foreign agent into Cuban counter-revolutionaries. Internationally, the object is to unite Cuba, the Cuban masses, and the Cuban Revolution with the overwhelming major-

ity of the peoples of Latin America who of course recognize that
they too are the objects of exploitation and domination by the
United States.

It is too early to say that either the United States or Cuba
is "winning" the political war between them. Each has made
certain gains. Washington seems to have succeeded in turning
North American public opinion decisively against the Castro
government. It has also gone a long way toward achieving its goal
of officially isolating Cuba from the other Latin American countries. Liberals like Betancourt in Venezuela, whose political power
is in considerable measure dependent on popular support, at first
tended to adopt a pro-Cuban policy, and several governments
indicated an intention to participate in the conference of underdeveloped countries scheduled to take place in Havana in September, 1960. Pressure from Washington, however, has largely overcome these tendencies, and it seems likely now that few, if any,
Latin American governments will be represented at the conference.

To offset these gains for Washington, the Cuban government
has very important achievements to its credit. First, it has effectively isolated the counter-revolutionaries internally. Reports
from objective observers in Cuba indicate that the pro-regime
demonstrations which took place all over the island on May 1
were tremendously impressive.* Further, it is clear that while
Washington has been winning over Latin American governments,
the popularity of the Castro regime and the Cuban Revolution
has been growing by leaps and bounds among Latin American
peasants, workers, and intellectuals. This, too, was demonstrated

---

* Since the United States press, including even the *New York Times* which
has been doing a fairly good job of reporting from Cuba since Herbert
Matthews visited Havana in March, deliberately underplayed the May 1
story, it is appropriate to quote from a letter received from Manuel Pedro
Gonzalez, retired Professor of Spanish-American Literature at the University
of California, Los Angeles. Professor Gonzalez was educated at the University
of Havana and is the leading authority on José Martí, Cuba's greatest
national hero. "On May 1st," he writes from Havana, "Fidel received at
least five or six times more votes than any president has ever received in
Cuba. More than a million men and women converged on the Plaza Civica
here in Havana alone. It was a magnificent demonstration of discipline,
civic spirit, and patriotic fervor."

on May 1 when large delegations from nearly all Latin American countries visited Cuba and expressed their solidarity with the regime and the Revolution. A Mexican observer who was present has written us that these delegations "included people of great political significance in each country."* Public opinion in Latin America, in truth, instinctively feels that the Cuban Revolution is in no sense a special nationalistic Cuban phenomenon but rather is the first stage of a great revolution which is destined to sweep over and transform the life of all Latin America. There is every reason to believe that this feeling will grow in intensity as time goes on and become an increasingly important factor in the total picture.

We do not suggest that the gains of either side in the political war between the United States and Cuba are likely to be decisive —at least not in the near future. But they undoubtedly are important in setting the stage for the use of other weapons of struggle.

This brings us to the economic aspect of the conflict. Cuba is particularly vulnerable at two points, and in discussing these we can cover the essential issues. The first point is exports of sugar to the United States which in recent years have accounted for about one third of all Cuban exports. The second point is imports of petroleum, which, while amounting to only about 5 percent of total imports, are of vital importance since (a) very little oil is produced in Cuba, (b) the Cuban economy is relatively highly motorized, and (c) all publicly sold electricity is generated from petroleum (the sugar industry generates most of its own power using bagasse as fuel).

The sugar problem is complicated, and only a few highlights can be touched upon here. In 1934, the Roosevelt administration, as a part of its agricultural stabilization program, enacted a control scheme for sugar. Very roughly—we will not burden the reader with exact statistics since they are of no importance to the main points we want to make—this provided that about one third of

---

* Those familiar with Latin American affairs will get an idea of what this means from the following list of signers of a manifesto issued by the Mexican delegation: Heriberto Jara (chief of the delegation), Ignacio Acosta, Alonso Aguilar, Fernando Benítez, Fernando Carmona, Jorge Carrión, Victor Flores Olea, Carlos Fuentes, Pablo González Casanova, Francisco López Cámara, Manuel Marcue Pardiñas, Mario Orozco Rivera, and David Alfaro Siqueiros.

the United States market should be reserved for domestic beet and cane producers, one third for Cuba, and one third for all others (Philippines, Hawaii, Puerto Rico, Mexico, Dominican Republic, etc.). Total supply was to be regulated by a quota system in such a way as to yield amply profitable prices for domestic producers—prices which of course are well above the so-called world market price. (We say "so-called" because in fact most countries have sugar control schemes to protect domestic producers, and only about 10 percent of the world's total production passes through the "world" market.) Cuban sugar of course sells in the United States market at the same price as domestic sugar and the tariff is quite low, so that Cuban producers realize a good price and correspondingly good profits on what they are permitted to sell in the United States. This was not in the least a matter of open-handed generosity on the part of Uncle Sam, however. Around half of the Cuban crop in those days was produced by American corporations, and in addition as part payment for her favored position in the American sugar market, Cuba was obliged to grant preferential import duties on a wide range of United States products. No one can prove which side got the better of the bargain, but there is at any rate absolutely no reason to assume that Uncle Sam was taken for a ride.

Since 1934, the sugar control scheme has been continued by successive acts of Congress, the most recent of which was passed in 1956 to run to the end of 1960. The scheme itself has remained basically unchanged, though Cuba's relative share of the market has been somewhat reduced. On the whole, it has worked very much as its original sponsors planned and expected, much more satisfactorily than the rest of the New Deal's agricultural support programs. Sugar prices have remained relatively stable for many years, and additional supplies were readily available from Cuba when they were most needed during World War II. None of the various vested interests involved in either the United States or Cuba has ever had much reason to complain about the working of the sugar scheme.

Now the question arises as to whether cutting the sugar quota can be used effectively as an economic weapon against the Cuban

Revolution. On the face of it the answer would seem to be obvious. As explained in Chapter 11, Cuba has a difficult balance of payments problem, and in order to carry out the planned industrialization of the country will need to sell as much as possible abroad for many years to come. The United States buys about 40 percent of Cuba's main export at favorable prices. Why not deal a heavy blow to the whole revolutionary program by excluding Cuban sugar from the American market, or at least reducing sharply the share of the American market allotted to Cuba?

The noisiest opponents of the Cuban Revolution in the United States have been asking this question for months now, and there need be no doubt that the will to do the maximum possible economic damage to Cuba exists at all levels and in all branches of the United States government. Nevertheless, no serious moves have yet been made to change the sugar scheme, and at the moment of writing (in May) it looks as though the most likely form of legislation at the present session of Congress is a simple one-year renewal of the sugar act, which expires at the end of the year. What accounts for this apparent paradox?

One part of the answer is clear: any monkeying with the Cuban sugar quota under present tense conditions between Washington and Havana would be instantly and overwhelmingly denounced throughout Latin America as a case of naked economic aggression. Even those elements in Latin America which are bitterly opposed to the Cuban Revolution would be forced to make common cause with Cuba on this issue, since every country knows that a similar economic weapon can be used against it. In short, cutting the quota would undermine and very possibly wreck the massive political and diplomatic campaigns which Washington has been waging in order to isolate Cuba from the rest of the hemisphere. This is a very weighty reason to go slow and probably accounts for the State Department's lack of enthusiasm for quota-cutting legislation.

But legislation is made in the Congress, not in the executive branch of the government, and Congress has never paid much attention to "subtle" arguments of this kind. What accounts for Congressional dragging of feet on this issue? The answer to this question was spelled out in a very revealing article in the *Wall Street Journal* of March 9, 1960, from which we quote as follows:

Should the United States punish Fidel Castro . . . by cutting Cuba's share of the U.S. sugar market and boosting the share held by sugar producers in the U.S.?

Strangely enough, just the suggestion of such a plan by some U.S. lawmakers fills most American sugar men with horror. "Naive and even bordering on the irrational," Richard W. Blake, chunky executive secretary of the National Beet Growers Federation, calls the proposal. Mr. Blake's organization represents 20,000 farmers in 12 states who provide the bulk of America's domestically grown sugar supplies.

This "let's not rock the boat" attitude stems mainly from concern that a short-lived boom in the sugar beet industry might well lead to costly over-expansion and over-production which could result in more long-range problems than short-run gains. . . .

Beet processors are no more enthusiastic about suddenly inheriting a big chunk of Cuba's U.S. sugar business. Of the 64 beet sugar refineries in the U.S., 24 are located in California and Colorado and most of the rest are west of the Mississippi. Transportation costs to eastern U.S. areas presently served by Caribbean sugar would absorb much of the profits from shipments from the West.

In addition, of course, the eastern refiners who process Cuban raw sugar are likewise unenthusiastic about cutting off their source of supply. All in all, it appears that vested interests in the United States sugar industry are overwhelmingly *against* any change in the present scheme, and it is of course vested interests that control the actions of the United States Congress.

We are not arguing that nothing at all will be done to exploit Cuba's present vulnerability in the matter of sugar exports. It would be quite possible, for example, to raise the tariff on Cuban sugar so that Cuba would actually realize no more on sales to the United States than she does by selling elsewhere at the lower world market price (with the nationalization of cane lands in Cuba, the objection to such a course from United States investors in the Cuban industry can be expected to decline rapidly). But it does appear to be unlikely that the United States will put extreme pressure on Cuba in this way in the near future. The situation is too complicated and there are too many conflicting considerations and interests involved. Cutting the sugar quota, in other words, is not the readily available and potentially lethal economic weapon which it appears to be. We do not believe that it will play any decisive role in the struggle between the United States and Cuba.

The situation in respect to petroleum imports is entirely different, of course, but, unfortunately from Washington's point of view, it seems to offer even fewer opportunities for effective economic warfare than does the sugar quota. This would not have been so a few years ago. The Cuban oil business has long been monopolized by a few major oil companies—notably Standard of New Jersey, Shell, and Texaco, all of which own and operate refineries in Cuba. Until quite recently, these companies could have simply cut Cuba off completely and made the private embargo stick. And they could have found ample excuse for doing so in the new regime's establishment of the National Petroleum Institute, headed by an experienced Mexican oilman, which is already a competitor of the international oil companies and obviously means to expand the nationalized sector of this industry as and when occasion offers. (The Institute will conduct all future exploration activity, already operates several small refineries seized from Batista henchmen, and is moving into the retail distribution field). When you recall how the oil majors shut down most of the Iranian oil industry in the period 1951-1953 and prevented the Mossadegh government from shipping a single barrel of its own oil to international markets, you can have few doubts that if conditions were still as they were then, the Cuban economy could be literally strangled in a few months' time. What a perfect solution from the point of view of the State Department! No need for awkward and embarrassing official measures to bring Cuba to her knees, just let the oil monopolies do it in the normal course of business.

Alas and alack, the good old days seem to be gone forever. The Soviet Union is now able and willing to supply Cuba's oil needs, and this means that the "position of strength" from which the oil companies have traditionally operated has completely crumbled. The story is well told by J. H. Carmical, petroleum editor of the *New York Times,* in that paper's edition of May 29:

Last week the Cuban government dissolved exclusive distribution contracts between the American oil companies and Cuban filling stations and fuel dealers and notified the foreign-owned refining companies they would have to refine Soviet crude oil. The explanation is that the steps were taken to break the hold of foreign companies on the Cuban oil market. . . . The companies have no intention of withdrawing from that market, in which they have been active for years, and the belief is that they will try to continue operations there as circumstances permit. . . .

Under Cuba's recently negotiated trade agreement with the Soviet Union, some 6,000,000 barrels a year of Soviet crude oil are to be sent to Cuba. This amounts to roughly one fourth the Cuban requirement, and the three principal refineries there, owned by Jersey Standard, Texaco Inc., and the Royal Dutch-Shell Group, are being asked to refine the oil. The products will be sold, probably at levels below those now prevailing, through Cuban oil dealers, most of whom now get their supplies from these companies. . . .

In recent years, the Soviet Union has been increasing its oil production and is in a position to supply all Cuba's needs if necessary. Anxious to get a foothold in the Western Hemisphere, the Soviet Union is thought to regard the price to be received for the oil as a minor consideration. With tankers in plentiful supply at ridiculously low rates, the movement of the oil from Black Sea ports is not an insurmountable problem.

The Cuban oil setup is perfect for the Soviet Union. With refining and marketing facilities already established, the cooperation of the Cuban government is all that is needed to establish the Russians firmly in the Cuban market. *And there is not much the oil companies can do.* If they refuse to run Soviet oil, the Cuban government could take over the refineries and bring in Soviet experts to operate them. (Emphasis added.)

It should be added that the setup is also perfect for the Cubans. They have now escaped from the stranglehold of the international oil cartel, "and there is not much the oil companies can do." Of course, it might be argued that the United States government is not quite so helpless, that given its obviously complete naval and air control over the Caribbean area it could institute a blockade of Soviet oil and thus bring Cuba back into the cartel fold. This is true. But a blockade would be an act of war, not a form of economic pressure. It is one of the military weapons which might be employed by the United States, a subject to which we shall return presently.

Before we do so, however, it is well to note that the oil situation admirably points up the role and importance to the Cubans of the Soviet trade and credit agreements negotiated on the occasion of Mikoyan's visit to Havana in February, 1960. The Soviet Union contracts to buy a million tons of sugar a year for the next five years at world market prices. This would yield Cuba no more than 20 to 25 percent of what she receives from the sale of sugar to the United States market. Quantitatively unspecified trade in other commodities is provided for, and Cuba is to be granted credits of $100 million, presumably also over approximately the five year period, which would work out to around $20 million a year or a little over 3 percent of Cuba's total imports in 1959. These quantities are neither very large nor startling, and Harry Schwartz was doubtless right to point out in the *New York Times* at the time (February 19) that "the agreements do not alter the fact that, barring major new developments, Cuba must continue to look to the West for most of her export markets and probably for most of her imports as well." But the quantitative aspect of the agreements is no measure of their importance to Cuba. We have already seen how this is so in the case of petroleum, and there is every reason to believe that the situation is basically similar in the case of other commodities which are strategically important to the functioning of the Cuban economy. An attempt to squeeze Cuba by cutting off supplies is foredoomed to failure since an alternative and potentially expandable source is now available. Under the circumstances, the attempt is not likely to be made. The Soviet agreements (and others which have been and are being concluded with Soviet-bloc countries) thus have the paradoxical consequence that trade between Cuba and Western countries, including the United States, is likely to continue uninterrupted and very possibly to expand in the years ahead as Cuba's ability both to export and to import grows.

A useful analogy to Cuba's position vis-à-vis the Soviet Union is provided by the postwar history of Yugoslavia. After the Yugoslav-Cominform break of 1948, Stalin thought he could bring

Yugoslavia to her knees by means of economic warfare. Yugoslavia countered by turning to the United States which provided the necessary trade and aid to enable the Yugoslavs to resist Soviet pressure. Eventually, Stalin's successors called the economic war off, and economic relations between Yugoslavia and her natural trading partners in Eastern Europe now appear to be developing normally. It is legitimate to hope that economic relations between Cuba and the United States will pursue a similar course, with Soviet trade and aid playing the same role in the Cuban case that United States trade and aid did in the Yugoslav case.

The Yugoslav analogy suggests something else, too. The fact that Yugoslavia became in a sense crucially dependent on the United States in the years after 1948 did not mean that the country was destined to become a satellite of the United States. Under a tough, seasoned, and intensely nationalistic revolutionary leadership, Yugoslavia showed that a country can accept whatever help is needed to survive without sacrificing its sovereignty or independence. We have no doubt that Cuba, under a leadership in many ways remarkably similar to that of Yugoslavia, can do as well.

The truth is that Soviet trade and aid, far from enslaving Cuba, is enabling her for the first time in her history to achieve a measure of genuine independence from *all* foreign powers. Since the time of Martí, this has been the fervent desire of every Cuban patriot. That it is now being realized in practice is surely one of the greatest achievements of the Revolution. And it is an achievement which will be treasured and fought for through thick and thin by the vast majority of the Cuban people.

If our analysis is correct and our judgment sound, Cuba should be able to weather the political and economic warfare which is being waged against her by the United States and its allies in Latin America. But we know from past history, and most recently from the experience in Guatemala, that the forces of imperialism and counter-revolution are always prepared to go beyond political and economic to military methods if and when they judge the chances of success to be favorable. The final question, therefore, the question on which the whole fate of the Cuban Revolution depends, is whether these forces, and more specifically the government of the United States which is their undisputed leader, will be able to devise a form or forms of military intervention in Cuba which stand a chance of success without at the same time involving prohibitive risks and costs.

We have already explained why it is absolutely impossible to "Guatemalize" Cuba: a strong and fervidly loyal army is the very backbone of the regime.

For the very same reason, however, *nothing short of a fullfledged invasion by the United States army, navy, and airforce could hope to achieve a military overthrow of the revolutionary regime in Cuba.* No expeditionary force of Batistianos or Latin American mercenaries, no matter how lavishly financed and equipped, would stand a chance against the Cuban army and the Cuban people. And no Latin American government would be foolhardy enough to send an army of its own citizens to fight against the Cuban vanguard of the Latin American Revolution.

No, if the deed is to be done it will have to be the United States itself that will do it. The role of the others can be, at most, that of the provocateur.

There are many people, in Washington and elsewhere, who are ready for the adventure, right now. And yet soberer heads in American governing circles hold back. Why?

Are they merely biding their time, working United States public opinion up to the appropriate pitch of hostility against Castro and Cuba, looking for the occasion and excuse which might seem to give some color of justification for an all-out effort to reimpose imperialist rule on Cuba?

Or are American governing circles perhaps deterred by weightier considerations, by the knowledge that the days of imperialist rule are after all numbered, that countries (like France) that try to hang onto insurgent empires lose much more than they gain, that if the revolutionary fire were squelched in Cuba it would only burst out more quickly and burn more fiercely elsewhere in Latin America? Are they beginning to understand what is undoubtedly a profound truth, that the Cuban Revolution is no mere local episode that can be controlled by guns and bombs and tanks but rather one of the great historic and prophetic events of our time—an event with which even a neighbor 30 times as populous, producing nearly 200 times as much wealth, and disposing over an almost literally infinitely greater fire power must sooner or later come to terms?

It is perhaps just as well that no one knows the answers to these momentous questions. There is still time for men of good will, both inside and outside the United States, to bring home to those responsible for making policy in Washington that an aggression against Cuba and the Cuban Revolution would be not only a crime against humanity but also a long step in the direction of self-destruction.

Meanwhile, the Cuban Revolution marches on, gaining strength and self-confidence as it proceeds, inspiring the young and the oppressed everywhere by its magnificent example, helping to blaze a new trail for humanity to a brighter socialist future.

EPILOGUE

Cuba Revisited

> *What lies ahead depends greatly on the United States. With the exception of our agrarian reform, which the people of Cuba desired and initiated themselves, all of our radical measures have been a direct response to direct aggressions by powerful monopolists, of which your country is the chief exponent. U.S. pressure on Cuba has made necessary the "radicalization" of the Revolution. To know how much further Cuba will go, it will be easier to ask the U.S. government how far it plans to go.*
>
> —Ché Guevara, in an interview with Laura Bergquist, *Look*, November 8, 1960

The foregoing chapters of this book were written after a three-week visit to Cuba in March, 1960. In the next few months, events moved with astonishing rapidity—both inside Cuba and in Cuba's relations with the outside world. How did these developments affect the Cuban Revolution? What changes have taken place in the Cuban economy and Cuban society? Are things going well or badly for the Cuban people? What is the outlook for the future?

We asked ourselves these questions as we read the daily headlines about Cuba, but we didn't find the answers in the stories that followed. Herbert Matthews told the American Society of Newspaper Editors last April that in his 30 years on the *New York Times* he had "never seen a big story so misunderstood, so badly handled, and so misinterpreted as the Cuban Revolution." Unfortunately, his fellow editors, including those on his own paper, paid no attention: reporting from Cuba, far from improving, had further deteriorated in recent months. So we decided to return to Cuba to seek the answers for ourselves. What follows is based on a second three-week visit to Cuba, in September and October of 1960.

Fidel Castro

First, let us attempt to answer some of the questions that
are most frequently asked about the leader of the Cuban Revolution, Fidel Castro. What manner of man is he? What are his
main drives? Above all, is he in his right mind, or is he, as
American pundits and Cuban defectors continually tell us, some
sort of madman?

We were lucky on this most recent visit to Cuba: we spent
two long evenings with Fidel, in relaxed surroundings and with
only a few others present; and we accompanied him on a day-
long inspection trip, with Fidel himself doing most of the driving, to agricultural establishments in Pinar del Rio, Cuba's
westernmost province. We listened, asked questions, discussed
all sorts of subjects, and watched him in his relations with people. There are lots of things we still don't know about him, of
course. But there are a few things we think we do know.

First and foremost, Fidel is a passionate humanitarian, not
in the fraudulent sense that he loves all humanity but in the
meaningful sense that he feels deep compassion for human suffering, hates injustice because it causes unnecessary suffering,
and is totally committed to building in Cuba a society in which
the poor and the underprivileged shall be able to hold up their
heads and enjoy a fair share of the good things of life. He treats
people within this framework—kindly, sternly, implacably, according to their actual or potential role in creating or hindering
the creation of the good society.

Two incidents will illustrate the quality of Fidel's hu-
manitarianism. On the way out of Havana he made a long de-
tour through the wealthiest residential streets of the Miramar
district. As he drove around, he kept saying, as much to himself
as to the rest of us, "Look at how they live"; and in that brief
phrase there was expressed not so much a feeling toward "them"
as a sense of outrage at a system that could enable a few to live
like kings while the great majority stagnated in ignorance, squalor, and often outright hunger.

The other incident occurred on the second evening. He
arrived in a subdued mood, and, on being asked the reason, said
quite simply, "I am sad." After a moment's silence he told us
why. A few hours earlier, a group of fourteen young prisoners
had broken out of jail in Havana. They were rebel soldiers who

had fought in the Sierra but later had become followers of Hubert Matos. Fidel felt sure that at heart they were good boys who had gone along with Matos only because he was their commanding officer: he did not believe that they were counter-revolutionaries like Matos himself. Fidel had therefore had them transferred from the Isle of Pines to Havana where they could see their families three times a week. One had been granted permission to leave prison to get married and had been provided a free room at the swank Havana Riviera hotel for the occasion. Fidel himself had frequently gone to see them, to talk to them, to get them to see the error of their ways. "And now today," he concluded, "they break out of prison. They will be caught. And then? I am sad." This attempted rehabilitation by the very busy leader of the Revolution, this deep personal concern for his former comrades-in-arms bespeaks not the power-hungry demagogue that Fidel is often pictured as, but a true humanitarian.*

Second, Fidel is a consummate politician. He has, probably to a greater degree than any other political figure alive today, the quality which sociologists, borrowing from the language of theology, call "charisma"—the inborn gift of being able to inspire in people a mixture of passionate love and blind faith. Accompanying him as he goes among his people, one not only sees it; all of one's senses are overwhelmed by it. To watch the faces light up as their owners suddenly recognized the driver of our car; to hear the delighted cries of "Fidel, Fidel"; to experience the rush of people, young and old alike, whenever the car stopped, even if only for a red light, people drawn like iron filings to a magnet, wanting to shake his hand, touch his sleeve, wish him well; to smell the sweaty bodies of hundreds of construction workers who swarmed around the car when it was halted by an obstruction in the road, pouring out to him their problems and urging that he take action to clear away obstacles to the more rapid completion of their project—these were indeed unforgettable experiences.

---

* The story may have an equally sad sequel. The boys were not caught; they escaped in a boat to Florida. It is possible that at least some of them will return to Cuba with one of the counter-revolutionary invasion forces that are being organized and dispatched from the mainland, and even more probable that they will then be caught. If and when that happens, they can expect no mercy, least of all from Fidel Castro.

But it is not only as the charismatic leader that Fidel can be said to be a consummate politician. He instinctively sees every problem as a political problem, that is to say, in its relation to the holding and fortifying of political power. He knows that the strength of a revolutionary regime threatened by powerful enemies lies in the unwavering support of the plain working people, their conviction that the Revolution is theirs because it serves their interest, their willingness to die for it because to go on living without it would be a betrayal of all they believe in. And he makes his decisions, big and little, only after taking full account of the probable effect on that support, that conviction, that willingness. From the outset, he has insisted that the masses must associate the revolution with immediate and tangible benefits; he has been bold, as in the role of cooperatives in the agrarian reform, where he felt sure the people would go along with him; and he has been cautious, as in the matter of the speed of industrialization, where he has not felt sure of the political repercussions. This is emphatically not to say that Fidel, like a bourgeois political opportunist, does only what he thinks the people want at any given moment. Far from it. His criterion is rather what the people can be taught to want, within the operationally relevant time period, by their own experience and the educational efforts of their leaders (hence those TV appearances in which Fidel talks directly to the people, always with a view to educating them to the tasks and responsibilities that lie ahead). Politics, it has been said, is the art of the possible. If so, Fidel's greatness as a politician consists not only in being a master of the art but also in knowing how ample and generous a meaning can be given to the "possible."

But is he in his right mind? Latin American statesmen are supposed to know their place in the world, and past experience seems to show that any who get uppish are soon taught a lesson. Isn't Fidel's defiance of the United States, both in word and in deed, a sure sign of mental derangement? Isn't his deviation from the norm of Latin American statesmanship too persistent and too blatant to be put down to anything but some form of insanity?

Our answer, we fear, will bring cold comfort to the powers that be in Washington. In their book, Fidel's disease is much worse than mere insanity. He defies the United States because he understands American imperialism. He deviates from the norm of Latin American statesmanship because he knows that those who adhere to it are selling out the interests of their own people. To put it bluntly and colloquially, Fidel acts the way he does because he knows the score. The disease from which he suffers, if you want to give it a name, is Marxism. Not that he calls himself a Marxist, or would claim more than a well-educated man's knowledge of the works of Marx and his followers: in these matters he is a remarkably modest man. But through his own rich experience, and by using his own sharp and fertile mind, he has arrived at an interpretation of the world of the second half of the 20th century which, in its essentials, is unmistakably Marxist. And he is acting on it in a way that would have made Marx himself proud to acknowledge him as a disciple.*

The Economic War

Early in June, 1960, the three big oil companies which had long dominated the Cuban oil market (Jersey Standard, Texaco, and Shell) flatly refused to refine the Soviet oil which was about to be imported by the government in accordance with the terms of the Soviet-Cuban trade agreement of the preceding February. It was a direct challenge to the authority of the government: failure to meet it head on would have meant the end of the Cuban Revolution then and there. Recognizing this fact, the regime acted promptly and decisively. When the Soviet oil began to arrive, the refineries were intervened and the oil put through. The companies immediately retaliated by cutting off further imports of oil from Venezuela. To this move Cuba replied by arranging to purchase substantially all of her petroleum requirements from the Soviet Union. A round of sharp blows and counter blows thus ended with Cuba the clear winner.

Meanwhile, the United States Congress had for many months been considering what to do about the existing sugar

---

* The following story, probably apocryphal, illustrates the point: Khrushchev is supposed to have been asked by Soviet newsmen after returning from his last visit with Fidel at the UN whether Fidel was a Communist. "I don't know whether he's a Communist," Mr. K. replied, "but I do know that I'm a Fidelista."

control scheme, scheduled to expire at the end of the current year. As late as the end of May it seemed—to us as well as to others better informed about what goes on behind the scenes in Washington—that no strong action would be taken with regard to the Cuban quota. A substantial cut would injure important vested interests in the United States and would be sure to arouse widespread opposition in Latin America. This estimate of the situation turned out to be quite wrong. The oil companies' dispute with Cuba galvanized Washington into action, and in almost no time the rest of Cuba's quota for 1960, some 700,000 tons, was abruptly cut off.

It is not clear whether this was a sheer spite action or whether those who conceived it really believed that they were dealing a mortal blow to the Cuban economy. If they thought so, they were soon to be undeceived. The quota was cut in the first week of July. Before the end of the month the Soviet Union had agreed to buy the 700,000 tons excluded from the American market during the remainder of 1960, and China had concluded a trade agreement with Cuba calling for purchase of 500,000 tons per annum for the next five years.* Moreover, the two countries, together with the other members of the socialist bloc, have given satisfactory assurances about the market for Cuban sugar in the years to come.

Thus, thanks to the prompt and generous assistance of the socialist countries, the great sugar-quota blow, which many had believed would be fatal to the Cuban economy, was successfully parried. The counter blow, promised by Fidel the very day that the quota was cut, was not long in coming. On August 6, a large part of United States investments in Cuba were nationalized, notably, the electric power company, the telephone company, the sugar mills, and the oil refineries. By the terms of the nationalization decree the United States itself could decide for or

---

* It is true that the Russians and the Chinese pay a lower price for Cuban sugar than the United States has been paying. But Cuban government economists told us that the Soviet Union and China also charge less than the United States for what they sell to Cuba. For example, Cuban sugar sold to the USSR buys about as much oil from the USSR as the same amount of sugar sold to the United States used to buy from the American and British oil companies. No exact calculation of the real purchasing power of Cuban sugar before and after the shiftover is available, but it is certain that Cuba's losses will be much less than a mere comparison of the United States and world sugar prices would suggest.

against compensation: part of the proceeds of all sugar above 3 million tons sold in the United States in future years would be devoted to paying off United States investors. So far, needless to say, the United States gives every sign of voting permanently against compensation.

Further counter blows followed: early in September the Cuban subsidiaries of the big United States rubber companies were nationalized as was the American-owned Minimax chain of grocery stores; a week later it was the turn of the branches of American banks. Before the end of the month, the first nationalization of a major Cuban industry occurred when the cigar and cigarette companies were taken over. This was followed on October 14th by the nationalization of some 400 companies, 20 of them United States owned and the rest comprising just about everything that could plausibly be called Cuban "big business."

On October 19th, the United States aimed another, and by this time long-anticipated, blow at the Cuban economy by applying an embargo on all exports to Cuba except medicines and certain foodstuffs. The Cubans had enough ammunition left for one more big counter blow: on the 25th of October, 166 American-owned companies were nationalized. This act, said the *New York Times* the next day, "virtually eliminated major investments of United States citizens in Cuba."

This is doubtless not the end of economic warfare between the two countries. The United States can shut off imports from Cuba, and in the case of tobacco it would hurt.* On the other side there are still a few American properties that can be mopped up. But in the nature of the case the big economic battles have already been fought; from now on the struggle will for the most

---

* Theoretically, the United States could also seize Cuban assets in the United States, certainly amounting to many hundreds of millions, if not billions, of dollars. The trouble is that almost all of these assets belong to counter-revolutionaries. The Cuban government would like nothing better than to have them seized: they provide the financial lifeblood of the counter-revolution. The United States, of course, is not likely to oblige. It is noteworthy, however, that in all public discussions of policy toward Cuba this subject is either avoided altogether or treated as of minor importance. Could that be because it might be hard to convince some Americans who have lost their Cuban holdings that they should forego a readily available source of compensation so that wealthy Cuban exiles can continue to live well and support the counter-revolution?

part have to take other forms. It is a good time to assess the impact on Cuba of what may be called the "five months' economic war."

The Impact of the Economic War

The effects of the economic war on Cuba can be conveniently discussed under the following headings: (1) the transformation of Cuba's trade relations; (2) the radicalization of the regime; and (3) the growth of counter-revolution. Let us consider them in turn.

(1) *Transformation of Cuba's Trade Relations.* Traditionally, of course, the United States has been far and away Cuba's leading trading partner, taking close to two thirds of Cuba's exports and providing three quarters of her imports. The socialist countries, on the other hand, have played a very minor role in the pattern of Cuba's trade. Now, within the space of a few months, this relation has been reversed: for the visible future it will be the socialist countries that take most of Cuba's exports and provide her with most of her imports, and it will be the United States that plays a minor role. It is important to know in what ways this shiftover creates problems and in what ways it does not.

The difficulties are definitely not of a financial nature. Cuba is in a position to buy abroad, not everything she could use but certainly enough to keep the economy going at a satisfactory level. Moreover, with regard to credits for new capital investment the Cubans already have been granted more by the socialist countries than the present state of their economic organization and planning permits them to make use of. Since Cuba enjoys an expanding market for her products in such areas as Western Europe, Canada, and Japan, and since the socialist countries evidently mean to go on supporting the Cuban economy, there is no reason to anticipate the emergence of financial (or balance of payments) difficulties. This, needless to say, is an enviable position for a country embarking on an ambitious development program to be in.

It does not, however, obviate serious economic and technical problems. Many adjustments and new procedures are necessitated by the substitution of socialist bloc for United States sources of supply. For example, in the past many kinds of goods have been shipped to Cuba in freight cars via the railroad ferry from New Orleans to Havana. A more or less continuous flow could be maintained in this way and the need for warehouse space kept at a minimum. When the same goods come to Cuba from an Eastern European port, they arrive in big discontinuous shipments and an entirely new system of reception and storage becomes necessary. There are many more problems of this kind and their solution will be more difficult and costly than the inexperienced layman would ever suspect.

Furthermore, most of Cuba's modern technical equipment —machinery, automobiles, rolling stock, tractors, etc.—came from the United States. To keep this equipment in operation there is needed a more or less steady flow of replacement parts. The United States export embargo means that these parts can no longer be acquired in the usual way. To develop alternative methods of meeting the need for replacement parts for American equipment is probably Cuba's No. 1 economic problem now and for some time to come.

There are various possibilities. Some parts can be bought from third countries that also use American equipment, some of which may be produced by American subsidiaries abroad. Washington will doubtless try to halt such traffic, but past experience, especially in wartime, suggests that the attempt is unlikely to be wholly successful. In some cases substitute spare parts can be produced by the Cubans themselves in their own machine shops. Fortunately, this seems to be true of most sugar mill machinery. Some crucially important but hard-to-make items—like control gear and catalysts for oil refining—will probably be supplied by the USSR (Czechoslovakia, East Germany) even if doing so is relatively very expensive. And in some cases— perhaps automobiles, jeeps, tractors, and equipment with similar economic and technical characteristics—it might pay the Cubans not to try to import replacement parts beyond a certain minimum level but rather to "cannibalize" the existing stock and to import wholly new units from non-United States sources from which it will also be possible to obtain spare parts in the future. Finally, it should be remembered that the Cubans expected the embargo for some time before it was applied and made strenuous and largely successful efforts to build up stockpiles of many needed replacement parts. This is particularly important in that it gives them time to work out alternative methods of meeting their requirements.

But even if, as seems likely, all these possibilities are exploited to the full, serious shortages and difficulties are almost sure to arise in the period ahead. The effect will be to slow down the pace of economic development, to divert brains and resources from positive, constructive tasks. Tight government controls will be needed, in some areas of the economy probably strict rationing; Cubans may have to learn to get along without some things to which they are accustomed, at least for a while.

None of these problems, however, is insuperable, and they are all essentially temporary. In the long run, moreover, their solution will bring enormous advantages to Cuba. After a more or less difficult and trying transition period, the Cuban economy will be fully insulated from further shocks emanating from the United States, and it will be closely integrated with the economies of the socialist countries. Since the latter are planned and not subject to the periodic disturbances of the capitalist business cycle, this realignment will enable Cuba, too, to plan her economic development without fear of the kind of man-made catastrophes which in the past have inflicted so much damage on the peoples of the underdeveloped countries. Looked at in historical perspective, the economic war between the United States and Cuba will be seen to have finally conferred on Cuba the most precious of all national liberties—the freedom to plan her own development in the interests of her own people.

(2) *Radicalization of the Regime.* The economic war has also had tremendous repercussions in the political field. On the one hand it has radicalized the regime and solidified its support among the working people; on the other hand it has increased and strengthened the forces of counter-revolution.

The process of radicalization has been complex and pervasive. When we arrived in Havana last March, it was generally taken for granted among supporters of the regime that the private sector of the economy would remain quantitatively predominant for a long time to come, and one of the liveliest subjects of debate was whether and to what extent planning could be effective under such conditions. One never heard Cuba referred to as a socialist country, nor was socialism even included among the ultimate goals of the Revolution. Except among

Communists, coolness toward the Soviet Union and the other socialist countries was widespread, and dogmatic anti-Communist attitudes such as are almost universal in the United States were frequently encountered even among loyal revolutionaries. Diplomatic relations had not yet been established with the socialist bloc, and technical or trade missions from the socialist countries were still a rarity. Many people of liberal, or even conservative, views held high positions in the government.

When we returned in September things were very different. The nationalization process was already far advanced, and everyone took it for granted that it would soon encompass all large and most medium-sized concerns. There was no longer any doubt about the necessity and feasibility of comprehensive planning: the only question was how soon it could start to operate effectively. We revisited the School City in Oriente Province,* and were gratified to have one of the headmasters explain to us that the Cuban Revolution is nationalist, anti-imperialist *and socialist*. Our own view that Cuba should already be considered a socialist society, which was novel when we advanced it in our book, we now found to be commonplace.** There may still be some anti-Communism among Cuban revolutionaries, but it is certainly much less marked than it was a few months ago, and a feeling of gratitude toward and friendship for the socialist countries, and especially the Soviet Union, is evident and freely expressed. Missions from the socialist countries are now frequently encountered, and several members of such missions told us that they were hospitably received not only

---

* See above, pp. 99-101. We would like to take this opportunity to correct an error. It was our earlier understanding that there would only be one school city. This was wrong. Plans call for an ultimate total of ten school cities, with at least one in each of the country's six provinces.

** Paradoxically, it is the Communists, both in Cuba and elsewhere, who have most stoutly resisted this view. See the report of Blas Roca to the August conference of the Popular Socialist [Communist] Party, an English abridgment of which appeared in *Political Affairs,* October 1960; also the review of our book by James Allen in the same issue of *Political Affairs.* Now that the big majority of the means of production are in public ownership, and the regime is rapidly developing a consciously socialist ideology, the Communist argument against classifying Cuba as socialist appears more and more clearly as mere verbal gymnastics. The reason for the Communists' adopting this position, however, is straightforward enough: they don't want to admit that it is possible for socialism to be built under non-Communist leadership.

by officials but also by the Cuban people with whom they came in contact. Finally, while there are still many moderates in government, they have been increasingly replaced in key positions at all levels by outspoken radicals.

All of these changes testify to the rapid radicalization of the regime during the summer months. But perhaps even more significant is the growing role of the militia, "the people in arms" of classical revolutionary theory. Not that everyone is in the militia, or even everyone who would like to be. It is an honor to be in the militia and only those are admitted who have good records and are considered to be trustworthy supporters of the Revolution. In addition, the duties and tasks of the militia are arduous and call for much self-sacrifice: there are naturally many who are unable or unwilling to assume them. Under the circumstances, the fact that the militia counts perhaps as many as 250,000 members and is still growing is an excellent indication of the depth and strength of the support the regime enjoys among the popular masses.* But not only is the militia large and growing, it is also playing an increasingly important role in the life of the country. In all cases of nationalization, militiamen have played a key part, assuming control of the nationalized installations and guarding them against any attempts at sabotage. In emergencies—for example the tremendous explosion that occurred in an ammunition dump in East Havana in July—it is the militia rather than the police or the army that takes over. But most important of all, the primary military responsibility for defending the regime against both internal and external attacks now rests with the militia. The regular army has actually had both its size and its budget *reduced* in the last few months, while the militia has been expanding and receiving new and more effective arms. The reasons for this shift are both military and political. Everyone in Cuba knows that it would be impossible to repulse an all-out attack by United States armed forces. In such an event, the problem would be first to make the attack as costly as possible and then to organize civilian and guerrilla resistance. For these tasks a militia is far better suited than a regular army. When it comes to coping with counter-

---

* It may help to lend perspective to the picture if we remind ourselves that a militia of comparable size in the United States would have more than seven million members.

revolutionary uprisings, whether organized on Cuban soil or coming by sea from abroad, it is necessary to maintain a continuous alert all over the island, and this can only be done by *local* militia units, with the army acting as a mobile reserve if and when needed. We were able to follow newspaper accounts of the recent operations in the Escambray mountains where the number of counter-revolutionary guerrillas, at its maximum, was probably in the hundreds. In every dispatch that came to our notice the loyalist forces were described as militia, and full credit was given to the militia for the final dispersal and mopping up of the counter-revolutionaries. It appears that in this case—the biggest battle against counter-revolutionaries to date—there was never any need for the regular army to take a hand.

In addition to purely military reasons for assigning the major responsibility for protecting the regime to the militia, there are also weighty political reasons. Knowing the history of Latin America and having come to power in a struggle against one of the worst of its military dictatorships, the Cuban revolutionary leadership has a strong instinctive preference for militias over standing armies. And last but most important, the leadership understands the tremendous political importance of entrusting the defense of the Revolution to the armed people. The result is to unite government and people by the closest and strongest bonds that can be imagined. Fidel does not indulge in idle rhetoric when he proudly points to the arming of the people as the best proof of the genuinely democratic character of the regime which he heads.

The rise of the militia and the (relative) eclipse of the regular army during the period of the economic war are facts of profound significance for the interpretation of the Cuban Revolution. In its initial phases—from the first establishment of a base of operations in the Sierra Maestra at the end of 1956 to roughly the middle of 1960—the Cuban Revolution had a peasant base. Real power, as we argued earlier,* rested with the rebel army which, owing to its origin in guerrilla warfare, was essentially a peasant army. Appropriately enough, the programmatic aspect of the Revolution during this period centered on the agrarian reform which was enacted into law in May of 1959 and remains even now the most important positive accom-

---

* See above, Chapter 8.

plishment of the Revolution. As of May, 1960, nationalization in the field of industry was largely confined to recovery of the ill-gotten gains of the Batistianos, and no plans had been made to extend the area of nationalization except through the necessarily slow process of establishing new industries under state auspices. It is possible to argue that this is about as far as a peasant-based revolution could be expected to go, that in the absence of outside shocks Cuba would have tended to develop into a mixture of agrarian collectivism and state-directed capitalism. If this had happened, it is more than likely that a degenerative process would sooner or later have set in, leading ultimately to the ascendancy of the private sector and the reduction of the state to the role of servant of business interests.

Actually, of course, events took a very different turn: the brutal intervention of the foreign oil monopolies jolted the Revolution onto a new track. Almost overnight, the area of nationalization was extended to include all the larger capitalist units in industry and commerce. Vast new problems and responsibilities confronted the Revolution. Most important from our present point of view, the whole relationship of the non-agricultural working class to the Revolution was transformed. No longer on the outside, as it were, facing their private employers, the workers now found themselves on the inside in possession of "their own" establishments. New functions and responsibilities were thrust upon them, new attitudes and institutional arrangements were needed. From being mere beneficiaries of the Revolution—through such measures as rent and price roll-backs, low-cost housing, health and education reforms, etc.—the workers suddenly became *participants* in it on the same level as the members of the cooperatives in the countryside. The full effects of this change are, of course, still in the future, and in the meantime one must beware of hasty generalizations. Nevertheless, we have the strong impression that the workers have responded positively to the challenge, that they are showing initiative and responsibility in coping with new and difficult situations, that new leaders are emerging and new institutional structures being built. Through shop committees, trade unions, and the workers' militia, the Cuban working class is increasingly pouring its brains and energies into the direct support of the Revolution. No longer can it be said, as it could be only a few months ago, that the Cuban Revolution is essentially a peasant revolution. No longer can it be said that the main support of the regime is the rebel army. The nationalizations of the summer and fall have swept the working class into the revolutionary process; and the militia, uniting all the working people of the island, has become both the backbone and the strong right arm of the revolutionary regime. To borrow an expression which the Chinese have used in a somewhat different context, the Cuban Revolution is now walking on two legs where before it was hobbling on one.

(3) *Growth of Counter-Revolution.* The radicalization of the regime is one side of the coin; the growth of counter-revolution is the other side. And the two, of course, stem from the same basic causes. Those who have lost their properties as a result of the nationalizations or whose business has shrunk or disappeared as a result of the United States export embargo have with few exceptions gone over to the counter-revolution. "They wanted revolution," said Fidel, "but not too much revolution."

In addition, the severing of ties between the United States and Cuba has driven many into opposition and has led to the defection of a number of government officials. Cuba's nearness to and dependence on the United States meant in the past that many Cubans had travelled to the States, not a few had lived and worked there for extended periods, the children of the well-to-do often went to school or college there. Moreover, a large part of Cuba's commercial products and almost all of its radio, TV, and movies came from the United States. It saddens many Cubans, middle class as well as upper class and even some from the lower classes, that these close bonds to the United States should be dissolved. Add to this the fact that Cubans have been long subjected to the same kind of anti-Communist propaganda that we in the United States have been subjected to and one can understand why the switch in trade and official affection from the United States to the socialist bloc should come as a shock to substantial segments of the population. The wonder is not that so many have gone over to the opposition—that was to be expected—but that so many have resisted the psychological pressures generated by the economic war and remained loyal to the Revolution.

No one knows exactly how large the opposition is or how

much of it can be accurately classified as counter-revolutionary. A number of non-official public opinion polls taken before the economic war showed overwhelming majorities in favor of the regime. For example, Tad Szulc reported in the *New York Times* of August 1: "A recent sample poll of the Institute for International Social Research, a United States private institution, found last spring that 43 percent of the Cubans were ardent supporters of the Revolution, 43 percent were 'moderate' supporters, 10 percent were against it, and the rest had no opinion." Unfortunately, no comparable polls seem to have been taken in the last couple of months, so that one can only guess that the opposition may have roughly doubled and may now amount to some 20 to 25 percent of the total population.

As to how much of the opposition is decisively counter-revolutionary, again no one knows. But in estimating the future outlook it seems prudent to assume that practically all of it is. All observers agree that there has been a hardening of attitudes on both sides, and what Mr. Szulc reported last summer is even more true today: "The Revolution is such an overwhelming fact of Cuban life that nothing else seems to matter. Virtually nothing else is discussed. Almost nobody can be neutral or detached about it."

How well organized are the counter-revolutionary forces? Those in exile are badly split, and while the same divisions do not seem to exist inside Cuba—at least not to anything like the same degree—nevertheless there is no convincing evidence of a well-organized underground movement. This is not surprising. It is one thing to organize and maintain an underground against an unpopular dictator like Batista and something entirely different to do so against a regime that has the loyal (and to a large extent fanatical) backing of three quarters or more of the population. The chances of discovery in the latter case are so great as to make failure only a matter of time. Under these circumstances, it is simply impossible to maintain a formal movement: oppositionists are forced to bide their time, waiting for more favorable conditions and in the meantime doing what they can to undermine and weaken the regime by means of individual acts such as bombings (which occur almost every night in Havana now), sabotage, and so on. This appears to be the present behavior pattern of the Cuban counter-revolution.

If our estimate of the situation is right, there is a serious counter-revolutionary potential in Cuba today, but no organized movement and certainly no threat to the regime. The big question, then, is under what circumstances the potential might turn into reality. What changes might take place that would allow the hard-core counter-revolutionaries to organize an effective movement and proceed to the offensive against the regime?

The answer to these questions is clearly to be sought in the economic sphere. If the economic development programs of the regime succeed, there is no reason to doubt that its popular support will be maintained and the counter-revolutionaries will continue to be frustrated. If on the other hand there are serious failures in the economic sphere, the opposition will grow and the enthusiasm of the regime's supporters will flag. Under such conditions, the threat of counter-revolution would become very real indeed. The fate of the Cuban Revolution, in other words, is crucially dependent on its economic success or failure. Let us therefore inquire which it is likely to be.

Myth and Reality

Anyone who relies for information on the American press may wonder why it is necessary to ask the question at all. For many months now, correspondents, commentators, and editors have been virtually unanimous in reporting the decline and fall of the Cuban economy. We select a couple of representative items, not from the yellow press but from *Business Week,* one of the country's most responsible and reliable economic periodicals. The first is from the issue of September 17th:

> Cuba's internal problems are becoming more acute.
>
> A "galloping" inflation has taken hold, unemployment is widespread, and revolutionary leader Fidel Castro is losing support even among the peasants, once his most ardent backers. Fuel and food are in short supply despite imports of Russian crude oil and Communist Chinese rice.

This might seem bad enough, but it sounds positively like prosperity compared to the shattering report in the issue of October 22nd:

> In the cities, black markets are thriving. Hoarding is general. Cuban officials admit that the country needs $250 million annually in import credits for consumer goods. They've asked the Communist bloc for them but so far little has been forthcoming.

The government can't collect taxes. Practically nobody has any real income anymore. Sugar workers now get 80 percent of their wages in script for purchases in government cooperatives.

A country in which "practically nobody has any real income anymore" is certainly in a bad way. In fact, not only is it in a state of complete economic collapse but its people are, by definition, starving to death. Unhappily for *Business Week*— and all the other wishful dreamers of the United States "power elite"—the plight of the Cuban people is not quite as bad as all that. They have their problems: unemployment still is widespread; there is no doubt that inflationary pressures exist; and shortages do occur. But for the rest, detailed examination of *Business Week's* picture of the Cuban economy shows that it is sheer fantasy:

Far from "galloping," inflation has been remarkably successfully contained by means of price controls.*

Peasant support for Fidel has never been stronger. We were able to verify this ourselves on a number of widely scattered cooperatives; and Professor Samuel Shapiro of Michigan State, an authority on Latin America who visited Cuba during the summer and made a special point of investigating the condition of the peasants who have received individual title to their land under the agrarian reform, reports that "all the landholders I talked to were pleased with the new order."**

Fuel is not in short supply: there is no rationing and one can buy all one wants. In fact, R. Hart Phillips reported in the *New York Times* of November 6, that Cuba is offering to *sell* "up to 5,000 barrels of gasoline daily" to Canada.

Food shortages are sporadic, not general, and are due either to (a) the fact that consumers are buying much more than they used to, or (b) special circumstances, as in the case

---

* Let the reader judge for himself. We have before us a copy of the newspaper *El Mundo* for September 29. In it there is an advertisement for an "end of the month" sale at the high-price Minimax supermarkets. Here are a few of the prices: T-bone and sirloin steak—57¢ lb; fresh lobster— 35¢ lb; froglegs—55¢ lb; soup meat—29¢ lb; condensed milk—19¢ can; "Pet" evaporated milk—43¢ 2 cans; Libby's purée of tomatoes—15¢ can; Kellogg's corn flakes—25¢ pkg; sugar—27¢ 5 lbs. (The official rate of exchange between the dollar and the peso is one-to-one.)

** Professor Shapiro's article, "Cuba: A Dissenting Report," appeared in the *New Republic,* September 12. It is an excellent piece of work.

of beans which have recently been scarce because a large part of last year's crop was used for seed (we were told by people who know the situation that after the next harvest there will probably be a glut of beans).

Black markets are certainly not "thriving": enforcement of price controls is strict and impartial, and there are not many who care to take the risk of black-marketing.

There is no evidence of hoarding.

It is absurd to say that officials admit that Cuba needs $250 million annually in credits to import consumer goods: Cuba can and does pay for the consumer goods it imports; it wants credit for capital goods; and it has got from the socialist bloc more credits for this purpose than it can yet use.

The government is collecting taxes much more efficiently than any prerevolutionary government ever did.

Practically everyone has enough real income to live on, which never used to be the case in Cuba.

Finally, since at the time the *Business Week* article appeared the sugar harvest had not yet begun, many sugar workers were unemployed and would have been starving, as they used to, if it were not for the credit allowed them at the "people's stores."

It is interesting to speculate on the reasons why *Business Week*—as well as the *New York Times* and the *Wall Street Journal,* not to mention the lesser lights of the American press—puts out such nonsense. No doubt the main reason is to help bamboozle public opinion about what is really going on in Cuba. But there is also another reason which should not be underestimated. A ruling class in decline is simply unable to look objectively at, and hence to recognize the truth about, anything that threatens its power and privileges. It is forced by the logic of its situation to substitute rationalizations for rational analyses, wish fulfillments for realities. It is only necessary to add that the Cuban Revolution certainly does constitute a threat to the power and privileges of the United States ruling class.

But whatever the explanation of the nonsense about Cuba poured out by the American press, one thing is clear: it *is* nonsense and can in no way be relied upon as a guide to what is likely to happen. The Cuban economy is not in decline or crisis. This is not to say that there are no problems, however,

or that future failures of a serious nature are impossible. To
form our own judgment about these matters, we need to have
a closer look at underlying forces and trends at work in the
Cuban economy. Let us begin with agriculture.

Progress in Agriculture

The first thing to be stressed, and in many ways the most
important, is that production of the "new" crops—that is to
say, crops other than sugar, tobacco, and coffee*—has continued
to expand as it did during the first year of the Revolution, and
gives every indication of going on expanding for the foreseeable
future. No statistics are yet available which would permit a
comparison of 1960 with 1959 and earlier years, but the basic
trends are clear and indisputable. All over the island, good land
which under the old system had lain idle has been and is being
brought into cultivation. We were fortunate to be taken on a
trip from Manzanillo to Belic to see the huge new cooperative
that is in the course of being established in the Niquero-Belic
area—and also to see the historic spot on the seashore where
the *Granma* landed that fateful day in December, 1956. Our
guide was Comandante René Vallejo, the surgeon who served
in the American army in Germany during World War II and
is now INRA chief for the province of Oriente, one of the most
important jobs in Cuba. Again and again as we drove through
the countryside, Dr. Vallejo pointed to vast tracts of land, now
fairly bursting with crops, that had previously produced nothing but *maribu*, the tough bush-like weed that quickly invades
untended land. He also told us of spectacular successes in increasing per-acre yields, especially in rice cultivation where Japanese
methods of transplantation are beginning to be introduced.

One could perhaps discount the testimony of Dr. Vallejo
and other government officials and economists (though it is not
so easy to do so when one is looking right at the object of the
testimony!)—it is certainly true that they are deeply involved in
a personal way and no doubt see things in the best possible light.
But one can hardly have similar reservations about the testimony

---

* With respect to these traditional mainstays of Cuban agriculture, the
problem remains, as before, one of markets rather than of production.
Cuba can produce more of these staples than she can sell. By the same
token, if markets should by any chance expand, there is no doubt that
production could be expanded to supply them.

of a distinguished foreign agronomist. René Dumont, Professor of Comparative Agriculture at the Sorbonne's Agronomic Institute and a leading authority on the agriculture of tropical countries, spent several weeks in Cuba in May and again in August. He was naturally given every facility to acquaint himself with the circumstances and achievements of Cuban agriculture, and the advice which he gave the government after his first stay has had a deep influence on agricultural policy (we shall return to this in a moment). Professor Dumont published an article in the Paris weekly, *L'Express,* after he returned from his second visit (September 22). The subtitle of the article reads: "After a month in Cuba, Professor Dumont tells how the Fidelist Revolution is in the process of winning its economic gamble." Here is the key paragraph:

Already from May to August I observed marked progress. There will naturally be some difficulties, but *underproduction was such, before the Revolution,* that Cuban agriculture cannot but advance, even if errors are still committed. One can now say that the Cuban Revolution is in the process of catching up on the economic plane with the very high level it had already attained on the political plane. (Emphasis in original.)

So much for the overall agricultural picture. It is one of rapid, and in some respects quite sensational, progress.

Agricultural developments, however, have by no means been limited to quantitative increases in production and yields. There have also been important qualitative changes, which in turn will be reflected in further quantitative changes in the future. These developments are in line with, and to a certain extent stem from, policy recommendations which René Dumont made to the government in May.

Dumont criticized the agricultural policy followed during the first year of the Revolution on the ground that it was excessively concerned with bringing new land into cultivation and too much oriented toward specialization by the individual cooperatives.* To remedy these defects, he recommended more

---

* He also expressed the view that INRA had unduly neglected the small peasant proprietors who, since the agrarian reform, constitute a third or more of the agricultural work force (though of course accounting for a considerably smaller proportion of total output). Dumont believes that if adequate technical assistance, advice, and guidance are provided, the individual-peasant sector can vastly increase its production.

intensive cultivation of land already in use and greater diversification within the individual units, especially the cane cooperatives which were then in the process of formation. Every cooperative should have its own livestock operation and should grow a variety of crops. Natural pasture should be widely replaced by pasture sown to pangola, a grass which Dumont believes can, in Cuban conditions, bring about a veritable forage revolution. This would release much present pastureland for crops and obviate the expensive necessity of opening up new lands. Capital investment should be directed less toward tractors and more toward fertilizers and irrigation. These and related measures would make possible the utilization of by-products which now often go to waste, permit each cooperative to supply a greater part of its own needs, give more and steadier employment to the workers, and above all expand output while lowering unit costs of production.

Given the right policies, in Dumont's view, Cuban agriculture has fantastic potentialities. Cultivated with the same intensity as South China, he says, the island could feed a population of 50 million! Meanwhile, the country has the enormous advantage of being able to operate under a kind of law of increasing returns. In this connection we can do no better than quote from a memorandum on economic planning prepared for the Cuban government (after a visit to Cuba in September) by Professor Charles Bettelheim, a colleague of René Dumont at the Sorbonne:

Cuba is a country with absolutely exceptional agricultural possibilities. Studies made by specialists in agriculture and livestock show that within a relatively few years (generally from 10 to 12) it will be possible to multiply the production of many commodities by a factor of 3, 4, 5 or even more, without any great investment effort. This is an unprecedented situation. All the other countries that have entered the road of planning have had to make great efforts to raise their agricultural output to a much more modest degree—whether because this increase could not be realized without prior important investments (as in the Soviet Union) or whether because it demanded much labor and a tremendous organizational effort (as in China). In Cuba, on the other hand, the system of large rural property and the domination of foreign capital have produced an immense underutilization of the relevant means of production. The latter could therefore be brought into operation immediately or almost immediately by essentially political and technical means.*

Who would have thought that the shameful, inhuman neglect of productive potential that the combination of feudalism and imperialism imposed on Cuba for so many years would be transformed, in a revolutionary Cuba, into a source of strength such as no other country has yet possessed? It would be hard to find a better illustration of the dialectical principle of the interpenetration of opposites.

To complete this discussion of basic agricultural policy, it is useful to quote what Dumont wrote after his second visit to Cuba: "Most of the ideas which I had developed in my report have been adopted, but only after Fidel had rethought and adapted them to the Cuban situation." (*L'Express*, September 22.)

One further agricultural development should be mentioned, the establishment of the first "people's farms" (*granjas del pueblo*) which are organizationally similar to the state farms (*sovkhos*) of the Soviet Union. The land and capital belong to the state which also gets the profits, if any. Housing and other amenities are furnished the workers free, and they get a regular wage on a year-round basis. Up to now, so far as we could discover, all the people's farms that have been set up are primarily breeding establishments: we visited a number of them (chickens, hogs, cattle, ducks, goats) in Pinar del Rio, with Fidel as guide. The reason why this new form of agricultural enterprise has made its first appearance in breeding is an economic one: in this field a very large initial capital investment in stock, buildings, and specialized mechanical equipment (incubators, feeders, etc.) is required, and it would make no sense to turn all this over to a cooperative and allow the members to reap the profits from it in the future. The investment is financed by the people's money, hence the farms are rightfully the people's farms.

The establishments we saw were very impressive, with their brand-new buildings, modern equipment, and mostly imported stock. Already, output is zooming up, and it is clear that in the

* *Memorandum sobre la planificación económica en Cuba,* Havana, September 19, 1960.

near future these new "factories in the field" will be pouring out the animals and poultry needed by cooperatives all over the island to make the new agricultural policy a reality. We were fortunately able to check our own impressions when we got back to Havana, for we found that staying in our hotel were two American cattle dealers (one of whom was also a teacher at an agricultural college in Tennessee) and an equipment sales-man: they happened to be doing business at one of the people's farms when we visited it. They were, as might be expected, completely non-political, and their interest in Cuba was of a purely professional and business nature. They had high praise for the Cubans with whom they had dealt—contrasting their honesty and efficiency with the corruption and red tape one of them had encountered on a similar mission to Mexico—and fully confirmed our own good opinion of the breeding farms we had visited. The one serious weakness in the program, in their view, was that the INRA Zone chief who was in charge of op-erations, a young engineer named Rolando Fernandez, was carrying an enormous load of work and responsibility without anywhere near enough qualified assistance. They were particu-larly impressed by the great number of new projects and the feverish pace with which they are being pushed. What skep-ticism they expressed stemmed from a characteristically Ameri-can source: would the money hold out until all these projects could be completed and put in running order? Speaking in our capacity as professional economists, we assured them that they could put their minds at rest on this score.

What is likely to be the future of the people's farm as a form of agricultural enterprise? Will it be confined to situations requiring a high initial capital investment, or will it spread to other types of agriculture where the cooperative now holds the field? In our judgment, it will spread. Fidel is a strong believer in the superiority of the people's farm over the cooperative, and what is even more important he thinks that the *guajiro,* given a choice, will prefer it. No one knows as well as Fidel what the *guajiro* wants.

To the extent that the people's farm spreads, it will solve the two basic social questions which the cooperative leaves un-solved: the problem of cooperative members versus hired work-

ers, and the problem of rich versus poor cooperatives.* On the
people's farm all workers have the same status, and since the
profits all go to the state, i.e. to the people as a whole, there
can be no richer or poorer people's farms.

Problems of Industry

So far as agriculture is concerned, then, all the talk about
declining production, imminent crisis, and the like is the exact
opposite of the truth. Cuban agriculture is progressing with
astonishing rapidity and gives every indication of continuing
to do so. There is no comfort for the enemies of the Cuban
Revolution here. The outlook for industry, however, is much
less clear. Here, if anywhere, trouble might develop.

We have already discussed the question of replacement
parts. On this account alone, a period of very real difficulties
lies ahead. But there are other and perhaps even more serious
problems.

The nationalization within a brief period of upwards of
700 large and medium-sized enterprises confronts the regime
with staggering management problems. In nearly every case,
the top management has to be replaced with reliable men, and
in many cases the necessity for replacement extends a long way
down the management ladder. But the regime's manpower resources are already strained to the limit to staff the Ministries
and INRA and the other agencies that are carrying out the
work of the Revolution in such fields as agriculture, public
works, education, health, and social welfare. There simply is
no pool of unemployed managerial talent to draw upon. It follows that the success of the nationalization program depends
crucially on the ability of the Cuban working class to throw up
from its own ranks the men and women with the necessary qualities of initiative and responsibility. We believe that the working
class will rise to the challenge, but there is no sense in under-
estimating the magnitude of the problem.

Perhaps even more serious, because more difficult to remedy, is Cuba's shortage of technical personnel. Most American
specialists, who of course played a very important role in the
United States-owned companies, have already left. We heard
from several sources that many Cuban engineers are leaving

---

* See above, pp. 121-122.

the country for better-paid jobs in the United States or other Latin American countries (whether there is a deliberate campaign to lure them out of Cuba we do not pretend to know). And all this comes on top of an already desperate shortage of qualified technical personnel for the new and mostly technologically advanced industries which Cuba must establish as part of her program of economic development.

There are various ways of meeting the shortage. Each available man has to do the work of several, not as well as it should be done but better than not at all. Foreign technical specialists can be brought to Cuba, and are being brought in increasing numbers—from the socialist bloc, from many Latin American countries, and even a few from the United States. The regime is sure to redouble its efforts to bring in foreign technicians, and much depends on its success. Finally, crash training programs can be instituted, designed to teach minimum necessary skills. (Wartime experience in the United States showed that astonishing results can be achieved in this way, provided the necessary teachers are available.) We believe that by a combination of these methods the regime will succeed in overcoming the shortage of technical personnel, but again nothing is to be gained by minimizing the seriousness of the problem.

Even this does not exhaust the list of difficulties facing Cuban industry. There are also grave organizational problems to be solved. No advance preparation had been made—or in the nature of the case could have been made—for handling the nationalized establishments. The industrialization department of INRA was set up to make plans for the new industries, most of which are still in the future: it has suffered from growing pains and inadequate leadership. Finally, the Central Planning Commission (*Junta Central de Planificación,* generally referred to as *Juceplan*), plagued with the usual shortage of qualified personnel, has been preoccupied with its own organizational tasks and in no position to take a constructive hand in the problems of industry. Chaos may be too strong a word to characterize the situation in this field but at any rate it is not too far off the mark.

Once again, however, there is no reason for despair: the regime is acutely aware of its shortcomings in this, as in other respects, and a remedial program is already in the works. Ché

Guevara has been President of the National Bank for just over a year now and in this period has succeeded in restoring the nation's monetary reserves to a healthy state. At the moment of writing he is on an important economic mission to the socialist-bloc countries. When he returns, which will probably be before this is in print, he will head up a new Ministry of Industry which will bring under one roof and one authority the problems of managing, staffing, and planning the development of Cuba's industry. Since the early days of the rebellion, Ché has had the reputation of being the man who gets things done. He is about to be handed the best opportunity yet to prove that the reputation is well deserved.

If you add up all the difficulties and problems confronting the regime in the industrial field—the establishment of new supply lines, the impending shortage of replacement parts, the need for a tremendous increase in management cadres, the still-growing scarcity of technically qualified personnel, the administrative disorganization at the top—you may well conclude that the situation *is* hopeless, that only a miracle can prevent the onset of a crippling industrial crisis. Here at last the counter-revolution would seem to have solid grounds for optimism. And yet history tells us that this conclusion, however logical, is completely wrong.

The truth is that all revolutions are faced, not once but repeatedly with "insoluble" problems. That's the reason their enemies invariably anticipate their downfall. But the problems are only insoluble by the standards of the past, and it is precisely the nature of revolutions to transcend those standards, to meet the challenges which confront them by new methods and with previously untapped resources. And by solving the insoluble problems they grow strong, drawing out the latent energies and talents of the classes which support them and steeling themselves against the onslaughts of their foes.

The Cuban Revolution has already shown that it stands squarely in the middle of this great tradition, It came to power only by solving any number of insoluble problems, and it has successfully met all the challenges that have since arisen. It has wonderful leadership; it has vast untapped resources in land and minerals and in its own people; and the magnitude of its potential support abroad, not only in the socialist countries but throughout the anti-imperialist world, is almost unlimited. Given these priceless assets, the Cuban Revolution most assuredly can master the difficult problems of industry with which it is now faced. And we have no doubt that it will.

The Outlook

If the United States would leave Cuba alone, the outlook would be excellent. As we have emphasized, the country has brilliant prospects: what it lacks is personnel and organization. With time and assistance from outside, these deficiencies can be made good. In perhaps five to ten years the Cuban national income could be doubled and the evil vestiges of the past—unemployment, illiteracy, filth diseases, slums, and all the rest—could be largely wiped out. With the counter-revolution worn down by attrition and despair, a new and genuine democracy could take root and flourish on Cuban soil. Cuba, in short, could become a showplace of socialism and a model for other under-developed countries to emulate.

But of course the United States will not leave Cuba alone. So much has been made clear by everybody concerned—the President, the State Department, and the President-elect. It would be too much to expect a return to sanity in Washington in the visible future. The relevant question is rather what the United States can do to Cuba.

When we were in Cuba in March, responsible government leaders believed that the chances of an all-out attack by United States armed forces were great. When we returned in September, they no longer thought so. They were convinced that Soviet Premier Khrushchev's pledge of rocket retaliation in case the United States should directly attack Cuba was wholly serious, and they did not believe that the United States would start World War III over Cuba. We have no idea whether this estimate of Soviet intentions is correct, and we doubt if Washington does either. Clearly, it *may* be correct, and that in itself is likely to be enough to deter a direct attack. Cuba's immunity from direct military intervention by the United States would now seem to be of approximately the same order as Turkey's or Iran's immunity from direct military intervention by the USSR. This, at any rate, would seem to be the logic of the situation. At the same time it is necessary to add immediately that American policy toward Cuba seems to be guided less and less by logic and more and more by fear and hatred. Under the circumstances, direct attack must be considered a definite possibility, with all its incalculable and possibly catastrophic consequences.

But other forms of intervention are possible and in fact are already being practiced. Small invasion forces composed of counter-revolutionaries and mercenaries have been sent to Cuba from Florida and Guatemala. Cuban charges that the Central Intelligence Agency is training large forces in Guatamela have been impressively backed by no less an authority than Dr. Ronald Hilton, Director of the Institute of Hispanic-American Studies at Stanford University (see "Are We Training Cuban Guerillas?", *The Nation,* November 19, 1960). So far these interventions have been successfully defeated, a large number of participants have been caught, and several have been executed. But further efforts are expected.

What is the theory behind these small-scale invasions? There are two possibilities. One is that the CIA believes what it reads in *Business Week* and the *Wall Street Journal,* that things are so bad in Cuba that a few pushes will topple the regime. The other is that what we have seen so far are mere probing actions designed to help prepare the way for something bigger to come. The Cuban government obviously holds this second theory—partly no doubt on the basis of its own intelligence reports but also because in a situation like this it is always prudent to expect the worst. This explains why it has brought the matter up in the UN and is currently making every effort to keep the world's attention focused on the question. Those who would invade another's territory prefer to operate under cover of night and cloud, not in the bright glare of publicity.

A larger-scale invasion would not necessarily have the strategic aim of taking over the whole island. United States military experts presumably know that the Cuban militia and army together constitute a formidable fighting force which could not be smashed by any conceivable expedition of counter-revolutionaries and mercenaries. The aim would presumably be a much more limited one, to establish a foothold on Cuban soil which could then become the seat of a rival Cuban "government." (The Isle of Pines, which is situated directly in the route of an invading force from Guatemala, would obviously be ideal

for such an operation, which no doubt explains recent newspaper reports of heavy reinforcements for the garrison there.)
Once this was accomplished, the next step would obviously be
recognition of the rival regime and the dispatch of aid to it,
much as Hitler and Mussolini sent aid to Franco. It would of
course be highly important to get the Organization of American
States to endorse the whole operation, thus lending it a sem-
blance of legality. From this point the strategy would presumably call for a war of attrition leading eventually to a collapse
of the government or its overthrow by an internal fifth column.
Once again, the example of the Spanish civil war comes to mind.

Another possible strategy, with which at the moment of
writing Washington appears to be actively experimenting, is to
attempt to involve Cuba in a war against Guatemala or Nicaragua or both. It is hard to interpret the latest naval maneuvers,
ostensibly designed to "protect" Guatemala and Nicaragua from
an alleged threat of invasion from Cuba, in any other way. If
such a war could be started, the United States, with OAS backing if obtainable, could then feed in arms and "volunteers."
This is essentially a variant of the German-Italian strategy
against the Spanish Republic in the 1930's. All in all, it would
seem that the closest analogy to what is being planned for Cuba
today is what Hiter and Mussolini actually did to Spain twenty-
five years ago.

Can the United States, in the 1960's, duplicate the fascist
success of the 1930's?

It seems unlikely. The Cubans are much better prepared
than the Spanish Loyalists were. Fidel was not idly boasting
when he recently told a graduating class of army officers that
"we have the morale, the technique and the enthusiasm, and
we have the arms" to destroy any invading force of mercenaries
that may be sent to Cuba. Without a Franco installed on Cuban
territory, the whole operation could never get off the ground.

But even if we assume an initial success for the counter-
revolution, final victory would be far from assured. The Cuban
people would certainly get more help than the Spanish Loyalists did, even if the allies of the United States should agree to
an equally shameful policy of "non-intervention." And it is very
doubtful whether the present political structure of Latin America, which provides the United States with a large numerical

majority of its allies, would survive a drawn-out war of intervention against Cuba. Suppressing the Cuban Revolution would be the aim of such a war; spreading the Latin American Revolution would more likely be the result.

No, Cuba is not Spain and the 1960's are not the 1930's. The world has come a long way since then. The relation of forces is far more favorable to peoples struggling to liberate themselves from the yoke of a feudal past and an imperialist present.

The United States may have the power to destroy the world; it does not have the power to enforce its will on the world. Cuba has already proven that. Fidel and his followers set out to make their country free and independent, a sovereign nation. They have succeeded. We have it on the best authority, out of the horse's mouth, as it were. Here is the testimony of Earl E. T. Smith, former Ambassador to Cuba, before the Senate Subcommittee To Investigate The Administration Of The Internal Security Act (the Eastland Committee) on August 30, 1960 (p. 700):

MR. SMITH. Senator let me explain to you that the United States, until the advent of Castro, was so overwhelmingly influential in Cuba that, as I said here a little while ago, the American Ambassador was the second most important man in Cuba; sometimes even more important than the President.

That is because of the reason of the position that the United States played in Cuba. Now, today, his importance is not very great.

Unlike Mr. Smith, who deplored this changed relationship, those of us who have the interest of the American people at heart, rejoice in the fact that the American Ambassador is no longer "the second most important man in Cuba, sometimes even more important than the President." We are for an end to colonialism, not only in Asia and Africa, but in Latin America, as well. And the success of the Cuban Revolution is the beginning of the end for imperialism in the Western hemisphere.

References

Page 2,   line 26.   Lowry Nelson, *Rural Cuba* (Minneapolis, University of Minnesota Press, 1950) p. 47.

Page 3,   line 11.   U.S. Department of Commerce, *Personal Income By States Since 1929* (Washington, D.C., 1956) p. 142.

            line 13.   U.S. Department of Commerce, *Investment in Cuba* (Washington, D.C., 1956) p. 184.

Page 4,   table.   *Ibid*, p. 187.

Page 5,   line 17.   Ray Brennan, *Castro, Cuba and Justice* (New York, Doubleday & Company, 1959) p. 273.

Page 6,   line 2.   Nelson, *Rural Cuba*, p. 236.

            line 17.   International Bank for Reconstruction and Development, *Report on Cuba* (Washington, D.C., 1950) p. 408.

            line 25.   *Investment in Cuba*, p. 181.

Page 8,   line 29.   Foreign Policy Association, *Problems of the New Cuba* (New York, Foreign Policy Association, 1935) pp. 73-75.

Page 10,   line 24.   World Bank, *Report on Cuba*, p. 168.

            line 30.   Foreign Policy Association, *Problems of the New Cuba*, p. 3.

Page 11,   line 29.   Quoted in Leland H. Jenks, *Our Cuban Colony* (New York, Vanguard Press, 1928) p. 7.

Page 12,   line 32.   *Ibid*, p. 27.

Page 15,   line 34.   Quoted in Scott Nearing and Joseph Freeman, *Dollar Diplomacy* (New York, B. W. Huebsch and Viking Press, 1925) p. 176.

            line 35.   Quoted in Jenks, *Our Cuban Colony*, p. 81.

Page 17,   line 8.   *Ibid*, pp. 80, 81.

Page 20,   line 9.   *Ibid*, p. 310.

Page 21,   ftnote,

            line 5.   Nelson, *Rural Cuba*, p. 148.

            ftnote,

            table.   *Investment in Cuba*, p. 37.

Page 22,   line 8.   Jenks, *Our Cuban Colony*, pp. 301, 302.

            line 21.   *Investment in Cuba*, p. 10.

Page 25,   line 22.   Quoted in Jules Dubois, *Fidel Castro* (Indianapolis, Bobbs-Merrill, 1959) p. 29.

Page 26,   line 23.   *Ibid*, p. 15.

Page 31,   line 2.   *Ibid*, p. 43.

           line 17.   *Ibid*, p. 45.

           line 25.   *Ibid*, pp. 45, 46.

Page 32,   line 15.   *Ibid*, p. 46.

Page 33,   line 3.   *Ibid*, p. 47.

Page 34,   line 24.   *Ibid*, pp. 47-49.

Page 47,   line 42.   Fidel Castro, *History Will Absolve Me* (New York, Liberal Press, 1959).

Page 49,   line 24.   Quoted in Dubois, *Fidel Castro*, pp. 88, 90, 91.

Page 50,   line 29.   *Ibid*, p. 103.

Page 52,   line 25.   *Ibid*, p. 138.

Page 53,   line 36.   Quoted in Brennan, *Castro, Cuba and Justice*, p. 106.

Page 55,   line 2.   Quoted in Dubois, *Fidel Castro*, p. 144.

Page 58,   line 10.   *Ibid*, p. 145.

Page 59,   line 15.   Brennan, *Castro, Cuba and Justice*, p. 113.

Page 62,   line 2.   Dubois, *Fidel Castro*, pp. 234-240.

Page 63,   line 36.   Quoted in Brennan, *Castro, Cuba and Justice*, p. 234.

Page 65,   line 25.   Quoted in Dubois, *Fidel Castro*, p. 282.

Page 66,   line 7.   *Ibid*, p. 271.

           line 35.   *Ibid*, p. 301.

Page 67,   line 29.   *Ibid*, p. 313.

Page 68,   line 19.   *Ibid*, pp. 296, 297.

Page 71,   line 25.   *New York Times*, April 22, 1960.

Page 79,   line 27.   Nelson, *Rural Cuba*, p. 166.

           line 30.   *Investment in Cuba*, p. 183.

Page 80,   line 7.   Nelson, *Rural Cuba*, pp. 166-168.

           line 20.   *Ibid*, p. 227.

           line 28.   *Ibid*, p. 174.

Page 96,   line 21.   *Investment in Cuba*, pp. 180, 181.

Page 97,   line 9.   Nelson, *Rural Cuba*, pp. 234, 235.

Page 108, line 28.   World Bank, *Report on Cuba*, p. 15.

Page 126, line 32.   *New York Times*, April 14, 1960.

Page 136, line 28.   *Cuba Economica y Financiera*, January 1960, p. 10.

Page 137, table.   *Ibid*, pp. 9, 18.

Page 145, line 24.   Text of Panel Interview, held in the Hotel Nacional, Havana, March 10, 1960.

           line 29.   *New York Herald Tribune*, May 8, 1960.